A Guide to Masonic Symbolism

Duncan Moore

First published 2009
Reprinted 2010

ISBN 978 0 85318 294 8

All rights reserved. No part of this book may be reproduced or transmitted in any form or by any means, electronic or mechanical, including photocopying, recording or by any information storage and retrieval system, without permission from the Publisher in writing.

© Duncan Moore 2009

Published by Lewis Masonic

an imprint of Ian Allan Publishing Ltd,
Hersham, Surrey KT12 4RG.
Printed by Ian Allan Printing Ltd,
Hersham, Surrey KT12 4RG

Code: 1008/A2

Visit the Lewis Masonic website at www.lewismasonic.com

Distributed in the United States of America and Canada by BookMasters Distribution Services.

Copyright

Illegal copying and selling of publications deprives authors, publishers and booksellers of income, without which there would be no investment in new publications. Unauthorised versions of publications are also likely to be inferior in quality and contain incorrect information. You can help by reporting copyright infringements and acts of piracy to the Publisher or the UK Copyright Service.

Contents

About the Author	4
Acknowledgements	5
Introduction	7
The Origins and History of Symbolism	13
The Symbolism of the Lodge Room	36
The First Degree	74
The Second Degree	117
The Third Degree	148
The Installation	176
Symbols no longer used	184
Endpiece	198
Bibliography	202
Index	203

About the Author

Duncan Moore

Duncan Moore grew up in Lancashire and was educated at Merchant Taylors' School, Crosby. He was bitten by the history bug at an early age and has been a lifelong student of that subject.

Initiated into Freemasonry in Cheshire in 1971, he now holds Grand Rank or equivalent in most Masonic Orders. He has been active in various degrees in several English Provinces. He is also a member of the Knight Masons of Ireland and active in Scotland and Belgium. His particular delight has been to witness the expansion of Masonry in the English District of Cyprus, where he was a founder of Mark and RAM lodges and two Rose Croix Chapters.

Duncan Moore has been a member of the Merseyside and Manchester Associations for Masonic Research and has given many papers to lodges and associations in the north of England. Having written many histories of Craft Lodges and other Orders, he is firmly of the opinion that it is vital to look behind the minutes, to the events on the local and world stage that will have affected the members and conditioned their Masonic membership.

In tackling this subject of symbolism, he has been careful to avoid the fantastic and to stick to interpretations of Masonic symbols that are generally acceptable and historically valid.

Outside Masonry, Duncan Moore now lives in Cyprus with his wife, Cathy. They have a large extended family, which necessitates regular visits to various parts of England. His non-Masonic recreations include cookery, history research, watching Rugby (preferably Rugby League, but he is prepared to look in on the gentler version as well) and trying to learn Greek.

Acknowledgements

I have to acknowledge a great deal of assistance and advice in producing this book and I sincerely hope that both enjoyment and instruction may be derived from reading it. I have been generously received wherever I have gone and all the brethren I have consulted have extended true Masonic generosity.

First of all, I should thank Lewis Masonic for asking me to write the book in the first place and for their unfailing help and courtesy during the course of its production. Many Freemasons have helped me with ideas and suggestions and have informed me of possible sources of information. Among them I am indebted to Bros Barry Dickson-Bate and Roy Willis of Cestrian Lodge No.425 in the Province of Cheshire for the conducted tour of their fascinating Masonic Hall at Queen Street in Chester, allowing me to photograph various of their artefacts and presenting me with a copy of their book, *The Origins, History and Possessions of the Cestrian Lodge No.425*. Bro Tom Prince PP Dep G Supt Wks (West Lancashire) of Liverpool Charter Lodge No.7650 pointed me at much Masonic symbolism in Liverpool Cathedral.

My thanks are also due to Bro Colin Denne PAGDC, formerly Provincial Grand Secretary of Staffordshire and now an Assistant Provincial Grand Master of that Province, for providing me with the photograph of the ceiling in Stafford Masonic Temple, and also Bro Joe Hunter PPrGW (Cheshire) and the Board of Birkenhead Masonic Guildhall Ltd for permission to photograph interiors there. I also took photographs at the Masonic Hall in Jerusalem Street, Limassol, Cyprus and am grateful to St Paul's Lodge No.2277 for permission to do so.

For help with photography, I am extremely grateful to my stepdaughter, Mrs Joanne Cunningham, and also to Bros Roger Quayle ProvDepGDC (Cheshire) and Peter van de Pol DistJGW (Cyprus). I must convey profound thanks to Royal Cumberland Lodge No.41 at Bath and to their Lodge Historian, Bro Dennis Mosley. My visit to their Lodge in October 2007 was an evening of pure delight, not only to me but to all of the first-time visitors who attended. I am also grateful to Bro Richard Parker PJGD for information about Union Lodge No.129 in the Province of Cumberland and Westmorland.

I would also like to thank two senior Freemasons from the Province of Yorkshire (West Riding), Bros James Bramley Morley and James Patterson Greenwood (now a neighbour of mine in Cyprus), for their assistance with the Chain of Union and other unusual aspects of symbolism in their Province. This book could not have been written without the efforts of many Masonic scholars, some living, some dead, whose work I have referenced. To them I shall always be indebted. Any errors made are mine.

Many of the smaller illustrations and line drawings are taken from the CD 'Just Perfect' produced by J.Styles Software and I am obliged to Bro Styles for permission to use it. I also have to thank many lodges up and down Britain, Ireland and abroad who have entertained me as a guest over nearly forty years in Freemasonry. When I first stood outside that temple door in Birkenhead back in 1971, waiting to be initiated into the Craft, I never imagined that one day I'd write a book about it, or about anything else for that matter, but wherever I have been in Masonry I have always been well-received – even on occasions when I was a total stranger to everyone present – and I would recommend membership of the Craft to anyone, both as a means of enjoying oneself but more importantly for making us better men.

Above all I cannot conclude these acknowledgements without thanking my wife, Cathy, for her unfailing support and encouragement. It is easy to lose heart and get blocks when one is writing a book, and I thank Cathy for helping me to stick at it.

Introduction

'The interpretation of the symbolic kind is useful in many respects; for it leads to theology, to piety, and to show the ingenuity of the mind, the conciseness of expression, and serves to demonstrate science.'
SAINT CLEMENT OF ALEXANDRIA (C.150-211 A.D.)

What is a Symbol?

Whatever we do in life we cannot get away from symbols – we encounter them on signs and notices, on products we buy, on our modes of transport, in our places of work – everywhere. When you wake up in the morning you may see figures on your alarm clock that SYMBOLise the fact that it is six am. You pick up a cardboard packet with a device on it SYMBOLising cornflakes. You get into your car and look at a gauge which SYMBOLises whether you have enough fuel to get to your destination – and so on through the day. I'll leave you to think of a hundred other examples you could encounter before you even get to your place of work.

Often we use the word emblem when referring to symbols. Is it always correct to do this? The Oxford English Dictionary defines a Symbol as *A thing conventionally regarded as typifying, representing or recalling something* or *A mark or character taken as the conventional sign of some object*. It defines an Emblem as both *A symbol or representation typifying or identifying an institution, quality, etc* and *A heraldic device or symbolic object used as a distinctive badge*. So is there a significant difference between the two words, or is it just a question of nit-picking semantics?

Sometimes Classical language roots provide a clue to the real meanings of words. Symbol comes from a Greek word συμβολον *(Sumbolon)* meaning a mark or token. Emblem is from another Greek word εμβλημα *(Emblema)* meaning an insertion. If nothing else this probably tells us that the two words were, originally at least, intended to convey different meanings. And don't forget, words are themselves SYMBOLS of the meanings behind those words!

The real difference between the two concepts was brought home to me one day when I was driving up the M5 motorway in the centre

An Ancient Egyptian Cross or Ankh

lane. To my left was a tanker lorry with a green diamond on the back of its tank. This I knew to be the SYMBOL of noxious liquid, regularly carried in that vehicle. In front of me, struggling to overtake the tanker, was an articulated parcel van, which bore a device of four square packages, the top right of which was slightly detached to represent the delivery of one of those packages to its destination. That, I realised, was both the EMBLEM of the company which operated the van and a SYMBOL of the fact that it delivers things.

Many symbols are very ancient. Consider, for example, the Cross. We think immediately of Christianity, and within that there are many types of cross – the Calvary Cross, the Greek Cross with both limbs the same length, the Coptic Cross, the Maltese Cross, the Russian Cross with an extra slanted piece denoting the penitent and impenitent thieves crucified with Christ. And there are many more varieties, but did you know that Ancient Egyptians used the symbol of a cross many years before the time of Christ and called it an 'Ankh', denoting the union of the male and female sexes and the union of Heaven and Earth? The Ankh or Hieroglyphic Cross has a circle on top of it and frequently appears in hieroglyphic illustrations. The cross is also the Chinese character for the number ten.

Now consider a Masonic example: The Square worn by the Worshipful Master on the end of his collar, used as a Working Tool in the Second Degree and placed with the compasses on the Volume of the Sacred Law, while the Lodge is open. In the first instance the Square is the EMBLEM of the Master's office; in the other two cases it has SYMBOLic meaning.

The Arms of the United Grand Lodge of England

To go a little further and look at something more complicated, consider the Arms of the United Grand Lodge of England. Outwardly these are emblems. Indeed perhaps they could be called emblems within emblems because those Arms are an amalgam of the Arms of the Moderns' Grand Lodge, also called the Premier Grand Lodge, which came into being in 1717 (the three castles or towers and a square) and the Antients' Grand Lodge which existed from around 1751 (the Ox, Man, Lion and Eagle).

When the two Grand Lodges came together in 1813 to form the United Grand Lodge of England this badge was devised. They did not actually become Arms as such until Grand Lodge applied for a grant of Arms in 1913.

8 A Guide to Masonic Symbolism

In the case of the Moderns, their Arms are thought to be derived from those of the London Masons' Company. I suppose they are also SYMBOLIC of the fact that Masons build great edifices and use the tools of their trade to accomplish that end. In the illustration above you can see the crest of the Moderns' Grand Lodge as depicted on the Master's Chair formerly belonging to Royal Chester Lodge No.80 and still in use by its successor, Cestrian Lodge No.425 at the Masonic Hall, Queen Street, Chester.

The Master's Chair, Queen Street, Chester

The chair is richly decorated and you can also see many other symbols. Apart from the Square and Compasses and the two columns which have obvious Masonic significance, there are also two oval crests. The one on the right bears the devices shown on the Royal Standard. This is hardly surprising in a city like Chester which has always been Royalist and was the last place to surrender to Parliament in the English Civil War; in fact one of the existing lodges in Chester is named Loyal City Lodge No.4839. The pendant on the left shows the three lions or leopards which are emblematic of England, together with the wheat sheaves of the county of Cheshire.

The device of the Ox, Man, Lion and Eagle used by the Antients will be well known to Royal Arch Masons, who will be aware of the symbolism behind each emblem. It is hardly surprising that the Antients selected this design, given that they were very fond of the Royal Arch, certainly to a much greater extent than the Moderns. But we can go even further in tracing the origins of the Antients' device. We can consider where the Antients' Grand Lodge got it from in the first place. The answer is undoubtedly the prophetical vision recorded in the Book of Ezekiel, Chapter 1, where the prophet sees a vision of the Chariot of God drawn by four winged creatures, each of which has four faces – that of an Ox, a Man, a Lion and an Eagle. So within those emblems within emblems, we have individual symbols with esoteric meanings.

But there is more than that. Consider the motto of Grand Lodge – AUDI, VIDE, TACE. In many parts of the world (notably in the Far East) the ape is seen as a symbol of wisdom. The motto – meaning Hear, See and be Silent – reminds us in our own culture of the three wise monkeys – hear no evil, see no evil,

Introduction 9

speak no evil. The full wording is 'Audi, vide, tace se vis vivere in pace' taken from a Latin proverb (Hear, see and be silent if you would live in peace). We have a sort of parallel in the motto of the Order of the Garter in Old French 'Honi soit qui mal y pense' (Evil be to him who evil thinks) and in Lancashire the saying 'Hear all, see all, say nowt' expressing the same kind of sentiment.

Perhaps after all that, we have arrived at a conclusion that a symbol is more likely to be of an abstract concept – danger, justice, strength or equality – or a general concept like cornflakes or a winding road. An emblem, on the other hand, represents something specific like the United Grand Lodge of England, Kelloggs or Shell Petroleum. But we could argue about that all day. Let's get on to what really interests us and that is what symbols there are in Freemasonry and how they relate to our Craft and the science behind it.

Symbols in Freemasonry
The Objective of this Book

We say that Masonry is *'veiled in allegory and illustrated by symbols'*. Some regard the Bible and particularly the Old Testament as a series of allegories. Others believe in its literal truth. This is not the place to consider that argument. The Hiramic legend in the Third Degree is a fictitious, allegorical story meant to teach us to meet death with equanimity and to be faithful to our trust. In some of the other Solomonic Degrees, there are similar legends – The Degrees of Select Master and Royal Master in the Order of Royal and Select Masters and the Degree of Grand Tylers of Solomon in the Order of the Allied Masonic Degrees have to be allegories because they are based on the hiding of secrets after the murder of Hiram Abif, which is in itself fictitious.

Some of our Degrees are based on stories which may be read in scripture and from which moral lessons are derived. The first two Degrees of the Order of the Secret Monitor are obvious examples. The object of this book is to provide a simple guide to elementary Masonic symbolism, concentrating entirely on the Craft. We start with a chapter on the Origins and History of Symbolism and then go on to examine the Symbolism of the Lodge room or temple. Then there is a chapter on each of the three Degrees in which we look at the symbolism within each in terms of the Preparation for taking the Degree, the symbolism inherent within the Degree, the Working Tools explained and the Tracing Board used. Next we look at the symbolism used within the Ceremony of Installation. The concluding chapter covers some of the symbols which may no longer be seen in current use, or are not used as they once were, but are still found on some of the older illustrations and artefacts thankfully preserved.

An understanding of the symbols we use is an essential part of the education of every Freemason. Without symbolism and allegory Masonry would merely be a series of sermons exhorting its members to love God and their neighbours, live a good life, educate themselves and know themselves. Whether the Craft in that form would have survived for nearly 300 years and spread all over the free world is questionable. For the Freemason, everything covered in this book is, as the ritual of the Mark Degree says, *'symbolical of sundry moral truths inculcated by Freemasonry'*. Put another way, that of the First Degree Tracing Board, *'there is not a character or emblem here depicted but serves to inculcate the principles of piety and virtue among all its genuine professors'*.

In Masonic symbolism it has to be admitted that there is some degree of overlap. The Volume of the Sacred Law, for example, is one of the Three Great Lights, but it is also itself symbolised by the Tracing Board, one of the immoveable jewels of the Lodge. The square is a moveable jewel, but it too is one of the Three Great Lights. I have tried to deal with each symbol within each heading under which it occurs.

A few moments ago, I quoted from the ritual the phrase *'veiled in allegory and illustrated by symbols'*. To illustrate means to throw light on, and so what Masonry is really about is the meanings behind those symbols. That is what this book attempts to cover.

Throughout the book I have referred to symbolic meanings outside Masonry, often in an attempt to indicate the reason they may have been brought into our Craft symbolism in the first place. It has been necessary to refer often to Christian symbolism and, in doing so, I mean no offence to my non-Christian brethren; the Craft was exclusively Christian in the early days and there are still many Christian references that we need to be aware of. For clues as to how symbols came into Masonry in the early days, I have also referred frequently to the ritual of the Royal Order of Scotland which claims to have been founded *'To correct the errors and reform the abuses which had crept in among the Three Degrees of St Johns* (i.e. early Speculative) *Masonry'*. The reason for doing this is not an admission that we have now got it wrong, but rather an attempt to throw ever more light on this complex but fascinating subject.

That said, many symbolic things have also come into Masonry from pre-Christian times and I hope to give a few examples of these when dealing with possible precursors of our modern Craft. I have also looked, in various places, at practices either not or no longer known in England but still used in Craft Degrees in other jurisdictions and obediences. This is an attempt to portray the symbolic 'big picture' and so aid understanding of the individual symbols that we use in English Lodges.

In doing so, I refer frequently to the 'Scottish Rite' and 'Rectified Scottish Rite' and these, I know, are terms many English Masons find difficulty in understanding – indeed some believe that because they contain the word 'Scottish' they refer to the Masonic Degrees as worked in Scotland. This book is about English Craft Masonry, but an understanding of these terms will help the reader's appreciation of Freemasonry worldwide, in part influenced by English Masonry but also with features that have influenced us. Put simply, Scottish Rite is a system of degrees worked in most European countries and in the United States of America, where it is big business. Continental Europe differs from the USA in that all the degrees of the Scottish Rite are worked (and it also has the Rectified Scottish Rite), whereas in the United States the first three (Entered Apprentice, Fellowcraft and Master Mason) are taken care of in what they call the 'Blue' (in other words Craft) lodge and one receives only the Higher Degrees in the Scottish Rite. I have been privileged to witness, and indeed take part in, some of these ceremonies in the French and Belgian Constitutions, and we now have a lodge in Cyprus, formerly under the Greek Constitution, that also works Scottish Rite.

With that potential source of misunderstanding cleared up, hopefully you will enjoy the book.

Duncan Moore
March 2009

The Origins and History of Symbolism

Where Did Symbols Come From?

Symbols are nearly as old as mankind. They began when man first learnt to communicate. The first types of symbols may well have been gestures made with the hands and other parts of the body. Recent research suggests that apes use the sign of an open hand to signify that they want food, and it was probably that way with humans as well.

In time, if one of our primitive ancestors wanted to tell his mate or his colleague something he would draw a picture. The first writing would have occurred in the form of symbolic pictures. If you wanted to tell others that there was food in the area, you would draw a picture of one or more animals. Arguably pictorial symbols could even pre-date speech. They would have started as crude diagrams of people, animals, weapons and so on and developed into the sort of complex, artistic pictographs which are found on the walls of caves and elsewhere.

Numbers will have come along fairly early – numbers, after all, are symbols in themselves – and the need to quantify things would have been essential to early man. All of this will have taken place long before there was any form of written language. There will also have been personal markings of a sort, perhaps so that one man could let others know he had been in a certain place – a sort of primitive 'Kilroy was here' but also a precursor of the Mason's Mark, which we will consider later in this chapter.

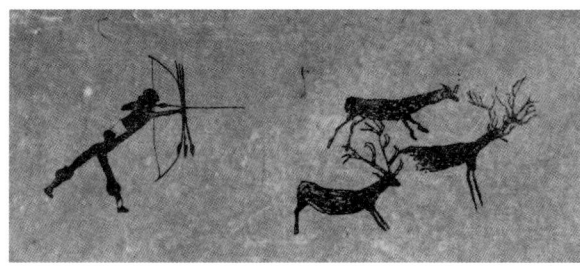

A Cave Painting

Forms of measurement would be needed as societies started to develop, and food and shelter had to be provided. Even the crudest building projects would need to be aware of the lengths and breadths of materials required. Early forms of measurement would probably have been based on the length of hands or arms (as, of course, was the biblical cubit), but it would soon become apparent that something more precise was required.

We know for a fact that the scribes of ancient Babylon, who used a cuneiform script, employed a numbering system with a sexagesimal base (as opposed to a decimal one like ours) which was capable of quite complex mathematics. Evidence has even been found of Babylonian algebraic equations as early as 1500BC (although what we now know as algebra was invented in India later on). The ancient Egyptians, who came after the Babyonians, were quite adept at calculating fractions. This, when you think about it, is not really surprising given that you cannot achieve much in life without the ability to number, calculate and count.

We know from the peculiar form of some Megalithic monuments like Stonehenge in Wiltshire, and many others throughout the world, that not only symbolism but ritualised forms of doing things were well known in prehistoric times, and that even Neanderthal man had set procedures for burying his dead. Stonehenge is a fascinating piece of work, built around 2500BC from 85 stones, some as heavy as 40 tonnes. And that wasn't the start of it; recent research suggests that the site was already being used as a burial ground five hundred years before that. The central axis of Stonehenge aligns with the rising Sun at the Summer Solstice on 21 June each year. Indeed the surrounding area contains many circular 'structures' – there are circular mounds and, of course, crop circles have become a source of fascination for some people in recent years. Stonehenge is older than the Pyramids, as carbon dating has proved, but the most remarkable thing to my mind is that some of the stones are thought to have come from the Preseli Mountains in West Wales, nearly 200 miles away, unless they were deposited by the action of glaciers at the end of the Ice Age, but this is considered unlikely. The bigger stones come from within a 25 mile radius. It has been established that Bronze Age man was

Stonehenge

capable of building barges substantial enough to carry the stones from Wales. Indeed one such vessel has been unearthed at Shardlow in Derbyshire. One wonders what knowledge our ancient British ancestors possessed which led them to believe that it was necessary to build a temple in that particular spot and how they would have known that there were stones at such a distance away that were the right ones to use. What, of course, we cannot now discover is precisely what our ancestors meant Stonehenge to represent. Clearly, they did not pile stones up in that particular fashion for no reason, but what it symbolised we can never know for sure.

Colours are, and always have been, symbolic. The First Covenant made by God with Noah was symbolised by a rainbow. Its colours: red, orange, yellow, green, blue, indigo and violet (often remembered by the mnemonic *Richard Of York Gave Battle In Vain*) form the basis of all the colours in the spectrum and these have been associated with various things, both spiritual and practical. From ancient times white has represented purity and innocence. It had that connotation within the Ancient Mysteries of Egypt and Greece, from which some aspects of Masonry – arguably – are derived. Green has indicated matters connected with the Earth. Red meant fire and war. Blue – a very important colour in Freemasonry – has connotations with the ancient Jewish priests, who wore blue tassels, as we read in the Book of Numbers, Chapter 15 v.38. In Christian terms the Virgin Mary is often portrayed wearing a blue garment.

We will look at colours in relation to our Masonic regalia a little later, but it is interesting to note how colour symbolism has persisted throughout the ages. Take black and white and think how often in films and pictures the good guys are portrayed as wearing white and the bad guys black. *Star Wars* with Luke Skywalker and Darth Vader (who turns out in the end to be Luke's father) is an obvious example. We have already seen that, from earliest times, 'a picture has told a thousand stories' and even today we see stained glass windows in churches, murals depicting a whole host of things, and heraldry, in the form of coats of arms, all conveying symbolic pictorial images.

But speech and language will eventually have demanded a form of notation – why draw a picture when you could simply write the word 'Ox' or whatever it was that primitive man called it? Of course, some languages, notably Chinese, still retain pictorial images in their

An Italian Mural

representations of words. By nature we are always looking for abbreviations and short cuts. There is nothing new in this. Ancient Semitic languages omitted vowels, as those of us who are in the Royal Arch remember. We ourselves write 'Dr' and know it to mean Doctor. A modern example is sending text messages. If I text to someone the words *'C U 2nite'* he can expect to meet me later. By the same logic other symbols developed like signs for monetary values, musical notation and mathematical formulae.

In the same way developments in numerical notation occurred to simplify matters. The adoption of Arabic numerals, instead of Roman ones, will have made things much easier for the mathematician (or indeed ordinary tradesman) who needed to multiply XCIV by XIX.

Once there was spoken and written language, the possibilities expanded. There will have been emerging forms of literature – books, plays, poems – which would have initially been written for the purposes of communication and entertainment but, as and when the human mind developed, will have contained symbolic messages as well. The Parables we read in the New Testament are allegorical symbols of the moral principles being communicated – love thy neighbour etc. Great novels like James Joyce's *Ulysees* are rich in symbolism. Figures of speech can likewise be symbolic. For example, Bro Robert Burns in *Tam o'Shanter* refers to midnight as *'That hour o' night's black arch the key-stane'*. The mental image that conjures up is a very real one. Indeed we could say that our ritual is itself a means of communicating the meaning of our symbolism.

Music, of course, is also highly symbolical. In Masonry, as one of the Seven Liberal Arts and Sciences and with a close and interdependent relation to the others, it has great significance. But its evolution from simple tunes played on crude instruments to the complexity of Bro Mozart has symbolism all the way. Martial music announced the arrival of anything from a platoon of soldiers to an entire army; if they had simply marched in without the music the impact would have been far less. Earlier composers wrote what their patron – maybe a king or an archbishop – wanted to hear. The kind of stirring, rather pompous music we would associate with, say, King Henry VIII or Queen Elizabeth I brings to mind power and authority. Later on, composers like Haydn and Mozart (both Austrian Freemasons) got more of a chance to express their own ideas. As an example from a little later, consider the famous opening bars of Beethoven's Fifth Symphony. The idea for that is said to have been put in the composer's head by his hearing a yellowhammer bird pecking at the side of a tree. Beethoven is using this idea to symbolise fate knocking on the door of a man's life, but it was also used to great effect by the Allies in World War 2 to represent the concept of freedom by saying 'whatever you may be undergoing, there is a free world, it is with you and this is it talking'. The Roman numeral V stood for 'Fifth' as in Fifth Symphony and also for Victory, giving Bro Churchill his famous sign. When you think about it, if Beethoven had encountered that bird later in life, when he was stone-deaf, the world may well have been deprived of both a fine piece of music and much symbolism.

Mozart

Moving on, consider music in things like film screenplays in which it is used to symbolise the effect of tension, danger, romance and many other concepts. Experiments have been tried by getting two groups of people to watch the same piece of speechless film, but with different music in the background. One group having listened to romantic music thought the film, which featured a man and a woman meeting on a river bank, to have been about a lovers' encounter. The other group, which had been played 'tension-type' music to the same film, believed that either some deep intrigue was going on or that the lady was about to be raped! The advertising industry is well aware of the potential symbolism of music, colours and other things in inducing us to buy things. For example, playing classical music in restaurants is thought to make us feel affluent and to want to eat and drink more expensively.

It always strikes me as remarkable that signs and symbols have developed across the world with no possibility of any overall co-ordination. This gave rise to much speculation at one time – and still does in some quarters – as to whether the Earth had been ruled and ordered by a race of space gods. Discounting the 'Was God an astronaut' school of thought because we are Freemasons and therefore believe in a living God, probably the first symbols to have developed in the abstract sense would have been connected with the Sun, Moon and stars. It is easy to see why primitive peoples worshipped the Sun. It gave them light and kept them warm. If it disappeared completely, as it did and does in Arctic climes, or if it was clouded over, the god was angry and they knew they had to appease him. Perhaps, given that the Sun was available to all the peoples of the Earth, this was the start of man's fixation with that which he could not readily understand. Having said that, certain other symbols also became common in divers parts of the world.

Take, for example, the Square and Compasses: we will look at them in a Masonic context later, but it is worth noting that they were known to the ancient Chinese as together representing a Yin-Yang balance of male and female principles, and also the unity of Heaven and Earth. The latter, as we shall see, is also what we are using them to represent. Mencius, the disciple of Confucius, wrote: *'A Master Mason, in teaching apprentices, makes use of the compasses and square'*. The Chinese also refer to the principle of acting on the square – and all this is in around 500BC.

Again, think about the Mosaic Pavement. Native Americans used the idea of the contrast of two colours in painting alternate lines round their totem poles to represent opposites (good and bad, light and dark, etc) assigning a similar symbolism to the way we think of the Mosaic Pavement in our lodge rooms. We have Mosaic Pavements because we know about Moses and are told by tradition that the floor of his Tabernacle and later the Temple of King Solomon at Jerusalem had chequered floors. But the Indians did not know about that until the 16th or 17th century at the earliest, when they came into contact with Christianity; yet the Tree of Life, as it is called, is known to have existed among Indians of North, Central and South America for over 1000 years.[1]

Julian Rees notes that many of these Native Americans, because of their familiarity with Shamanism (traditions and beliefs based on communication with the spirit world; Shamanic cultures are found in places as far apart as North America, South Africa and Siberia), readily embraced Freemasonry, when they got the chance.[2]

So given that we understand the vital part symbols have played in the development of humanity, how did symbols come into Masonry in the first place? Why should we, as Masons, need to study symbols to help us understand what our Craft is about? Freemasonry is by no means the first society of its kind, so it will perhaps help if we look at some of our possible antecedents. Whilst it would be rash to claim a direct descent to Masonry from any of them, we can probably discern something of a system which may have influenced our early forebears.

Ancient Egypt

From around 3000BC the God Thoth was worshipped in Ancient Egypt. Thoth was credited, among many other things, with the invention of hieroglyphics and the introduction of writing, which we know occurred during the 1st dynasty (c.2925-c.2775BC). He may well have been responsible for the introduction of writing in Egypt, but earlier forms were known to have existed in China and elsewhere – the oldest being the Jiahu script dated 6600BC.

Among Thoth's other titles were: Logos, Measurer, Reckoner of Heaven and Earth, Lord of Hermopolis, Lord of Maat* (death), Judge of the Two Combatant Gods (Horus and Set), Inventor of All Arts and Sciences and Scribe of the Gods. In a way, I suppose, we could also confer on him the title of the *'Father of symbolism'*. A further known title of Thoth is that of Great Architect of the Universe (although many people ascribe the origin of that phrase to the Swiss Protestant Reformer, John Calvin) from which perhaps the Masonic notion of God is derived.

The Fraternity at Hermopolis in Egypt – established to study and practise the teachings of Thoth, who was also known as Hermes Trismegistus, or Thrice Great Hermes – had an initiatory rite of three degrees, like Freemasonry. The significance of the name Hermes needs first to be explained, because we shall consider it again later.

These three grades or degrees of the rite at Hermopolis – Mortals, Intelligences and Beings (or Sons of light) – had a ritual with charges

---

* Maat, the Egyptian word for death, is an interesting one. Not only is it the root of our two alternative words in the Third Degree, but it is also encountered in the game of chess. Chess probably originated in India, but what we play today is a modified version devised in Persia. The final removal of the King piece signifying the end of the game was accompanied by the declaration that the king is dead – 'Shah Maat' or 'Checkmate'!

and other features that would be to some extent recognisable to us. From the Lecture on the First Degree Tracing Board we learn that, among the ancient Egyptians, their *'systems of learning and polity were couched under signs and hieroglyphical figures',* and that those to whom they were communicated were *'bound under solemn oath to conceal them',* a custom passed on to the Pythagoreans. From this we know that they had symbols and a form of obligation. The First Degree Tracing Board Lecture also tells us *'The Blazing Star or Glory in the Centre refers us to the Sun, which enlightens the Earth and, by its benign influence dispenses its blessings on mankind in general'* – a reference no doubt to Ra, the Egyptian Sun god. This then informs us definitely of one symbol that was in use at Hermopolis and is still in use in our lodges, though not as a god but as *'the glory of the Lord'.*

Legend has it that Thoth played draughts with the Moon. The game of draughts obviously brings to mind the Chequered Pavement: the chequered existence with its due proportions of pain and pleasure, and indeed the command to Moses, Aholiab and Bezaleel to lay out the first Tabernacle with what has come to be known as the Mosaic Pavement.

Mark Grand Officer's Collar Jewel

Within the worship of Thoth-Hermes, there was also a symbolism of fire and a Mystic Rite of the Flame. Ordeal by fire and water is used by Mozart in *The Magic Flute*, which refers to his experiences in 18th century Austrian Masonry, and those elements still play a part in the Initiation ritual of Scottish Rite Masonry, as practised on the Continent of Europe. The caduceus carried by Hermes-Mercury, messenger of the Gods, and referred to in connection with Hermes-Thoth, the Vizier of Osiris, is still symbolised in Masonry, notably in English Mark Masonry, in which it is the insignia of the office of Deacon.

It is interesting to note that Masonry, often considered as the successor to the Egyptian Mysteries, continues this mode of teaching through symbols and allegories.

Pythagoras

What they effectively had at Hermopolis then, was a fraternal grouping, dedicated to self-improvement through the study of the teachings of Hermes-Thoth. Beyond doubt this school had a great effect on others which followed notably the Pythagoreans and the Essenes. Pythagoras spent several years in Egypt, at Hermopolis, and later always refused to sacrifice a white bird (the ibis being a white bird and the symbol in the worship of Hermes-Thoth of purity and innocence). Indeed his very name is supposed to signify 'he who worships Ptah', another name for Hermes-Thoth. It is also worthy of note that in his society at Croton in Italy, Pythagoras also instituted a system of three degrees, or grades.

Pythagoras was born in about 580BC. Having established a community on the Greek island of Samos, he feared persecution by the tyrannical rulers there for his beliefs and moved to Italy in about 532BC. He made many converts and, as at Hermopolis, there were certainly similarities between his society at Croton and modern-day Freemasonry. There were also similarities with monasticism as practised in early Christian times, and to some extent today. Communal living and eating in mess halls, owning no property, poverty, and obedience are all features of the devout life.

Rather like Freemasonry, we see a fraternity at Croton which, whilst not apolitical and indeed eventually having an influence on the politics of the city of Croton, was to some extent rising above direct political involvement in everyday affairs. Furthermore, the society at Croton, whilst religious, was, like Masonry today, not a substitute for established religion. They had principles and tenets, embodied in oaths, which they took, and which expounded the numerical doctrines of their Master. They were sworn to secrecy, although some violated it. Also rather like Masonry, their secrets were not covert plotting and scheming, but rather things appertaining to the different stages of advancement within their society. All of it was unknown to the profane world, most was unknown to the novices and only those who had advanced to be *Illuminati* were privy to the most esoteric matters.

There was a charitable aspect to their work, and also the typical day of the Pythagoreans can to some extent be compared to a meeting of a Masonic lodge. As they went for walks in the early morning to clean their psyches ready for the philosophical tasks of the day ahead, so when we gather before the lodge opens, we are expected to realise that, for the time being, we have left the profane world and should concentrate our minds on higher things. We have a time to discharge the administrative affairs of our lodge, just as they spent time in the mornings focusing on the political and economic life of their city and their world. They shared a common meal at the end of their labours as we have our Festive Board. This latter may vary around the world as anything from a five-course meal to a burger in a bun, or even just a drink, but the principle is the same – brethren getting together after labour to 'chill out' and discuss anything pertinent, or perhaps even just get to know one another better.

It was usual for Pythagoras' followers to wear white, and Masonry also regards white as a symbol of innocence and purity. They memorised their lessons whilst walking at the end of the day, much as we learn our ritual and are exhorted to make a daily advancement in Masonic knowledge. They even had a final libation before the end of the day, rather like the Tyler's Toast!

Eleusis

Another initiatory rite of three degrees was the Eleusinian Mysteries, which were practised in Ancient Greece. Some claim that this is where we derive the word Lewis. The Mysteries were founded by Orpheus, who was said to be a reincarnation of Thoth, and the whole concept may well have been imported either from Egypt or Persia. Pythagoras' system was an offshoot of the Orphic schools, although we have seen that he was also profoundly influenced by Egyptian ideas. Orpheus was a minstrel who taught by song and gathered disciples, working on their astral and mental bodies. Eleusis maintained this tradition in ceremonial form with the addition of the legend of Demeter, Pluto and Kora or Persephone.

The story runs that Persephone (or Kora) was the daughter of Demeter (some versions say of Demeter and Zeus) and as she was gathering flowers with her friends in a meadow, the earth opened and Pluto, god of the dead, appeared and carried Persephone off to be his queen in the underworld. Holding her torch, the sorrowing Demeter looked throughout the world for her daughter and when she didn't find her she prevented the earth from bringing forth any crops. For a year no corn or anything else grew, with the result that Zeus had to step in and intervene with Pluto. The latter agreed to release her on condition that Persephone ate a pomegranate seed so that she would not be able to stay away from him permanently. So it was arranged that she should spend two-thirds (according to later authors, one-half) of every year with her mother and the heavenly gods, and should pass the rest of the year with Pluto beneath the earth. This, of course, is one of the mythical explanations for why we have summer and winter.

Although the two legends are totally dissimilar, I suppose the fact that the Eleusinian Mysteries introduced a legend into their ceremonies is a point of similarity with Masonry, given that we have the legend of Hiram Abif in our Third Degree. In both instances it is the use of a fictional symbolism, in our case to teach a moral lesson.

In the days when the Mysteries were confined to the town of Eleusis, initiation was a prerequisite to citizenship. After Eleusis was annexed to Athens, the Mysteries became available to every Athenian, and eventually to every Greek, with many famous names amongst the Greeks, such as Sophocles, and later on also Romans like Plutarch seeking initiation. By this time, a tribal rite of manhood had changed into a more social thing, which provided an opportunity, by its mystical nature, for men and women to undergo religious experiences not offered by the mainstream religions of the day. Drugs were used – notably a hallucinogenic gruel called Kykeon.

Again, there were three stages – Lesser Mysteries, Greater Mysteries and a further 'degree', known as the 'Path of Holiness' for future leaders. The Lesser Mysteries were received in Athens, but the Greater Mysteries had to be conferred in Eleusis. The Hierophant (or revealer of light) bears comparison to the Worshipful Master. Other office-bearers like the Dadouchos (Torch Bearer) and Herald still exist today in some Masonic Orders (notably the Red Cross of Constantine) and fulfil the same functions.

At Eleusis there was also a stress on communal eating and drinking, which we are used to after our Lodges today. Secrecy was of the essence and oaths were taken in the name of the Divinity which might result in a divine retribution if the trust was betrayed. In practice the betrayer would also attract the opprobrium of and be ostracised by his fellows. We maintain this in Masonry today in the First Degree where we say that such a betrayal would result in the perpetrator being *'branded as a wilfully perjured individual, void of all moral worth and totally unfit to be received into any lodge or society of men who prize honour and virtue above the external advantages of rank and fortune'*. The word 'branded' used in this sense, of course, means categorised, just as a new kind of washing powder might be branded with a certain name; it is not a statement of intention to brand in the physical sense as in some dire medieval penalty.

Punishment would also be meted out to intruders (or cowans, of whom more later), even if such intrusion was accidental or through ignorance. In Modern Masonry, the degrees of Grand Tilers of Solomon (Allied Masonic Degrees) and Select Master (Royal and Select Masters) are based on just such a circumstance.[3] If, for a moment, we consider the following passage from Hippolyto Joseph da Costa's *Sketch for the History of the Dionysian Artificers* (see below), in which he refers to the Mysteries of Eleusis, we may discover some more similarities:

'The mysteries of Eleusis, the same as those of Dionysius or Bacchus, were supposed by some to have been introduced into Greece by Orpheus: they may have come there from Egypt, but Egypt may have received them at a previous period from the Persians, and these again from the Scythians; but taking them only as we find them in Greece, we will give here an outline of their ceremonies. The aspirant for these mysteries was not admitted a candidate till he had arrived at a certain age, and particular persons were appointed to examine and prepare him for the rites of initiation.

'Those, whose conduct was found irregular, or who had been guilty of atrocious crimes, were rejected; those found worthy of admittance were then instructed by significant symbols in the principles of society.

'At the ceremony of admission into these mysteries, the candidate was first shown into a dark room, called the mystical chapel. There certain questions were put to him. When introduced, the holy book was brought forward, from between two pillars or stones; he was rewarded by the vision: a multitude of extraordinary lights were presented to him, some of which are worthy of particular remark.

'He stood on a sheep skin; the person opposite was called the revealer of sacred things and he was also clothed in a sheep skin or with a veil of purple, and on his right shoulder a mule skin spotted or variegated, representing the rays of the sun and stars. At a certain distance stood the torch-bearer, who represented the sun; and beside the altar was a third person, who represented the moon.'[4]

First of all the statement that *'The aspirant for these mysteries was not admitted a candidate till he had arrived at a certain age, and particular persons were appointed to examine and prepare him for the rites of initiation'* rings true of Masonry. We only admit mature individuals over 21 and of good character. Going on to the second paragraph we learn that *'those found worthy of admittance were then instructed by significant symbols in the principles of society'* – this sounds like a peculiar system of morality, veiled in allegory and illustrated by symbols!

The dark room called the mystical chapel may not be familiar to English Masons but, in the chapter on the First Degree we refer briefly to the Initiation ceremony in Continental European Scottish Rite Masonry in which it is a familiar concept. In the next paragraph we really are on familiar ground where da Costa says *'When introduced, the holy book was brought forward, from between two pillars or stones; he was rewarded by the vision: a multitude of extraordinary lights were presented to him, some of which are worthy of particular remark.'* This says to me that he was blindfolded, stood between two pillars and took an obligation on a holy book. On restoration to light he is shown extraordinary lights. We do not know the precise symbolism involved, but it would be fair to assume, at least to some extent, that it would be similar, if not identical, to our own.

All the things in the final paragraph are familiar to us, when you think about it. *'He stood on a sheep skin'* – the lamb has been since time immemorial the universally accepted emblem of purity and innocence – and at one time English Masonic aprons were made from sheepskin and some still are. It should be noted that the inclusion of the sheep in the Eleusinian Mysteries was also connected with the Zodiac sign of Aries which we will look at later. The candidate also wore a sheep skin and a veil of purple – the significance of that regal colour being also well known to us. The spotted or variegated mule skin we may not know about, except inasmuch as the word 'variegated' is applied in the Lecture on the First Degree Tracing Board to the Chequered Pavement in our lodges. But we are told what the mule skin symbolised *'the rays of the sun and stars'*! These are familiar decorations on Masonic ceilings.

Lastly, if we consider that the candidate is being instructed by three people, we can draw a parallel with the Master and his two Wardens because the first is the *'revealer of sacred things'*, the second represents the Sun and the third the Moon!

The Dionysian Artificers

The Dionysian Artificers are an interesting group of people who originated in mainland Greece and then colonised an area of modern Turkey which they named Ionia in honour of their homeland. The society was named after the Greek god Dionysus who was known to the Romans as Bacchus. This may bring to mind bacchanalian drinking orgies, but that was a later development. Among other things, Dionysus/Bacchus was the patron of theatres and it was the building of theatres and other edifices that was the concern of the society. They appear to have been skilled in the arts and sciences and particularly in astronomy and architecture/geometry. They, or at least their leaders, may well have received the Eleusinian Mysteries.

We do not know too much about the Dionysian Artificers because, of course, they never wrote anything down. We know that labour from the city of Tyre was used in the building of King Solomon's Temple – mainly because the Jews themselves were not particularly good at building and King Hiram of Tyre, in addition to supplying the cedars of Lebanon (an image of a cedar tree appears on the flag of Lebanon to this day), also provided much of the manpower. There is a suggestion (perhaps a way-out one) that some of these men were Dionysian Artificers – but this is a long way from being a proven fact, and even if it were, that does not establish a link with modern Freemasonry because there were no lodges in the Masonic sense in those days.

The Essenes

The Essenes lived in the Holy Land, and were known to teach morality through symbolism and to espouse such doctrines as the immortality of the soul. Sadly we know little of their actual ceremonial and the symbolism used. They came into being in around 152BC and lasted until the destruction of the Temple by the Romans under Titus in AD70 which Royal Arch Masons will know about. More has been learnt about the Essenes since the discovery of the Dead Sea Scrolls between 1947 and 1956. Their headquarters was around Qumran on the western shore of the Dead Sea, where the scrolls were found, but there were many Essenes in cities and villages all over Palestine.

I believe it is important not to go 'over the top' about possible Essene influence, which I think is more likely to have been on the monastic life, rather than on Freemasonry, with their property held in common, celibacy (to some extent anyway) and their emphasis on healing and teaching. Some have gone further and suggested that Jesus Christ was a member of the Essene Sect – a claim I find faintly ridiculous.

But what we can look at is the fact that the Essenes had a knowledge system based on the hidden mysteries of nature and science. Again, they wore white – the emblem of purity and innocence – much of the time, and we can point to other things such as the practice of the Four Cardinal Virtues and a charitable aspect in teaching and healing, if not in actually giving money. Beyond doubt the Essenes were influenced by Hermes Trismegistus and Pythagoras. There was an initiation ceremony (available only to those over 21) with an oath of secrecy strictly enforced. There were also communal meals with a form of grace being said before and after them. They made great play on entertaining guests, as we do.

They also believed in one God, Creator and Sovereign of the Universe, and that all men are equal (for which reason they kept no servants). The idea of a 'poor' candidate in a state of darkness (ignorance) could have come from this source as well as from the Apocalyptic story of the Shepherd of Hermas used in the early church, which among other things talks about the wearing of aprons as working dress, although, as we shall see later on, aprons have a much earlier origin than that.

Knights Templar

Of course, some would argue strongly that the Knights Templar who were a communal society with oaths, initiation rites and symbols not only influenced Freemasonry but were the forerunners of it. We can look, for example, at the Mosaic Pavement and note that it reflected the Beauceant standard of the Knights Templar. When the Order was suppressed, so the story goes, its substantial fleet disappeared, and it is worth noting that the anchor (see the chapter on Symbols no longer used) came into Masonry as a prominent symbol. We also know from the legend that the one country in which the suppression was ineffective was Scotland and that was where many Templars went. Indeed that fact is borne out by Templar gravestones which can still be seen in Scottish churchyards.

But I need to sound a note of caution with all these possible forerunners. As Frederick Smyth points out, the similarities are there but so are the differences, and what is lacking is any form of hard evidence. [5] And, of course, we need to remember that of all those groups mentioned only the Dionysian Artificers were actually builders!

I prefer to think of it as Masonry having been 'done before' in the form of many societies of good men that preceded it. Those of the societies (and in particular the Dionysian Artificers) who were connected with construction may well have had symbols and emblems connected with the building trade, but given that the tools used in that trade are pretty universal, is that sufficient proof that Masonry is actually a direct descendant?

Operative Masonry

Moving on a considerable number of years, Alex Horne and others have questioned whether our Operative forebears assigned any symbolism to the tools they worked with. The Old Charges which governed their trade do not mention it.

Pick and Knight go further in suggesting that there is no real evidence to suggest any descent to modern Speculative Freemasonry from the Operative practitioners sometimes claimed to be its predecessors – the Roman Collegia of Artificers, the Italian Comacine Builders or the German Steinmetzen – but point out that the last of these – the Steinmetzen (or stone-cutters) did have a 'greeting' (possibly a type of formula rather than a word, as in Scotland) and also an obligation, following which a grip was communicated and a mark chosen.[6]

Horne, in fact, quotes Knoop and Jones in *Masonic History Old and New*, saying:

> 'There is no evidence to suggest that masons themselves (i.e., operative stonemasons) moralised upon their tools. Though the Regius Poem is full of moral precepts, and the Cooke MS rather less so, in neither of these early manuscripts, nor in later versions of the MS Constitutions, those peculiarly Masonic documents written about Masons for masons, is there any sort of symbolism based upon masons' tools. Had the masons made use of such symbolism in their teachings, one would have expected some reference to it in surviving documents.'[7]

Albert Pike seems to agree with this when he says: '*The symbolism of Masonry is the soul of Masonry. Every symbol of the lodge is a religious teacher, the mute teacher also of morals and philosophy… It is not known that the original Ancient Craft Masonry had any symbols at all. If it used any they were only the actual working tools, and they had only the most trite and common explanations, if any.*[8]

There is, however, one piece of evidence of Operative moralising in the Baals Bridge Square discovered near Limerick in Ireland in 1830, and now in the possession of Ancient Union Lodge No.13, in the Province of North Munster. This has been dated at 1507 and is a mason's set square, no doubt used for checking right angles in the stones used to build the bridge. The square is engraved on both sides: on one side is '*Upon the Level by the Square*' and on the other '*I will strive to live with love and care*'. Now this points to a very definite symbolising of particular Operative working tools. The question, of course, remains: where did this form of moralising come from, how widespread was it among Operative masons and did those who contrived Speculative Masonry know about it? We may never know.

Ireland was in those days something of a backwater, geographically far removed from the great cathedral building sites of Europe, where stonemasons usually practised their art. The mason who caused his square to be incorporated into the fabric of the bridge may not, of course, have been Irish. He wrote the inscription, or had it written, in the English language (little spoken in Limerick in those days), but that was possibly so it could be read by those who found it. He may have been a journeyman mason from England just over in Ireland to build the bridge, after which he could have gone anywhere. The point I am making is that, whoever that mason was, he had been schooled in the idea that the tools he was working with had symbolic meanings.

The Baals Bridge Square

Alex Horne also quotes an author simply known as Gwyllim who wrote a treatise called *Heraldry* in 1611, in which he comments that '*the level and plumb rule denote Equity and uprightness in all our actions, which are to be levelled and rectified by the rule of reason and justice*'.[9]

So here we have clear examples of moralising and symbolising of Operative masons' working tools long before the known advent of Speculative Masonry.

Salisbury Cathedral

But there is more to it than that. If there are two things about Operative masonry that set it apart from all other trades, the first is the mobility of the craftsman and the second is the involvement in ecclesiastical building works. After he had finished working on a particular church or other building, the mason had to move on if there was no more work for him in that place. We know, for example, that in the twenty years following the Norman Conquest, no fewer than 5,000 churches were built in England, and so it went on throughout the Middle Ages. Many of them were very beautiful, particularly in places that had prospered from the wool trade, such as Kendal in Westmorland, and throughout East Anglia.

Building of churches, cathedrals, monasteries and similar establishments did not tail off until the Dissolution of the Monasteries in the 16th century. Of course, it would not just be 'new-build'; there would be maintenance work as well. For example, Salisbury Cathedral was begun on its present site in 1220 (replacing an earlier Norman cathedral at Old Sarum), but the spire was not completed until 1333 and has had to be renovated and repaired many times since. Another spire, at Ormskirk Parish Church in Lancashire, was first built in 1430, blew or fell down in 1731 and then had to be rebuilt in 1790, 1826 and 1886. So stonemasonry is an ongoing process just as Freemasonry is a progressive science. But, to get back to the point, a mason who finished work in Salisbury and then heard of new work and made his way to, say, Exeter, would be received by the lodge or guild there and would be expected to prove his competence.

York Minster

We know that such organizations existed at major ecclesiastical building sites because there are historical records at places like York Minster which show that to be the case. The lodge was initially a lean-to building at the side of the major edifice in which tools and equipment were kept

30   A Guide to Masonic Symbolism

and in which meetings could be held to discuss points relevant to the building operation. The new man had to prove he was what he said he was. Written references would not avail in an age when illiteracy was the norm and so he would have to demonstrate familiarity with the trade secrets he had begun to learn as an apprentice and of which his knowledge will have increased as he advanced in the trade. We cannot now find out what these were, because they were trade secrets never to be revealed, but if we accept that the concept of a sign, token and word must have come from somewhere, perhaps this was it.

In the course of their ecclesiastical building works, Operative masons would not only come into contact with but work in close harmony with the monks and other clergy who were based in these buildings. This would obviously mean that these ecclesiastics would try to influence the working men in moral terms and this provides a possible source of symbol moralising such as we saw with the Baals Bridge Square above. One example of this influence may be found in one of the oldest extant documents relating to Operative masonry – the Cooke Manuscript. Dated around 1425, the original manuscript is in the British Museum, but there is a copy at the Masonic Hall, Queen Street, Chester, which belongs to Cestrian Lodge No.425. Historical evidence suggests that much of the content of that manuscript comes from the Polychronicon, a history of the world in seven volumes, written by Ranulf Higden, a Benedictine monk at the Abbey of St Werburgh in Chester in the early 1300s. This certainly implies a close working relationship between the church and Operative masonry. Another obvious facet of this is, of course, the mystery plays that were regularly performed in Chester, York and other places by members of the stonemasons and other trade guilds.[10]

And then, of course, there were masons' marks. These were the means Operative masons used to mark the stones they had worked on, so as to point out to their overseer that they had done that piece of work and wanted to be paid for it. This is obviously a different kind of symbol, one used not for moralising but for the everyday function of earning one's living. Marks were obviously very useful means of identification in the days

Chester Cathedral, built on the site of the Abbey of St Werburgh

The Origins and History of Symbolism   31

Masons' Marks at Birkenhead Priory

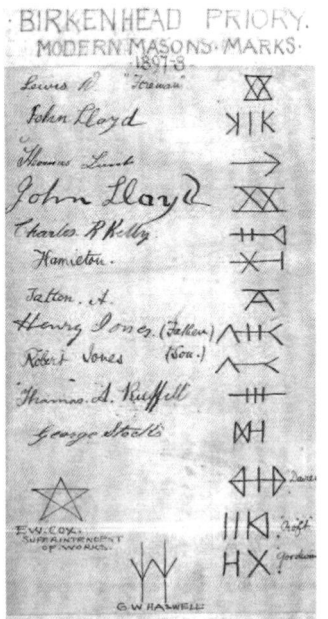

before working people would have been able to read and write, but it is interesting to note that they continued to be used long after everyone in England was required by law to have some kind of elementary education. The Priory of St James in Birkenhead, Wirral (now generally known just as Birkenhead Priory) has existed since 1150. There are few medieval masons' marks still visible, but there are plenty from the refurbishment of the building in 1898. The illustrations below show the marks – most of which are still present – and the men to whom they were assigned. It is interesting to note that the Superintendent of Works, Mr E. W. Cox, has selected the five-pointed star, which, of course, appears on the jewel worn by the Grand Master of the United Grand Lodge of England, as his personal mark.[11]

The five-pointed star is sometimes called the Pentangle and this, of course, has special significance for Speculative Masonry, as we shall see later.

What is perhaps strange is that by 1898 all of these men should have been able to read and write. Compulsory primary education was enforced by law from 1876 and so they could, presumably, have placed their names or initials on the stones. Obviously they preferred to stick to the tradition of their trade or perhaps they found marks the best way of avoiding confusion. As a matter of interest, masons were not the only trade to have a system of marks to identify who had done what. The Trade Rolls of the city of Aberdeen record that they were even used in the 14th century by bakers (then called baxters).[12]

Early Speculative Masons

In the 17th century, well before the establishment of the Premier Grand Lodge in 1717, Elias Ashmole and Sir Robert Moray became the first known Speculative Masons in England and

Operative Masons at Birkenhead Priory, 1898

Scotland respectively. Why was it that these men found themselves inclined to join a society based on a trade guild serving a trade which they had never practised?

Kirk McNulty has said that the reason Ashmole and Moray joined was because of their interest in matters Alchemical and Rosicrucian. Both were known to have been interested in Hermeticism and the Kabbala. Ashmole certainly was; he published various treatises on Alchemy, which was his passion, and there is evidence that Moray, as Master of the King's Ordinance, would have shared that interest. He was the son-in-law of Lord Balcarres who was keen on mystical matters and later became the patron of Thomas Vaughan, a well-known Rosicrucian.[13]

Later Mediaeval Hermeticism was the survivor of what we have looked at in Egypt, at Croton in Italy under Pythagoras and in Greece during pre-Christian times, and was one of the greatest intellectual movements of the Renaissance. It is thought, through the influence of men like Ashmole and Moray and others like William Schaw (author of the Schaw Statutes which governed the

Craft of Masonry in Scotland) and Alexander Seton, to have had a direct influence on the emerging science of Freemasonry.

Moray was initiated in 1641 into the Lodge of Edinburgh (Mary's Chapel) No.1. The first extant minute of that Lodge, written in 1598 some 43 years before Moray's Initiation, was about a brother being disciplined for allowing a cowan or unskilled person (possibly the origin of the word 'cowboy' when used to mean a workman whose standards are not of the highest) to work on a chimney stack. Hardly high-flying intellectual stuff, but Moray was probably nearer to Operative masonry than is immediately apparent because it was part of his job as Master of the King's Ordinance to plan and lay out army camps, with all the building work that involved.[14]

Ashmole, on the other hand, was initiated at Warrington in 1646, into an *ad-hoc* lodge formed to initiate him and another, and consisted, so far as we can tell, totally of non-Operatives, as was the Scottish lodge at Haughfoot near Galashiels which existed from 1702 to 1763. Both Ashmole and Moray later became founder members of the Royal Society. The other thing they appear to have in common is that both are recorded as attending no more than two lodge meetings during the course of their lives (although they may have attended many others which are not recorded). But what is significant about Moray is that he appears to have been the first Speculative Mason to choose a mark and that mark was the Pentangle. I wonder if Mr (or Brother) Cox, the Superintendent at Birkenhead Priory, knew that?

The reason I am asking that question (and also whether Mr Cox may have been a Freemason) is this: the five-pointed star symbolised the five extremities of the human body – the head and the four limbs, the five senses, five fingers on the hand and the Pythagorean concept of being the sum of the feminine number 2 and the masculine number 3 and therefore the Perfect Number symbolising marriage. It is also said to represent the five wounds of Christ – the crown of thorns, the nail through the feet, the two nails through the hands and the spear through the side. Going further, it has been suggested, but in no way conclusively proved, that this figure is symbolic of the Five Points of Fellowship. We will deal with the Pentagram/Pentangle more fully in the chapter on the Second Degree.

To sum up then, whilst we might not be able to pinpoint where exactly Masonic symbolism came from, it is clear that a variety of things could have influenced the framers of Freemasonry who imported it: the Egyptian Mysteries, Pythagoras, the Greek Mysteries, the Dionysian Artificers, the Essenes, the Knights Templar, Operative masons and the Rosicrucians. All of these used symbols of various sorts; many were common to more than one of them and it is therefore not surprising that we end up with a system that is *'veiled in allegory and illustrated by symbols'*.

---

1 Heike Owusu – *Symbols of Native America*
2 Julian Rees – *Through Ritual to Enlightenment*
3 C. W. Leadbeater – *Freemasonry and its Ancient Mystic Rites*
4 Hippolyto Joseph da Costa – *Sketch for the History of the Dionysian Artificers*
5 Frederick Smyth – *A Reference Book for Freemasons*
6 F. L. Pick and G. N. Knight – *The Pocket History of Freemasonry*
7 Alex Horne – *Sources of Masonic Symbolism*
8 Albert Pike – *Esoterika*
9 Horne, op. cit.
10 R. Willis and B. Dickson-Bate – *The Origins, History and Possessions of Cestrian Lodge No.425*
11 Wirral Borough Council – *Sources on Birkenhead Priory*
12 *Trade Rolls of Aberdeen – AQC 11 1888*
13 W. Kirk McNulty – *Freemasonry, Symbols, Secrets, Significance*
14 David Stevenson – *The Origin of Freemasonry*

The Symbolism of the Lodge Room

We 'adn't good regalia; An' our Lodge was old an' bare,
But we knew the Ancient Landmarks; An' we kept 'em to a hair.
RUDYARD KIPLING (1865-1936) – THE MOTHER LODGE

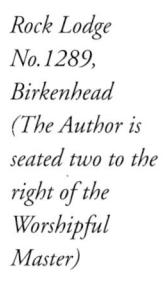

Rock Lodge No.1289, Birkenhead (The Author is seated two to the right of the Worshipful Master)

The Layout of the Temple and the General Furnishings

Before we can understand the symbolism of our ceremonies, we need to look at what is symbolic about the rooms in which we meet. Some temples may be more opulent than others, but the end result is the same.

There are certain items, all of them symbolic, which must be present in any and every lodge and these are covered in this chapter. The First Degree Tracing Board Lecture teaches that the form of the Lodge is a *parallelepipedon*, which the dictionary defines as *A prism of which each side is a parallelogram*. Going on from there, it defines a parallelogram as *A four-sided rectilinear figure with opposite sides parallel*. On that basis Dr Oliver's description of the form of the Lodge as *'an oblong square'* becomes inadequate.

Good! But, as we all know from school maths, before we can put that to the test we need to know what we are measuring. The

36   A Guide to Masonic Symbolism

First Degree Tracing Board says that the depth of our four parallelograms descends to the centre of the Earth and the height reaches to the very Heavens.

So what does the temple itself symbolise? There are three possible ways of looking at this.

Firstly, it is said to represent a stone-yard in which either biblical or the later medieval Operative stone masons would have worked. Remember that no actual cutting of stone was done at the site of King Solomon's Temple – it was all done in stone-yards and then carried into Jerusalem to be assembled without the sound of metal tools (1 Kings, Chapter 6 v.7). We know that the casting was done in the clay ground between Succoth and Zaradatha and we may assume the hewing and shaping of stones would be done in what are now referred to in Jerusalem as King Solomon's Quarries. Because our lodge has a celestial ceiling we may think of it as being under the open sky, which, of course, would have been the ceiling of these early stone yards.

Secondly, the lodge room may be said to symbolise King Solomon's Temple itself. In former times, and still today in some places, one enters a Masonic temple between two pillars, such as are described in 1 Kings, Chapter 7 vv.15-22. Wherever possible the replicas of these pillars will be placed in the west of the lodge room, but where this is not practical (in Gateshead, for example, where they are actually situated at the north-west corner) at the nearest possible point. The eastern end of the temple – the place of greatest light – symbolises the Sanctum Sanctorum or Holy of Holies – of King Solomon's Temple. It is also worth remembering that King Solomon's Temple (and indeed the Tabernacle tent before it) was in the form of a perfect cube.

Thirdly, the temple represents the sphere of the Universe. We saw above that it reaches from the centre of the Earth to the Heavens and is covered by a Celestial Canopy, representing the latter. Bro Albert Pike goes further than this in suggesting that the form of the lodge equated to the shape of the known world in those days, covering an area from Arabia in the east to the Pillars of Hercules (or Strait of Gibraltar) in the west.[1]

Gibraltar

The Symbolism of the Lodge Room 37

Directions East, North, South and West

These are crucial to the layout and understanding of what a Masonic temple is about. Primarily the direction of East represents the rising Sun, the West the setting Sun and the South the Sun at its meridian, or the noonday Sun. The Worshipful Master, of course, sits in the East, the Senior Warden in the West and the Junior Warden in the South. In the North, in the English Constitution, there is normally a table for the Treasurer and Secretary to sit, as the administrative officers of the lodge, and this is largely a matter of convenience with no symbolism implied.

In other obediences – for example, the Scottish Rite and the Rectified Scottish Rite in Continental Europe, these administrative officers sit in the East on a raised platform at the side of the Worshipful Master – usually the Treasurer is in the South East and the Secretary in the North East. There is also an additional office of Orator which is rather interesting, if only because it is proposed at the time of writing to reintroduce that office in our own Constitution. The office of Chaplain is not usual in the Scottish Rite and the Rectified Scottish Rite, but the Orator does not replace the Chaplain. He is there to instruct on points of the ceremony and to state his conclusions on the outcome of ballots etc. Potentially, I believe Orators could contribute much to the understanding of what the ceremonies are about and a far deeper knowledge of the science of Freemasonry.

In these Continental jurisdictions, the ritual is read, not recited, and it can, of course, be argued that reading and understanding is more to the point than learning by rote, because 'parrot fashion'

The Interior of the Temple at Ostend, Belgium, looking west

The Interior of the Temple at Ostend, Belgium, looking east

recitation does not convey real understanding. I realise I am on dangerous ground here, and there is obviously room for more than one sincerely-held opinion in this connection.

It is interesting to note from the photograph above, that in European obediences both Wardens sometimes sit in the West. In the 18th century, that was also the case in some places in England. We still retain this custom at our Festive Boards.

The North of the Lodge is used as a place for Entered Apprentices to sit, because it is the place of the least light.

For the same reason, few people were buried on the North side of churches. Being the place of least light, it was reserved in earlier times for the graves of suicides or unbaptised children.

A Festive Board at Kendal Masonic Hall, Cumbria

There is a further symbolism in that the East represents Wisdom; the West, Strength; and the South, Beauty. In this sense the North continues to represent Darkness. When, therefore, an Entered Apprentice is placed in the North East to hear what in some lodges is called 'The Address in the North East Corner', the position in which he is placed symbolises the fact that he has come from darkness and is aspiring towards the East, the place of greatest light.

Colin Dyer points out that the candidate's progress is gradually more towards the East. The Charge in the First Degree is given with him standing in the West alongside the Senior Warden's Pedestal, the Lecture on the Second Degree Tracing Board has him in the centre of the lodge, and the Third Degree Tracing Board is explained (in Emulation Ritual at least) with the candidate standing before the Worshipful Master's pedestal, in the East. This movement through the Degrees symbolises advancement in knowledge and the acquisition of greater light.[2]

The First Degree Tracing Board tells us that our lodges are situated due East to West and for this three reasons are assigned. Briefly these are that the Sun rises in the east, learning began in the East and spread its influence westward and that Moses was instructed to lay out the Tabernacle of the Lord in that manner and for that reason churches and other places of worship are usually so laid out.

The north side of Ormskirk Parish Church, Lancashire

The initiate enters the lodge and begins his spiritual journey in the West. To return to the

The Symbolism of the Lodge Room 39

comparison with Church practice, most baptismal fonts are situated at the West end of churches and so the West is also where we begin our journey through the Christian life.

We have to remember that our movement round the lodge, in terms of our perambulations and other 'official' movements like the conduct of ballots and the collection of alms, is usually in a clockwise direction. This is because that is the direction of the Sun, and the reasons for it are of great antiquity and far from being restricted to Freemasonry. At the Buddhist Shrine in Lhasa, Tibet, pilgrims circumambulate in a clockwise direction, and there are many other examples.

Anticlockwise movements also occur particularly when dealing with the spiritual, rather than worldly realm. In the Great Mosque at Mecca pilgrims circumambulate the Ka'aba in an anticlockwise direction. In Roman Catholic and some Anglican churches, the movement around the Stations of the Cross on Good Friday is also anticlockwise. For the reason stated of movement within the spiritual realm, movements round the temple in the Royal Order of Scotland are also made 'widdershins' or anticlockwise.

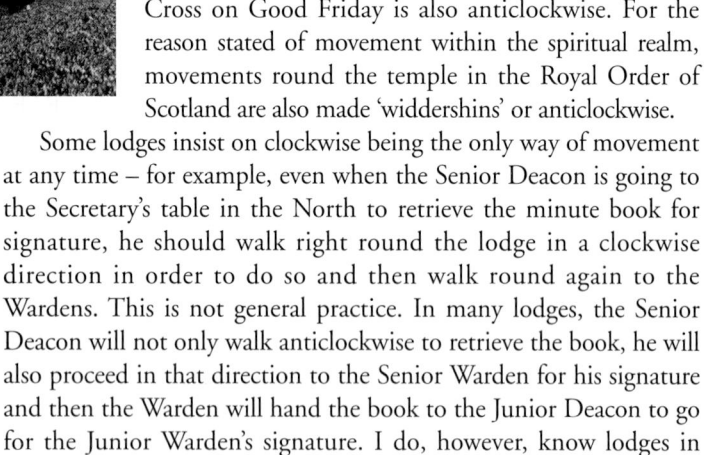

Mecca

Some lodges insist on clockwise being the only way of movement at any time – for example, even when the Senior Deacon is going to the Secretary's table in the North to retrieve the minute book for signature, he should walk right round the lodge in a clockwise direction in order to do so and then walk round again to the Wardens. This is not general practice. In many lodges, the Senior Deacon will not only walk anticlockwise to retrieve the book, he will also proceed in that direction to the Senior Warden for his signature and then the Warden will hand the book to the Junior Deacon to go for the Junior Warden's signature. I do, however, know lodges in East Lancashire where not only is every movement clockwise but as the officer, be he a Deacon or the Director of Ceremonies, who is called on to proceed round the lodge passes the Master or one of the Wardens he pauses and salutes.

Custom and practice vary considerably. In West Lancashire outgoing processions are formed so as to leave the lodge in a clockwise direction. In Cheshire they are not. Some Masonic authors have decried this adherence to 'clockwiseness' as 'tedious

40   A Guide to Masonic Symbolism

and a waste of time', but I do not feel qualified to criticise the procedure or traditions of any lodge.

That is not to say that I cannot identify anything which is palpably superfluous. A good example, taking us back to the signing of minutes, is the practice of receiving the signatures of the Wardens and then taking the book back to the Master so he can see their signatures. What is the point of that, when he has just sat and watched them do it? This I believe to be a recent development and we should get rid of it. We will consider clockwise movements again when we look at the Second Degree.

The Letter 'G'

One of the first things that strikes non-Masons when they visit a Masonic temple is the large letter 'G' often, but not always, in or suspended from the ceiling. The origin of the use of that letter is debatable. Some say it signifies 'Geometry'; indeed one of the lectures says:

Q: Why were you passed to the Second Degree?
A: For the sake of Geometry, or the fifth science.

It would appear then that the letter has more to do with the Second Degree than anything else. In Stafford Masonic Hall there is a large 'G' in the ceiling in the form of a light which is illuminated when a lodge is at labour in the Second Degree. It is also referred to in the closing of a Fellowcrafts' Lodge as the sacred symbol situated in the centre of the building.

Colin Dyer and others have noted that Greek letter 'G' is Γ (Gamma) and this is, of course, our Square. This is curious because the Square does not represent God. It represents other things which I have described elsewhere but not God. Some commentators have believed that, because the word for God only begins with the letter 'G' in Germanic languages (God, Gott, etc) that it would be meaningless in France (Dieu) or Spain (Deus). These languages evolved from Latin (Deus) and Greek (Theos).

However, Jacques Huyghebaert points out in *Reflexions Regarding The Three Pillars* that the word g-o-d is formed from the

The Ceiling of the Temple at the Masonic Hall, Gaol Square, Stafford

The Symbolism of the Lodge Room 41

initial letters of the Hebrew words *Gomer*, *Oz* and *Dabar* – meaning wisdom, strength and beauty.

The Pedestals

The pedestals used by the Worshipful Master and his Wardens are not really symbolic. They are a vestige of the large tables (usually about 5 or 6 metres long) round which the proceedings of the lodge were conducted before the Union of 1813. When these tables were dispensed with, it became convenient for the Principal Officers to have somewhere to put their gavels, papers, etc.

Having said that, most lodges today administer the Obligations of the Three Degrees with the Bible open on the Master's pedestal. The pre-Union custom was for those Obligations to be given at a separate altar in front of the Master's pedestal, so that the Master had to leave his pedestal for that purpose. This is still done in other Degrees and in Obediences abroad (see the chapter on the Symbolism of the First Degree).

The Junior Warden's Pedestal, Birkenhead Masonic Hall

The Lewis

The word 'lewis', we learn from the First Degree Tracing Board *'denotes strength and is hereby depicted by certain pieces of metal dovetailed into a stone forming a cramp, which enables the operative mason to raise great weights to certain heights with little encumbrance and fix them on their proper bases. Lewis likewise denotes the son of a Mason, his duty to his parents to bear the heat and burden of the day which they, by reason of their age, ought to be exempt from, to assist them in time of need and thereby render the closing of their days happy and comfortable.'* It goes on to say that *'his privilege for so doing is that of being made a Mason before any person however dignified'*. This in recent times has usually meant that if a member proposed his son into a lodge, the son would be initiated before and in preference to any other candidate who might be waiting to come in. I can remember in the 1970s this resulting in some lodges having three- or four-year waiting lists. Earlier on there were many examples of sons being initiated as young as 18, relying on this privilege, and it still happens in Scotland.

42   A Guide to Masonic Symbolism

Symbolically, then, the Lewis is about rendering aid and support to those less fortunate than ourselves, but Bernard Jones and W. L. Wimshurst both have an interesting theory about the derivation of the name. As we saw in the Introduction, the Ancient Greek Mystery School at Eleusis can be seen to have influenced Freemasonry in many ways. It is from the word 'Eleusis' that our Lewis is said to be derived. We will come back to the Lewis when considering the First Degree Tracing Board.

Wands

Wands are carried by the two Deacons, the Director of Ceremonies and his assistant. The ADC is a fairly recent creation (1911), but the others have a common root from the Church. Before the Union, the wands were carried by the Wardens because Deacons were not universal then, although the Antients' lodges did have them. As we have seen, after the Union of 1813, the long tables round which lodges used to meet were removed and Deacons were appointed in all lodges. The one exception to this was the Lodge of Sincerity which broke away after the Union to form its own Grand Lodge in Wigan. They came back to the fold of United Grand Lodge as Sincerity Lodge No.3677 in 1913, but in the intervening years had continued to do everything as it was done before the Union, including meeting round a 16ft table.

A Deacon fulfils the function of a messenger, which is why his jewel was formerly an image of Mercury, messenger of the Gods (see below). The Senior Deacon waits upon the Worshipful Master and the Junior Deacon waits upon the Senior Warden and between him and the Junior Warden. In former days in the Church of England there were two churchwardens, known as the Vicar's Warden and the People's Warden. They carried wands, certainly on special occasions, and the Vicar's Warden had a metal representation of a Bishop's mitre on top of his, the People's Warden's wand being similarly topped with a crown. I can remember that from my own parish church in the 1960s, but long before that time the Vicar also carried a wand as a symbol of his authority.

In Speculative Masonry, the wands carried by the Wardens passed to the Deacons, and the Master's wand passed to the Director of Ceremonies. Bro Neville Barker Cryer notes that at a Masonic Hall in Keighley one can still see clips on the Worshipful Master's pedestal where his wand was formerly secured, and that in

Selby there are batons on the Wardens' pedestals which are the remnants of the wands which they ceded to the Deacons.[3]

In considering the symbolism of wands, there are two questions to be answered. Firstly, what do the wands themselves symbolise and, secondly, what is the meaning of crossing the wands, as is done in most lodges at certain points?

The ritual itself is silent on the purpose of the wands. When investing the Deacons, the Worshipful Master simply says *'I entrust you with/place in your hand this wand as a badge of your office'*. This is because a wand has always been seen as a symbol of authority. Some Jewish legends date this association back to the Tree of Knowledge in the Garden of Eden, from which Adam cut a staff to assist him on his way into the world. From thence wands, known variously as staffs, rods, sceptres and batons have always been seen as proclaiming the holding of office, whether it be because of magical qualities such as Aaron's Rod which blossomed and bore fruit and then was laid up in the Ark of the Covenant (see the chapter on Symbols no longer used) or office-bearers such as the Gentleman Usher of the Black Rod in Parliament today.

The question of crossing the wands is a tricky one and nobody has yet come up with a categorical answer. Harry Carr in *The Freemason at Work* suggests several possibilities. Firstly, the placing of the Deacons' wands is in the form of a square so that the candidate is taking his Obligation or being prayed over within the square. Secondly, they could also be forming a triangle (the floor or the kneeling stool being the base) which is a symbol of the Deity. In some lodges, the Deacons in addition to holding their wands also join hands, which I suppose is another way of forming a triangle. I have seen instances of the Director of Ceremonies joining in so that there are three wands poised over the candidate. Finally, those who claim a pedigree from the Knights Templar would perhaps see a link to the Arch of Steel, formed in that Degree and also in the Order of the Secret Monitor which resembles a double line of swords, as seen at military weddings. Indeed Carr points out that a French exposure of 1751, called *Le Maçon Démasqué*, shows a candidate being brought in under 'la voûte ferrée … des épées croisées' (a vaulted arch of swords). Some rituals in France to this day make great use of swords, with every brother (or certainly those in the front row of seats in the North and South of the temple) having access to one and rattling it at appropriate parts of the ceremony. It seems to me that the wand, in England, has now substituted for the sword and this is further borne out by the custom in some English (and Scottish) Provinces of crossing wands to form an arch under which the Master and distinguished guests enter or leave the temple.[4]

The Pillars

The nature of the pillars and their correlation with the columns is a subject that gives rise to much confusion.

In *Reflexions Regarding The Three Pillars*, Jacques Huyghebaert says this:

> '*The pillars are also said to represent our first three Most Excellent Grand Masters, Solomon King of Israel, Hiram King of Tyre and Hiram Abif. The pillar of Wisdom is said to represent Solomon King of Israel, as it was by his wisdom that the mighty edifice was erected which immortalised his name; the pillar of strength is said to represent Hiram King of Tyre, who made an agreement with King Solomon to pay the craft their wages, if any be due, that none may go away dissatisfied, harmony being the strength and support of all societies, especially of ours, and the pillar of beauty is said to represent Hiram Abif, the widow's son, who was the architect of the work, and whose duty it was to call the craft from labour to refreshment at high twelve, which is the beauty and glory of the day.*'[5]

This statement summarises the functions of the pillars today, but in former times the Wardens are known to have both sat in the West, symbolising the two great pillars at the porchway or entrance of King Solomon's Temple. We have already seen that the positions of the Wardens at our Festive Boards still reflect this arrangement. The Temple pillars are now represented by the two columns on the Wardens' pedestals (see below) but it is worth looking at this previous symbolism, which was in use in Moderns' lodges of the 18th century in which the Three Great Lights were the Sun, the Moon and the Worshipful Master. This changed, in line with former Antients' practice, at the Union of 1813 so that the Three Great Lights are now the Volume of the Sacred Law, the Square and the Compasses, whilst the Three Lesser Lights are the Sun, the Moon and the Master of the Lodge.

It is relevant to distinguish here between the pillars and the columns. Confusion might well arise because the Second Degree Tracing Board refers to what we know as the columns on the Wardens' pedestals as *'Those Pillars'*.

The Columns

We have looked at the pillars and their symbolism above; what we are considering here is something entirely different.

Jointly the Warden's columns *'point out Masonry Universal'* and were considered finished *'when the network or canopy was thrown over them'*. They were placed at the porchway or entrance as a symbol to remind the Israelites, entering the Temple, of the pillars of fire and cloud which assisted the flight of their ancestors from Egypt.

So there is joint symbolic meaning, but there is also individual meaning because the left-hand pillar symbolises Boaz, the great grandfather of David and the right-hand pillar symbolises Jachin. Jachin, by the way, was not the Assistant High Priest who officiated at the dedication of the Temple, as the ritual tells us. The Dedication was performed by King Solomon and by him alone, although contemporary records show that there was a priest called Jachin, and he was important enough to head one of the Divisions of Priests recorded in 1 Chronicles, Chapter 24. The word simply means 'to establish' as the ritual points out and is conjoined with Boaz (meaning 'in strength') to give the joint meaning stated in the ritual.

However, there is possibly also a symbolism implied from a previous age. The Jewish chronicler, Flavius Josephus, tells of two pillars erected by Enoch – 'the seventh from Adam' – on which were engraved all the knowledge of the arts and sciences extant in his time.

In *Jewish Antiquities*, Josephus says this: *'Upon Adam's prediction that the world was to be destroyed at one time by the force of fire, and at another time by the violence and quality of water, they made two pillars; the one of brick and the other of stone: they inscribed their discoveries on them both, that in case the pillar of brick should be destroyed by flood, the pillar of stone might remain and exhibit those discoveries to mankind; and also inform them that there was a pillar of brick erected by them. Now this remains in the land of Siriad to this day.'* [6]

Josephus was born in AD37; the date of his death is not known for certain but it is obviously some time after he published *Jewish Antiquities* in AD93-4. What he seems to be implying here is that the pillar of brick was destroyed in Noah's Flood and that the pillar of stone alone remained in Siriad. This is borne out by the use of the words 'this remains', rather than 'these remain'.

So where does this leave us with the pillars of King Solomon's Temple? Quite simply by the fact that the concept of two pillars was established in Jewish folklore it is perhaps not too fanciful to suggest that instead of (or perhaps as well as) representing the pillars of fire and cloud in Egypt, they also brought to mind the earlier pillars erected by Enoch.

The ritual claims those pillars housed the 'Constitutional Rolls' (a claim which some scholars have described as ridiculous), but does not elaborate further. This to my mind is possibly a confusion on the part of the compilers of our ritual. However, I suppose it could be some sort of mistranslation or veiled reference to the knowledge of the arts and sciences engraved on Enoch's pillars. In some Masonic temples today, the Columns are placed in the West as one enters, but in others they stand at the Master's Pedestal.

The Main Temple, Birkenhead Masonic Hall

The Candles

Bernard Jones in his *Freemasons' Guide and Compendium* points out that the 18th century Grand Lodge of the Moderns (or Premier Grand Lodge) *'regarded their three big candles carried in high candlesticks as the three great lights, the purpose of which was "not only to show the due course of the sun which rises in the east, has its meridian in the south and declension in the west, but also to light men to, at and from their labour" and also to represent "the Sun, Moon and the Master of the Lodge".'*[7]

In other words, Jones is saying that the candlesticks today usually placed at the side of the Master's and Wardens' pedestals are what remains of the three pillars. Others concur in this opinion. The Antients' Grand Lodge had a different take on this regarding – as today – the Three Great Lights to be the Volume of the Sacred Law, the Square and the Compasses, and the three candles to be the Lesser Lights.

Jones thinks that towards the end of the 18th century, Moderns' lodges were beginning to follow this practice. He is

The Symbolism of the Lodge Room 47

probably right because certainly the further one got from London, and particularly in Lancashire, Moderns' lodges were adopting practices of the Antients such as working the Royal Arch, Mark and Knight Templar Degrees in their Craft Lodges. Peace and Unity Lodge No.314, at Preston in West Lancashire, lists Mark and KT equipment in its inventory even after the Union. In other words, the Moderns were behaving like Antients and adjusting their practices accordingly.

The Lodge of Promulgation, which existed between 1809 and 1811 with the remit of paving the way for the Union of 1813, effectively had the task of bargaining to see how far they had to go in accommodating Antients' practices. The fact that Moderns' lodges were now following the Antients' custom of Great and Lesser Lights would doubtless have been of persuasive effect, so that when the Lodge of Reconciliation came along after the Union to regularise the ritual, it was formally adopted.

Candles would, of course, have been necessary in 18th and 19th century lodges to provide illumination in the days before electricity, but, that aside, it is interesting to note that Scottish Rite and Rectified Scottish Rite lodges in Continental Europe have their three major candlesticks placed around the Tracing Board in the South West (representing the Sun), the North East (the Moon) and the South East (the Master of the Lodge).

The Regalia and Jewels of the Lodge
APRONS AND COLLARS

Aprons
Aprons were known in ancient Egypt and in Mexico. Given that Adam and Eve made aprons out of fig leaves to preserve their dignity when they realised they were naked, I suppose the apron could be considered the oldest garment in the world. Since 1814 we have standardised our aprons in England, and lodges under the Grand Lodge of Ireland also have a standard apron which changes only by the addition of gold braid for holders of Grand and Provincial Grand rank – the main body of it remains light blue. In Scotland, however, each lodge has its own regalia which leads to some very colourful assemblies.

The first apron we receive as Freemasons is that of the Entered Apprentice at our Initiation. It is plain white and tied with apron strings. In some lodges, the top flap is lifted up. The apron is made from the skin of a lamb and we are taught that there is great symbolism attached to both the lamb itself and the colour white.

As we progress to the Degree of a Fellowcraft the apron acquires two rosettes, symbolising the fact that it was once folded up and held by buttons.

In the Third or Master Mason Degree, a further rosette and a border of light blue appears, together with two sets of silver tassels. Harry Carr claimed that the old way of tying apron strings was to gather them at the front so the ends of the strings hung down. This, Carr says, together with the ornamental fringe customary on 18th century aprons, was the 'ancestor' of today's tassels. There are, of course, seven tassels on each hanging, but we will consider the symbolism of the number seven later.[8]

The Entered Apprentice and Fellowcraft aprons are normally loaned to us by our lodge as we progress through the Degrees. When we become Master Masons, however, we are expected to buy our own (unless we are lucky enough to be given one). At this stage the apron strings disappear and are replaced by a webbing belt, fastened by a representation of a snake biting its tail. Now, those of us who are old enough will remember, as boys, wearing snake belts and not giving them a second thought. But the snake, or serpent, is a symbol of wisdom – the wisdom we are acquiring as we gain more and more light in Masonry.

Early Scottish Aprons

When we are Installed as Worshipful Master of our lodge, the rosettes change to levels. Many commentators have declined to speculate on what the levels mean. One possible explanation can be had by looking at the position of the Wardens' columns. When the Lodge is open the Senior Warden's column is placed in an erect position, but the Junior Warden's column is lowered. It has been suggested that the level signifies the juxtaposing of these two columns, giving us the apron level.

If we are lucky enough to attain to Metropolitan, Provincial or District Grand rank – or indeed Grand Lodge rank – the outer border of our apron changes to Garter Blue (except, of course, for Grand and Provincial Grand Stewards, whose outer border is red). The tassels become gold. Why are there all these different colours, especially

The Symbolism of the Lodge Room   49

An 18th Century Masonic Apron before standardisation in 1814 (Photograph reproduced courtesy of the Library & Museum of the United Grand Lodge of England)

when one also remembers that the Scottish Grand and Provincial regalia has a green outer border and in Ireland that border is light blue and gold?

To start off with the English aprons: originally they were all completely white. The light blue adopted was the then colour of the Order of the Garter, which changed in around 1745 to what we now know as Garter Blue. The red of the Grand Stewards is taken from the Order of the Bath. The Scottish Green corresponds to the colour of the Order of the Thistle (and some say the House of Stuart) and the Irish to the Order of St Patrick, instituted in 1788.

We are taught that whatever the outer colour, and whatever the badge or emblem of rank shown on the skin, the skin itself remains the white skin of a lamb. Even in the 18th century, when brethren made their own aprons, often richly decorated with various Masonic symbols, the basic colour was still always white.

But there is also a deeper meaning: if we look at the apron we see that it consists of two triangles, the one made by the flap and the other by the triangle of the three rosettes or levels. These triangles symbolise the inter-penetration of two of the four elements of the Universe. This is a complicated concept so let me explain that these four elements are earth, fire, air and water. In this instance we are concerned with two of them – fire and water. So we have fire (the triangle of rosettes or levels) penetrating water (the triangle of the flap), but what does this mean? Fire is the symbol of the Divine Spark and water symbolises the soul of man.

Then we have a further symbolism in that the two triangles are contained in a square – the symbol of matter. So, within the matter of the human body the Divine Spark has penetrated the human soul. In the case of the Entered Apprentice this has only begun to happen so the flap of the First Degree apron used to be

50 A Guide to Masonic Symbolism

always turned up (it still is in some lodges) to indicate this. The Entered Apprentice has no rosettes on his apron, so the flap has nothing yet to penetrate. With the Fellowcraft some progress had been made because Masonry is a progressive science and so his apron has two rosettes. The Fellowcraft apron has the flap turned down, but the triangle of the Divine Spark has yet to attain its fullness. This shows that wisdom has started to penetrate and that body and soul are in unison, so all that is lacking is spirit.

It is only in the Master Mason Degree (and this is one reason why Wimshurst should have described the Third Degree as the true initiation – see elsewhere) that the two triangles become complete and the true union of body, soul and spirit is achieved.[9]

Collars

In the chapter on the First Degree, I cover the significance of the cable tow. Some have suggested that it represents a halter placed round the neck of slaves and prisoners, symbolising that the candidate is enslaved to the outside world. When he receives light, that cable tow may be dispensed with. It is also thought that the collars worn by Masons remind them of the cable tow that they wore when they came into Masonry for the first time.

Collars also vary with the rank of the wearer. The only collar an Entered Apprentice, Fellowcraft or Master Mason will wear is a lodge officer's collar to denote his position in the lodge. Some lodges still insist that nobody should hold even the office of Steward (normally the lowest in the lodge) before he has received the Third, or Master Mason, Degree. Even the Worshipful Master of a lodge only wears a lodge officer's collar, for indeed he is still an officer of the lodge, albeit the principal one.

A Craft Past Master's Collar

A Past Master will wear a light blue collar with a silver stripe running down the middle. From this he will suspend his Past Master's collar jewel of the 47th Problem of the Book of Euclid (see below). Provincial, Metropolitan and District officers wear a collar of Garter Blue, bordered with gold Masonic lace. Grand

Officers' collars are similar (all collars are 4in wide) but have the additional symbolism of ears of corn and acacia, which are dealt with in the chapters on the Second and Third Degrees.

The Lodge Officers' Jewels

Most of these can be seen merely as emblems of the office concerned, but in some cases there is symbolism behind them which deserves examination. The names of our officers weren't invented by us. City livery companies had Wardens, as did Operative guilds and synagogues. Deacons are known in some churches and the various Trade Incorporations in the City of Glasgow are headed by Deacons. Many other officers' titles – secretary, treasurer, almoner, etc – can be found in a multitude of organizations. In an earlier chapter, I pointed out that the officers' jewels are emblems of their office and where the emblem on a jewel also signifies something else (for example, the Square which also functions as one of the Three Great Lights and as a Working Tool), I have directed the reader to the longer explanation in the interests of time and space.

The Worshipful Master
the Square

See below –
The Moveable Jewels of the Lodge

The Past Master
the 47th Proposition of the Book of Euclid

The 47th Proposition states: 'In a right-angled triangle the sum of the squares of the base and perpendicular is equal to the square of the hypotenuse – i.e. the line that connects the other two sides'.

Well, we learnt this at school but knew it then as Pythagoras' Theorem, and indeed it was Pythagoras who made the discovery and was so conscious of its significance that he sacrificed a hundred oxen to celebrate it! From the point of view of the builder it does represent a good way of checking whether a corner is square or not but it is also the foundation of the geometry of right-angled triangles.

Harry Carr in *The Freemason at Work* points

out that although the 47th Problem was known in the early days of the Premier Grand Lodge, it was not formally adopted as the Past Master's Jewel until after the Union of 1813, when the 1815 edition of the Book of Constitutions stipulated it as the correct jewel to be worn by a Past Master. Before that time Past Masters wore a variation of a jewel showing a pair of compasses mounted on a segment of a circle with an irradiated sun in the centre. I say a variation because some of those jewels also had a square beneath the compasses and others had emblems associated with the Royal Arch Degree, then frequently worked in Craft Lodges.[10]

The 47th Problem, although contrived by Pythagoras, was incorporated in the 1st Book of Euclid (who lived about 200 years after Pythagoras). It is suspended from a square, which we will consider later, but it is worth recording here that some squares are shorter on one side than on the other. This is because the theorem is solved by having a square with sides 3cm (or inches) and 4cm long. Between the two points is the hypotenuse which will then be 5cm long. So we have the square of the shortest side – 3 x 3 = 9cm^2 – added to the square of the other arm of the square – 4 x 4 = 16cm^2 – equalling the square on the hypotenuse – 5 x 5 = 25cm^2 and Bro Pythagoras is proved. It is sometimes called 'the Egyptian string trick' because the Egyptians used to create right-angles when measuring their fields after the Nile had flooded, washing out their boundary markers. Pythagoras, having studied in Egypt, probably began his interest in right-angles there.[11]

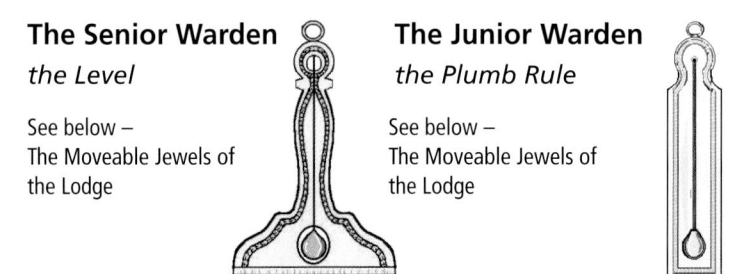

The Senior Warden
the Level

See below –
The Moveable Jewels of the Lodge

The Junior Warden
the Plumb Rule

See below –
The Moveable Jewels of the Lodge

The Chaplain –
the Open Book

The book is, of course, the Volume of the Sacred Law, with all the symbolism that entails (see below – The Furniture of the Lodge). It is interesting to note that, on the Chaplain's collar jewel, the book is mounted on a triangle, which we will look at in a moment, and then on a Blazing Star (see below – The Ornaments of the Lodge) and the only other jewel to be so mounted is that of the Most Worshipful Grand Master, although as I mentioned in the section on the Past Master's jewel above, those jewels before the Union also featured the Blazing Star. The triangle on which the Chaplain's book is mounted is a symbol of the deity – as we have already seen.

The Treasurer
a Key

No address is given to the Treasurer when he is invested at the Lodge Installation. His duties are not further explained, as being fairly obvious, so we presume no further symbolism is implied other than that he should keep his money under lock and key!

The Secretary
Crossed Pens

A similar principle applies here. The jewel merely denotes the duty of the Secretary to record the proceedings and maintain records.

The Director of Ceremonies
Crossed Wands

We have dealt with the symbolism of wands elsewhere, but it is interesting to note that, in some lodges, when wands are being crossed over the head of the candidate, the Director of Ceremonies also holds his wand, forming a three-way arch. This is custom and practice in some places, but the reason for it is not known.

The office of Director of Ceremonies has been recognised as an Additional Office only since 1884 (although the appointment of a Master of Ceremonies was allowed from 1841). Having been a Director of Ceremonies in many Orders and for many years, I am left to wonder who people blamed for everything before that time!

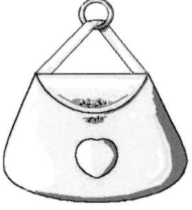

The Almoner
a Purse

Like the Treasurer and Secretary, no symbolism seems to be implied here. There is no address to the Almoner at the

54 A Guide to Masonic Symbolism

Installation, and the purse seems to signify no more than a container for the largesse he will hopefully be able to dispense amongst needy cases.

The Charity Steward
the Trowel
This is one emblem which could be described as truly symbolic. The builder's trowel spreads the cement which holds the building together and so the Charity Steward's trowel is to spread the 'cement' of kindness and brotherly love linking *'separate minds and separate interests that, like the radii of a circle which extend from the centre to every part of the circumference, the principle of universal benevolence may be diffused to every member of the community'*.

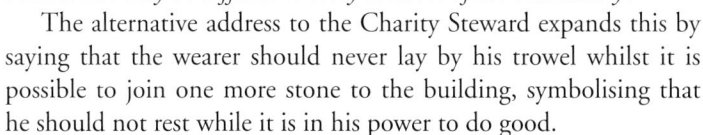

The alternative address to the Charity Steward expands this by saying that the wearer should never lay by his trowel whilst it is possible to join one more stone to the building, symbolising that he should not rest while it is in his power to do good.

The Deacons
the Dove
The Dove is another post-Union innovation. Prior to 1813, not all lodges had Deacons. They were more common among lodges working under the Athol or Antient Grand Lodge than among those owing allegiance to the Moderns. The common symbol for a Deacon before 1813 was the figure of Mercury, messenger to the Gods, which is still used by Deacons in the Mark Degree. Known in Greek as the *Kerykeion*, the caduceus is is a winged staff entwined by twin serpents and is known in many cultures as a symbol of harmony and balance.

So why the dove? Remembering the story of Noah, after forty days and forty nights, a raven was sent out to see if it could find dry land. It never returned. Next a dove was despatched and returned bearing an olive branch in its beak: a message or, if you like, a symbol that the waters had abated. In this sense the dove was a faithful messenger, as the deacon should be.

The Dove does have other symbolic meanings – purity, fidelity, chastity (see the Broken Column below) and timidity and, of course, the Holy Spirit descending on Christ at His Baptism. In Cyprus on the day of τα φοτα (Ta Fota) or Epiphany there is a ceremony where a Bishop or Archbishop throws his cross into the sea and young men dive in to attempt to retrieve it, bringing them good luck for the year if they succeed. I understand this was once tried at Brighton and the cross was never found! Two white doves are released in Cyprus to symbolise the Holy Spirit.

For Protestants, the dove symbolises the Holy Spirit, to the Jews peace. On gravestones, where doves appear, a dove ascending to heaven is transporting the soul, a sitting dove is guarding the soul, and a dove descending from heaven is an assurance of a passage to heaven.

The Organist
the Lyre

The lyre is something of an unexpected symbol. One might be excused for thinking that, as a musical instrument, it would be no more than a convenient emblem to denote a musician (even though in these days when Organists are not plentiful, the lodge Organist may be doing little more than pushing buttons on a CD player). However, music is one of the Seven Liberal Arts and Sciences which we look at in our consideration of the Second Degree and has been defined as the '*Concord of sweet sounds*'. The lyre is a symbol of the Concord, more usually described as harmony, which is an essential feature of our lodges and which none may disturb with impunity, and we are taught from the beginning that we must either settle our differences with others or not sit in a lodge with them if to do so would disturb that harmony.

The Inner Guard
Crossed Swords

There is more symbolism in the duties of the Inner Guard, particularly in the admission of candidates, than in the office itself which, as Harry Carr points out, is of comparatively recent origin, having only been introduced after the Union of 1813. For that reason one would think that the only reason the Inner Guard has crossed swords is because the Tyler has only one!

The Stewards
the Cornucopia

The cornucopia is the symbol of plenty (in Latin it means 'horn of plenty'). It is in the form of a spiral-shaped basket laden with fruit. Its

56 A Guide to Masonic Symbolism

origin is probably in Greek myth: the story is told that the infant Zeus accidentally broke one of the horns off the goat that suckled him. His nurse, Amalthea, promptly filled it with an inexhaustible supply of food and drink. There is an alternative version that, as one of his 12 labours, Hercules fought Achelous with the latter in the guise of a bull, whose broken horn was filled with good things by the Naiads.

The cornucopia is also reckoned as a phallic symbol and when empty is considered feminine and receptive. It is also associated with 'Mother' Goddesses like Fortuna and Demeter, whom we looked at in connection with the Eleusinian Mysteries.[12]

Masonically, this symbol underlines the exhortation given to Stewards when they are invested at lodge Installations: *'See that the tables are properly furnished and that every Brother is suitably provided for'*. In the Province of Cumberland and Westmorland there is a Provincial Grand Stewards' lodge called *Custodes Copiae*, the meaning of which is 'Guardians of the Plenty', although it is locally and irreverently referred to as 'Custard Pie'.

A cornucopia is also the collective noun for a group of slugs, but I'm sure there cannot be any connection there!

The Tyler
the Sword

The Tyler's sword is symbolic of the sword he actually carries *'to enable him to keep off all cowans and intruders to Masonry and to suffer none to pass but such as are duly qualified'*.

In 18th century lodges, Tylers actually began by carrying swords and standing outside the inn where the meeting was being held. Because a sword is an offensive weapon some of them later exchanged the sword for the trowel, but when the arrangements were later altered so that the Tyler moved inside the building the sword was again adopted. They also wore a uniform, of which there is an excellent example in the Museum at Congleton Masonic Hall, in Cheshire.

In the pre-Union Bottomley ritual used in the Liverpool area, there is an additional clause inserted in the address given at the investiture of the Tyler at Installations:

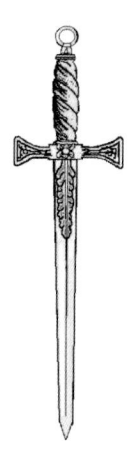

'Brethren, the sword in the hand of the Tyler teaches us to set guard upon our tongues, and place a watch at the entrance of our thoughts, thereby excluding every unqualified thought, word or deed, and endeavouring to preserve a conscience void of offence towards God and Man.'

Other Items

White Gloves

White gloves have a long history. Albert Pike notes that:

'In the continental rites of Masonry, as practised in France, in Germany, and in other countries of Europe, it is an invariable custom to present the newly-initiated candidate not only, as we do, with a white leather apron, but also with two pairs of white kid gloves, one a man's pair for himself, and the other a woman's, to be presented by him in turn to his wife or his betrothed, according to the custom of the German masons, or, according to the French, to the female whom he most esteems, which, indeed, amounts, or should amount, to the same thing.

'There is in this, of course, as there is in everything else which pertains to Freemasonry, a symbolism. The gloves given to the candidate for himself are intended to teach him that the acts of a mason should be as pure and spotless as the gloves now given to him. In the German lodges, the word used for acts is, of course, handlungen, or handlings, "the works of his hands," which makes the symbolic idea more impressive.

'Dr Robert Plott – no friend of Masonry, but still an historian of much research – says, in his Natural History of Staffordshire *that the Society of Freemasons, in his time (and he wrote in 1660), presented their candidates with gloves for themselves and their wives. This shows that the custom still preserved on the continent of Europe was formerly practised in England, although there as well as in America, it is discontinued, which is, perhaps, to be regretted.'*

But white gloves go back much further than that. There are records of gloves being presented as expensive gifts to Kings, Princes and Bishops. There was obviously the symbolism of the clean and covered hand in these presentations. It was also common to present perfumed gloves to a lady. Of course, the symbolism of throwing down a glove as a challenge to fight a duel was also well known.

Leon Zeldis notes in his essay on *The Place of Gloves in Freemasonry* that they were also used by Operative masons:

'The use of gloves by medieval masons is confirmed by documentary evidence. In the year 1322, at Ely (a cathedral city of England), the sacrist purchased gloves for the masons engaged in the "new work", and in 1456, at Eton College, five pairs of gloves were presented to the "layers" of the walls, "as custom may have required".

'Another document indicates that in Canterbury College, at Oxford, the Head Steward noted in his accounts that "twenty pence were given as glove money to all the masons occupied in rebuilding the College".

'In the year 1423 at York (England) ten pairs of gloves were supplied to the masons ("setters") with a total cost of eighteen pence.

'There are numerous reports of gloves being supplied to "hewers" and "layers" in Scotland, from 1598 to 1688.'[13]

Of course, that is not to say that the masons wore those gloves whilst engaged in their trade. We have seen that people often made a present of gloves and, in these instances, they may have given as a thank-you for doing the work, rather than as a piece of protective industrial equipment.

In early Speculative Masonry we see the use of gloves continued and when candidates joined lodges they were required to supply not just their own gloves but a pair of gloves for every member of the lodge. In 18th century France this was also applied to the wives of those members and the woman whom the candidate *'most esteems'*. To some extent this custom persists; a German-speaking lodge in Cyprus presents each initiate with a pair of white gloves – for his wife, not for himself.

Bro G. W. Speth was convinced that white gloves had been *de rigueur* from the beginning of Speculative Masonry in England.[14]

The ritual tells us that the fifteen trusty fellowcrafts who went in search of Hiram Abif were *'Ordered to attend his funeral clothed in white aprons and gloves as emblems of their innocence'* This may well be more of a reference to the symbolism of the colour white than to the gloves themselves. As Leon Zeldis points out, there is no evidence of gloves being worn in biblical times, possibly because Israel is a hot country and covering the hands might not be very comfortable.

Having said all of this, any additional symbolism, other than signifying purity and innocence, would now appear to be lost.

Breast Jewels

In the Craft it is customary to wear an optimum of two breast jewels. The most common is the Royal Arch breast jewel, signifying that the wearer is a Companion of the Holy Royal Arch (indeed if he is, he will be improperly dressed without it). The colour of the ribbon will vary according to the wearer's status in the Royal Arch: white if he is a Companion, red if he is a Principal and tricolour (dark blue, light blue and red) if he is a Grand, Metropolitan, Provincial or District Grand Officer.

A Royal Arch Breast Jewel

The other very common jewel is a Past Master's jewel from which will be suspended the 47th Problem of the Book of Euclid which is described in detail above. The jewel will also bear the name and number of the Lodge and often a depiction on an enamel plaque of the lodge logo or crest. Older lodges will have Centenary Jewels, which are of a standard pattern varying only in the name and number of the lodge and the year of Consecration. Very old lodges will add a Bicentenary bar.

Bro Tomlinson of Combermere Lodge

Many English Masons wear Charity jewels, particularly if their Province is engaged in supporting a Festival for one of the major Masonic charities. In former times many brethren who were members of different Masonic Orders wore the jewels of those Orders with their Craft regalia. The picture below of Bro Tomlinson, a member of Combermere Lodge No.605 in the Province of Cheshire, illustrates this. I should add that many of his jewels appear to be connected with various Charity Festivals, and I'm sure he was a very generous man.

This practice is no longer encouraged. However, many brethren in recent years have taken to wearing multiple lapel pins, proclaiming their membership of various Masonic Orders.

60   A Guide to Masonic Symbolism

The Forget-me-not

This little flower could, I suppose, be described as a modern Masonic symbol. Whilst some would probably say that it should not be included in a book like this, I disagree because its importance in symbolising Masonic membership has been very much to the fore since World War 2 and it is held in great affection by Freemasons throughout the world.

The following brief account of the adoption of the Forget-me-not was taken from a presentation card issued by the American Canadian Grand Lodge AF & AM within the United Grand Lodges of Germany.

Forget-me-not Flowers

'As early as the year 1934, soon after Hitler's rise to power, it became apparent that Freemasonry was in danger. In the same year the German Grand Lodge of the Sun of Bayreuth (one of the pre-war German Grand Lodges), realised the imminent problems facing them and elected to wear a little blue flower, the forget-me-not, in lieu of the traditional Square and Compasses, as a mark of identity for Masons. It was felt the new symbol would not attract attention from the Nazis, who were in the process of confiscating and appropriating Masonic Lodges and property. Masonry had gone underground and it was necessary that the Brethren have some readily recognizable means of identification.

'Throughout the entire Nazi era, a little blue flower in a lapel marked a Brother. In the Concentration Camps and the cities a little blue Forget-Me-Not distinguished the lapels of those who refused to allow the light of Masonry to be extinguished.

'In 1947 when the Grand Lodge of the Sun was reopened in Bayreuth by Past Grand Master Bayer, a little blue pin in the shape of a forget-me-not, was proposed and accepted as the official emblem of the first annual convention of those who survived the bitter years of semi-darkness, bringing the Light of Masonry once again into the Temples.

'At the first Annual Convent of the United Grand Lodges of Germany AF & AM, in 1948, the pin was adopted as an official Masonic emblem honouring those valiant Brethren who carried their work on under adverse conditions. At the Grand

Varosha, the 'Ghost Town' in Famagusta, Cyprus (It has been uninhabited and deserted since the invasion of 1974)

Masters Conference in the United States, Dr Theodore Vogel, the Grand Master of the newly formed VGLvD, AF & AM, presented one of the pins to each of the representatives of the Grand Jurisdictions with which the VGLvD, AF & AM, enjoyed fraternal relations.

'Thus did a simple flower blossom forth into a meaningful emblem of the fraternity and perhaps the most widely worn pin among Freemasons in Germany. In most of our Lodges in Germany, the forget-me-not is presented to new Master Masons, at which time its history is briefly explained.'

The flower, or badge, is now universally worn as a Masonic emblem in the coat lapel to remember all those that have suffered in the name of Freemasonry, and specifically those during the Nazi era. As a matter of interest, the forget-me-not is also the symbol of the Alzheimer's Society of Canada and the state flower of Alaska. In Cyprus it is known as a symbol of memorial of those who died in the Turkish invasion of 1974.

The Broken Column

This is another symbol which has appeared in England comparatively recently. Claimed to have been of American origin, the Broken Column is said to have been issued to Masonic widows whose husbands did not return after the American Civil War. Eventually its use became general throughout the United States and Canada.

Later, it was introduced into England by a member of the Earl of Chester Lodge No.1565 and it is intended to identify Masonic widows, especially when travelling, so that Masons who see the brooch would *'extend those courtesies which are due, along with the assistance to which she is entitled'*.

The real symbolism is of the continuing concern felt by and the honour accorded to the widow of *'a brother whose name has added lustre to the Craft'*.

The Broken Column is by no means the first symbol adopted to denote widowhood. In 17th century Holland, the tulip had that significance. The dove was once the symbol of chaste widowhood because doves do not mate again when their partner dies.

The Broken Column

62   A Guide to Masonic Symbolism

As far as I can tell, the Broken Column is one symbol peculiar to Masonry alone.

The Ornaments of the Lodge
The Mosaic Pavement
There are two derivations of the word 'Mosaic'. One implies 'derived from Moses' – so we get terms like Mosaic Law in referring to the Ten Commandments and the other God-given commands contained in the Pentateuch – the first five books of the Old Testament, also known as the Books of Moses.

In the ritual of the Royal Order of Scotland the Mosaic Pavement is said to represent the Law delivered by God to Moses on Mount Sinai. We learn that the Trestle-Board representing the Way of Salvation laid out for us in the Book of Glad Tidings will be placed on the Mosaic Pavement. The Royal Order of Scotland is, of course, a Christian Masonic Order and what is being shown here is the Christian covenant being placed on top of the earlier one made by God with Moses.

It has also been suggested that Mosaic could be derived from the Greek word *Mousa*, meaning a muse and therefore something artistic. There are nine muses who polish and adorn human nature – Calliope, Clio, Euterpe, Melpomene, Erato, Polyhymnia, Terpsichore, Urania and Thalia. This also figures because Mosaic work such as was common from Roman times is indeed artistic.

The symbolism of the Mosaic Pavement is intended to convey to us the concept of contrasts between light and darkness, good and evil, night and day, etc. As the ritual says: *'The Mosaic Pavement may justly be deemed the beautiful flooring of a Freemasons' lodge by reason of its being variegated and chequered. This points out the diversity of objects that decorate and adorn the creation – the animate as well as the inanimate parts thereof.'*

I was watching a video of the 275th Anniversary of Grand Lodge – a glittering occasion held at Earls Court which no one who was present will ever forget. My son walked into the room and, seeing the brethren moving round the chequered carpet, said: 'Ah, human chess!'

Well, strangely enough the game of chess, played normally on a board with 64 squares of variegated colours, is rich in symbolism.

The game probably originated in India and the board itself (I could write another book on the symbolic meanings of the pieces and their moves) is said to be the mandala (or symbolic design) of the Hindu goddess Siva or Shiva, which is intended to symbolise the same fundamental dualities (night and day etc) as the Mosaic or Chequered Pavement in Masonry.

Some, of course, who support the theory of an origin of Masonry from the Order of Knights Templar are quick to point out that the Templar Beauceant standard was, and is, a black and white one.

Well and good, but there is still something not quite right here. If the ceiling of the temple represents the heavens, or in other words the sky, why do we content ourselves with a Mosaic Pavement flooring? Should this not be a representation of the Earth in all its fullness, like the apron of the Order of Free Gardeners? Yes, but as we saw at the beginning of this chapter, the temple symbolises three things: the Operative masons' stoneyard, King Solomon's Temple and the Universe. The Chequered Pavement is certainly appropriate to the second of these.

Apron of the Order of Free Gardeners (Photograph reproduced courtesy of the Library & Museum of the United Grand Lodge of England)

The Blazing Star

There is more than one opinion about the significance of the Blazing Star. The First Degree Tracing Board says: *'The Blazing Star, or Glory in the Centre, refers us to the Sun, which enlightens the earth and by its benign influence dispenses its blessings to mankind in general'*. The Royal Order of Scotland sees it differently, defining the Blazing Star as representing *'The glory of God appearing on Mount Sinai at the deliverance of that (Mosaic) Law'*.

Colin Dyer quotes from John Browne's *Master Key* which came out at the turn of the 19th century. Browne was a Freemason in the Moderns' Grand Lodge and it is thought his work reflects the practice of the Moderns at that time:

64   A Guide to Masonic Symbolism

'*The Blazing Star, the Glory in the Centre, reminds us of that awful period, when the Almighty delivered the two tables of stone containing the ten commandments to his faithful servant, Moses, on Mount Sinai, when the rays of His Divine Glory shone so bright, with such refulgent splendour and unparalleled lustre, that none could behold it without fear or trembling.*

'It also reminds us of the Omnipresence of the Almighty, overshadowing us with His Divine Love and dispensing His blessings amongst us; and by being placed in the Centre, it ought also further to remind us that, wherever or however assembled, God the Overseeing Eye of Providence is always in the midst of us, overseeing all our actions and observing the secret intents and movements of our hearts.' [15]

This sentiment is, of course, reiterated in the Prayer of the Second Degree: *'Let us remember that wherever we are and whatever we do He is with us'* etc. The omnipresence of God is depicted in our lodges, these days by the letter 'G' usually situated in the ceiling of a Masonic temple. Evidence from 18th century exposures suggests that the letter 'G' then appeared on the floor within a diamond shape or within a Blazing Star. As we saw above, the Royal Order of Scotland symbolises the Blazing Star as the *'glory of God'* etc, yet the First Degree Tracing Board says: *'The Blazing Star, or Glory in the Centre, refers us to the Sun, which enlightens the earth and by its benign influence dispenses its blessings to mankind in general'*. Are we then sun-worshippers?

My own belief is that the Blazing Star was once a representation of the Divine Shekinah which appeared over the Ark of the Jewish Covenant, and that in the process of making Freemasonry amenable to men of all religions, it was written into the lectures as representing the Sun. On modern Tracing Boards, the Blazing Star appears at the top of Jacob's Ladder as a sort of bright aura.

The Indented or Tessellated Border

The First Degree Tracing Board says: *'The indented or tessellated border refers us to the planets which, in their various revolutions, form a beautiful border or skirtwork round that grand luminary the Sun, as the other does round that of a Freemasons' lodge'*. Bear in mind that the Tracing Board is a representation of the lodge and the border is

The Symbolism of the Lodge Room 65

The Indented or Tessellated Border

intended to be just what it says – a border. As far as Emulation Ritual is concerned this definition looks like it is intended to be the end of it. Indeed the Sixth Section of the First Lecture in the Emulation Book of Lectures does not define it further.

In the Royal Order of Scotland we learn that what is there called the Tasselled Border is associated with the Mosaic Pavement and the Blazing Star to portray aspects of the Law delivered by God to Moses on Mount Sinai. In this regard the Tasselled Border represents *'The ornaments of a well-spent life lived in conformity to that law'*. I am assuming 'Tasselled' and 'Tessellated' to mean the same thing here, but see below under Tassels.

The Tracing Board is a replacement for the original practice of drawing the requisite symbols on the floor of the lodge in chalk, which was done by the Tyler and is still done in some lodges in France (although there it is done by the Deacon) and then getting the candidate (be he ever so noble!) to erase them with a mop and bucket when the meeting was over. In those times the drawing would be bordered by a rope or cord with lovers' knots at intervals, known in French as 'la houpe dentelée' or a cord forming true lovers' knots, marking the boundary of the lodge board – a possible origin of the custom of 'Squaring' the lodge, so as not to step on the Tyler's handiwork!

Early First Degree Tracing Boards, like the ones painted by John Browne and Josiah Bowring, have a border that consists of such a cord with tassels at each corner. Later ones – notably by

John Harris including the Board he did for the Emulation Lodge of Improvement in 1845 which is still in wide general use today – still have the tassels, but they are attached to an indented or machicolated border.[16] The indented or tessellated border is used outside of Freemasonry – in Heraldry as a border for a shield.

The Tassels

The First Degree Tracing Board Lecture says of the Tassels:

'Pendant to the corners of the lodge are four tassels, meant to remind us of the four cardinal virtues: Temperance, Fortitude, Prudence and Justice…'

These virtues are first mentioned in the Old Testament, but why are they called cardinal? The word 'cardinal' comes from the Latin *cardo* meaning a hinge. The definition of the word in English implies 'most important', so for once it is perhaps appropriate to substitute the modern word 'pivotal' to get the sense of it.

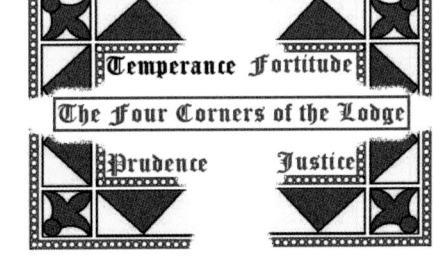

Some Masonic authors have suggested that the tassels further symbolise the four elements of earth, fire, air and water, themselves representing four spirits balancing and adjusting the affairs of man to prevent injustice.[17]

In English Masonry, the four elements are better known in the Royal Arch than in the Craft, but we will come back to them later.

'The cord surrounding the tracing board and connecting the four tassels was obvious intended to impress upon the candidate that the Lodge members surrounded and protected him while he remained within the teachings of Masonry. This cord has now disappeared from our tracing boards and Dr Oliver, who has been called the father of Masonic research, suggested that it has been replaced by the "indented skirting that surrounds the pavement" with the implication that the skirting is part of the pavement. Dr Oliver gives his opinion that this is a confusion brought about by the similarity of the words "tassel" and "tessel", this latter word meaning a small stone as indicated by the term tessellated or mosaic pavement, a pavement of small

The Symbolism of the Lodge Room 67

stones. If this idea is correct it would appear that the indented skirting is really a diagrammatic or conventionalised form of the wavy cord.'[18]

In parts of Yorkshire, and probably in many other places, there is a delightful custom of forming the 'Apprentices' Chain' at the part of the Festive Board when the health of the candidate is drunk. The brethren will form a circle, crossing their arms and swaying from side to side while the Master or a Past Master explains to the candidate that he has now become part of a Chain of Union. We will look at this again in relation to the Festive Board in the chapter on the First Degree.

The Furniture of the Lodge

The Volume of the Sacred Law

Freemasonry, as we often point out, is not a religion but is a system of morality based on *'that religion in which all men agree'*. The Sacred Volume is always open in our lodges, and although never read in open lodge, it is often quoted from. Perhaps the most substantive quote is given in some lodges in the Third Degree and is from Ecclesiastes Chapter 12, vv.1-7, describing the process of growing old.

Because we stipulate that our members must have a religion – i.e. we do not have atheists – the presence of a holy book is if course appropriate, but of all the faiths represented in Masonry, the Old Testament covers only two of them and it would be equally proper to have the Vedas or the Koran, or indeed any of half a dozen holy books of other faiths. Customarily when a candidate is initiated, passed or raised, lodges will arrange for him to take his Obligation on the book of his faith.

The ritual describes the Volume of the Sacred Law as that which *'Governs our faith'* and then more elaborately as *'That great light in Masonry which will guide you to all truth, direct your steps in the paths of happiness and point out to you the whole duty of man'*. The Emulation Lectures tell us that *'Were we as conversant in the doctrines contained in that holy book and adherent thereto ... it would bring us to Him who would not deceive us, neither will He suffer deception'*.

Of what then is the Volume of the Sacred Law symbolic? As well as being an item of the Furniture of the Lodge, it is also one of the Three Great Lights. As the Furniture of the Lodge it is described in the Lectures as being *'Derived from God to man in general'*. The use of the Bible to symbolise the sincerity and truth of the person swearing by it is, of course, well known outside Masonry, the obvious example being its use with sworn statements given in Court.

There are also instances of its use in the Old Charges of Operative masons. In the Grand Lodge Manuscript, dated 1585 and translated from the Latin:

'Then one of the elders holds out a book and he or they (that are to be sworn) shall place their hands upon it and the following precepts shall be read'. Again, in the Colne Manuscript No.1, dated around 1685: *'One if the elders taking the Bible shall hold it forth that he or they which are to be made Masons may impose and lay their right hand upon it and then the Charge shall be read'.*[19]

The term 'Three Great Lights' did not come into use in English Masonry until around 1760. By then there were two Grand Lodges in existence, as we have seen elsewhere, and the term had a different meaning within each.

Jewels

The Moveable Jewels

The moveable jewels are the Square, Level and Plumb Rule. They are said to be moveable because they are worn by the Master and his Wardens and are transferable to their successors on the night of Installation. Fine, but that only makes them emblems of the offices those brethren hold. What is the symbolism behind them?

The Square

We are looking at the Square in other places – as one of the Three Great Lights and as one of the Second Degree Working Tools, but in this instance the oldest known symbolism of the Square applies.

The Square was known to virtually all the ancient civilisations as a symbol of the Earth as opposed to the Circle, representing Heaven. Thus the Square and the Compasses combined (because compasses are used to draw circles) portrayed Heaven and Earth.

As to its use as the Master's jewel, the *Complete Dictionary of Symbols* says: '*The Square was once an emblem of the Chinese Emperors as lords of the Earth, which was conceived in Chinese cosmology as square. In more recent times, the square has become the symbol of the Lodge Master in Freemasonry, the square's right angle symbolising a Mason's duty to uphold moral righteousness, justice and truth.*'

The Level

The Level was known to the Ancient Chinese as a symbol of equality and justice and was used to represent magistrates and other pillars of the community.[20] I have referred to the Level before in connection with the inscription on the Baals Bridge Square, which shows that whilst as a practical working tool it would obviously be known to our Operative forebears, it was also symbolised by them as well.

The Extended version of the Second Degree Working Tools says: '*The level demonstrates that we are all sprung from the same stock, partakers in the same nature and sharers in the same hope and that, although distinctions among men are necessary to preserve subordination, let no eminence of situation make us forget that we are all brothers and that he who is placed on the lowest spoke of fortune's wheel is equally entitled to our regard, for a time will come, and the wisest of us know not how soon, when all distinctions among men shall cease and death, the grand leveller of human nature shall reduce us to the same state.*'

So when Bro Kipling in *The Mother Lodge* says: '*We met upon the level an' we parted on the square*' we may presume he means because we are in lodge we meet as equals and, having performed our Masonic duties, we go back into the profane world determined to uphold moral righteousness, justice and truth.

The Plumb Rule

It is interesting to note that the Plumb Rule has been associated with the Level long before any Masonic connotation that we know about, in that both were seen as the archetype of all works and the symbol of transcended knowledge. The Plumb Rule was also associated with St Thomas.[21] Unlike in Freemasonry where our symbols are explained in our lectures and elsewhere in the ritual (albeit sometimes not as comprehensively as we would like), symbols used in other connections do not have to be explained; they are merely recorded as having been symbols.

The Extended Second Degree Working Tools say that *'The infallible Plumb Rule, which like Jacob's Ladder connects heaven and earth, is the criterion of rectitude and truth. It teaches us to walk justly and uprightly before God and man, neither turning to the right nor the left from the paths of virtue, not to be an enthusiast, persecutor or slanderer of religion, neither bending towards avarice, injustice, malice, revenge nor the envy and contempt of mankind but giving up every selfish propensity which might injure others. To steer the bark of this life over the seas of passion without quitting the helm of rectitude is the highest perfection to which human nature can attain; and as the builder raises his column by the level and perpendicular, so ought every Mason to conduct himself towards this world, to observe a due medium between avarice and profusion, to hold the scales of justice with equal poise, to make his passions and prejudices coincide with the just line of his conduct and in all his pursuits to have eternity in view.'*

Wise and deep words.

The Immoveable Jewels

These are the Tracing Board and the Rough and Perfect Ashlars, which are said to lie open and immoveable in the Lodge for the brethren to moralise on.

The Tracing Board

What is a Tracing Board, other than a pictorial representation of the symbols of the Degree being worked? The ritual compares the Tracing Board to the Volume of the Sacred Law of which the First Degree Tracing Board Lecture says this: *'As the Tracing Board is for the Master to lay lines and draw designs on, the better to enable the brethren to carry on the intended structure with regularity and propriety, so the Volume of the Sacred Law may justly be deemed the Spiritual Tracing Board of the Great Architect of the Universe, in which are laid down such Divine Plans and Moral Laws that were we conversant therein and adherent thereto would lead us to an Ethereal Mansion not made with hands, eternal in the Heavens'.* I've always had a problem with this because the Master does not lay lines and draw designs on the Tracing Board. It is a finished product, lying there for anyone to look at and then explained in the course of the ceremonies and lectures.

But it was not always thus. In the 18th century the lodge board, as we have already seen, depicting the symbols of the degree being worked was physically drawn on the floor of the lodge room. The first ever reproduction of a lodge board appeared in Prichard's *'Masonry Dissected'* in 1730.

Then and even today there is no 'regulation' Tracing Board. Obviously, inappropriate symbols or those not relevant to the Degree the board is supposed to represent would be discouraged, but, aside from that, we have a free hand. In practice these days we buy our Tracing Boards and have them framed so the end result is fairly standard.

Neither is it mandatory for the Tracing Board to lie in the middle of the floor – although in most cases it does. In Barrow-in-Furness (geographically in Cumbria but Masonically in West Lancashire), for example, the Tracing Boards are on the wall: the First Degree Board behind the Junior Warden, the Second behind the Senior Warden, and the Third behind the Master. They are covered by curtains. When the lodge is opened in a particular degree, the Director of Ceremonies will go to the appropriate part of the lodge, give a court bow and the brother nearest will open the curtains and switch on a light to illuminate the board.

The Ashlars

The Rough and Perfect Ashlars represent the raw material and the finished product. The Rough Ashlar is the newly-admitted Apprentice who has little knowledge but will gradually, by improving his Masonic competence, evolve into the symbolic representation of the Perfect Ashlar.

We are taught that we are going to take a stone, rough and unhewn as it would be found in the quarry, but that is not completely true because it does have some shape; it just needs to be smoothed and formed into a perfect cube. Similarly the man who comes into Masonry is not as the ritual says *'in his infant or primitive state'*. He is a mature adult and must have something we can mould into a moral individual or (hopefully) he would not have been proposed into Masonry in the first place.

As the stonemason then chisels away at the rough ashlar, eventually producing a finished, cubic perfect ashlar, so we hope that the teachings of Masonry will operate on our candidate. There were ashlars in biblical times. They are the hewn stones referred to in the Book of Amos (although they are not actually called that in the Scriptures). Because a plumb line was used to test the squareness of the perfect ashlar the Volume of the Sacred Law is open at that Book in the Second Degree, as we shall see later.

We also come across hewn stones in the story of the construction of the Temple: *'And Solomon's builders and Hiram's builders did hew them, and the stonesquarers: so they prepared timber and stones to build the house'* (1 Kings, Chapter 5 v.18).

Mud bricks were used extensively in the Holy Land, where wood was scarce and therefore expensive. These bricks were made of mud and straw and, of course, we get the Bible story of Pharaoh refusing to provide straw to the Children of Israel to make his bricks: *'Ye shall no more give the people straw to make brick, as heretofore: let them go and gather straw for themselves'* (Exodus, Chapter 5 v.7). Once made, the bricks, which measured approximately 40cm square and 12cm high, were placed in a wood frame and left to dry in the sun. When iron tools arrived it became possible to produce dressed stone known in Hebrew as *gazits* – or in English, ashlars.

---

1 Albert Pike – *Esoterika*
2 Colin Dyer – *Symbolism in Craft Freemasonry*
3 Neville Barker Cryer – *I Just Didn't Know That*
4 Harry Carr – *The Freemason at Work*
5 Jacques Huyghebaert – *Reflexions Regarding The Three Pillars*
6 Flavius Josephus – *Jewish Antiquities* (Whiston Translation)
7 Bernard Jones – *Freemasons' Guide and Compendium*
8 Carr, op. cit.
9 Eric Place – *The Most Ancient Garment in the World*
10 Carr, op. cit.
11 David Lettelier – *The 47th Problem of Euclid*
12 J. C. Cooper – *Traditional Symbols*
13 Pike, op. cit. and Leon Zeldis – *The Place of Gloves in Freemasonry*
14 G. W. Speth – *AQC 11 1889*
15 Dyer, op. cit.
16 T. O. Haunch – *Tracing Boards, Their Development & Their Designers*
17 Charles William Leadbeater – *Hidden Life in Masonry*
18 A. H. Pullinge published in *The Tracing Board*, GRS; 1981
19 Carr, op. cit.
20 Cooper, op. cit.
21 Ibid.

The First Degree

No one can attain to truth by himself. Only by laying stone on stone with the co-operation of all, by the millions of generations from our forefather Adam to our own times, is that temple reared which is to be a worthy dwelling place of the Great God.
FROM WAR AND PEACE BY LEO NIKOLAYEVICH TOLSTOY (1828-1910)

The First Degree, or Ceremony of Initiation into Freemasonry, is the first contact we make with the Craft and its importance is therefore crucial. The ceremony obviously signifies a beginning, but it should also be thought of as a going *inwards*, in other words going below the superficial value of things into what lies behind them.

The term 'Entered Apprentice' is first heard of in Scotland in 1598 – the year of the first extant minute of The Lodge of Edinburgh (Mary's Chapel) No.1. Its first appearance in England appears to have been in Anderson's Constitutions of 1723. Dr James Anderson was, of course, a Scot; he was a Presbyterian Minister who had a church in Swallow Street, Piccadilly, and was also Chaplain to the Earl of Buchan. His father had been a member of the Lodge of Aberdeen and he may have been initiated in Scotland himself.

The symbolic importance of the First Degree lies in the fact that the candidate is leaving the profane world and entering the esoteric one. Put plainly this means that he has agreed to lay aside material things for the time he is going to be in lodge and has opened his mind to consider higher things. That is not to say he won't have already done just that in another sense. He may be a regular attender at his church, synagogue or mosque and have given considerable thought to matters spiritual. That is fine because the last thing Masonry wants to do is in any way interfere with his religious beliefs. They can be whatever they are and Masonry will do no more than complement them.

As a ceremony and as an experience, the First Degree has been described in a number of ways. It is said, in itself, to represent the physical or material being, what the philosopher Carl Jung would describe as 'individual consciousness', entering from the profane world on to the ground floor of the temple. I am not going to go too far down that route; there are far better books about Jung and his ideas than I could ever write. So, let's concentrate on the symbolic nature of the ceremony and the experience and what it teaches us.

But, first things first; we can't do anything until the lodge is open. What symbolism is involved in that? The answer is probably very little because much of the Opening is a rehearsal of where everyone sits and what they do. What turns a room, albeit a room with various special properties, into a temple is what happens at the end of the Opening. The truly symbolic aspects are the opening of the Volume of the Sacred Law and the placing of the other two Great Lights – the Square and the Compasses – upon it and the opening of the Tracing Board, which together symbolise the fact that this is now a Masonic lodge and that Heaven, in the form of the Compasses, is united with the Square of Earth. The other significant symbolic thing is the raising and lowering of the Wardens' columns. This is done to indicate which Warden is in charge of the lodge; while the brethren are working it is the Senior Warden, but once they go to refreshment the Junior Warden takes over and his column is raised, while the Senior Warden's is lowered.

By raising the Senior Warden's column we proclaim to the brethren that the lodge is at labour. When we call off or close the lodge, we are at refreshment and that period is under the supervision of the Junior Warden as the *'ostensible steward of the lodge'*, and so his column is raised. I'm afraid this is another pet hate of mine; the dictionary defines ostensible as *'Apparent, seeming or pretended'*. The Junior Warden is none of these things. He is the officer charged with superintending the brethren whilst at refreshment. He doesn't appear or seem to do that and he certainly isn't pretending to do it. Most of the people who use this inappropriate word probably do not appreciate its use in this context, so why don't we substitute the word 'chief' or 'superintending'? I'm sure there are many other words that would also suit.

In the District of Cyprus we call off at every meeting after the Degree ceremony has been worked and then call back on to complete our routine business. However, calling off is rare in some places, although it is becoming more common now because some Masonic authorities are insisting that wherever a 'Practice' ceremony (as opposed to one in which there is a real candidate) is worked, the lodge must be called off. Some years ago, I was told that the lodge I was speaking to must be called off because I was delivering a lecture on Mozart, on the basis that Mozart was not an English Freemason. Presumably that would have also applied had I been talking about Robert Burns, but not had my subject been Rudyard Kipling. Strange!

But back to the Ceremony of Initiation: the candidate, of course, is totally unprepared for any of it. He has come along to join what he has been told is a society of men dedicated to high ideals and charitable purposes. He may have read some of the excellent pamphlets and other preliminary material produced by Grand Lodge, but the manner of his preparation, his entrance into the lodge and what happens afterwards is bound to take him by surprise. He will arrive at the meeting place, usually a Masonic Hall. He will probably have been there before to be interviewed by the Lodge Committee; he may have been invited to a Ladies' Evening or Festival so he could get to know people prior to joining. Previous to that, it will have been a building he walked or drove past from time to time, with no idea what took place inside it. Now, all that is going to change.

*Kendal
Masonic Hall*

76   A Guide to Masonic Symbolism

A synopsis of the Degree can be given in sixteen separate stages, as follows:

1 The Candidate is prepared
2 The Candidate seeks admission
3 A Prayer of Dedication is said
4 The Perambulation round the Lodge
5 The Master questions the Candidate
6 The Candidate moves from West to East
7 The Obligation is taken
8 The Candidate is restored to Light
9 The Greater and Lesser Lights are revealed
10 The Candidate learns the Secrets
11 The Wardens test the Candidate
12 The Candidate receives his apron
13 The Charity address in the North East corner
14 The Working Tools are presented
15 The Charge is delivered
16 The Tracing Board is explained

Of all these things the candidate will remember very little. Indeed this may be all he sees because Freemasonry is not for everyone. Instances of people dropping out after the First Degree are mercifully rare, but it does happen – probably the best-known examples are former US President Lyndon B. Johnson and a former President of Cyprus, Tassos Papadopolous.

From my own Initiation, notwithstanding the fact that it was in 1971 and therefore a long time ago, I can particularly remember coming in, the Clothing and the Charge. That was possibly, in the case of the last two, because they were both done by the Senior Warden of the Lodge, Bro Harry Kidd, who, despite being a simple man with a great sense of humour (he was also as a matter of interest an Operative mason), took his ritual very seriously and delivered it extremely well. No, the candidate is likely to have to see the Ceremony of Initiation several times before he begins to comprehend what it is all about. To understand the process thoroughly may take years. Many lodges have small differences in the way they do things; I'm all for that, but please understand your traditions!

Find out why you do things in a particular way and pass it on to those who come after you. In one lodge I visited, as the candidate enters, someone repeatedly strikes the Rough Ashlar with a mallet and chisel. I asked what the origin of this practice was, to be told 'We don't know why we do it but we always have done'. Not really good enough that, is it? That lodge was nearly two hundred years old and the reasons for why they do things are no doubt lost in the mists of time. It may well even have been that the custom was adopted from Operative masonry to simulate the environment of a stoneyard. That is quite possible because the lodge in question met on the borders of Lancashire and Yorkshire and, as members of the Allied Masonic Degrees may recall, certain Operative traditions were imported into Masonic ceremonies in that area.

I firmly believe that we owe it to those who follow us to be able to explain the origin of customs like that because they are an essential part not just of the history of our lodge, but of Freemasonry in general. A lot of symbolism has been lost in the past and, with it, a lot of moral lessons. I have devoted a chapter at the end of this book to Symbols no longer used. When you have read it just pause and imagine how much richer our ceremonies could be if that symbolism were still woven into them at appropriate points. Let's go through the Ceremony then, following the synopsis given above. The first stage is the preparation and admission of the candidate, or initiate.

Preliminaries

The very word 'initiate' requires some consideration. It derives from the same source as initial and therefore signifies a beginning. Although Bernard Jones suggests that the first mention of the word is in the Books of the Apocrypha (*The Wisdom of Solomon*), written by a Hellenic Jew in around 50BC and translated from the Greek in the 16th century AD, we do come across it in reference to the Ancient Mysteries. It really means anyone coming into the first stage of something from the outside world.[1]

'Candidate' is another word we should consider. Coming from the same root as the word 'candid', it implies an openness and clarity of mind and a willingness to learn. In other words, here is one without knowledge, but seeking it. In Roman times, candidates for office in the Senate wore white togas and indeed the word is derived from 'being clothed in white'. We know that contestants in our elections are still known as 'candidates', although their function is vastly different from that of one seeking admission into Freemasonry.

The requirement to wear white is only generally practised today inasmuch as we still tend to wear white shirts to our meetings, but in Amphibious Lodge No.258 in the Province of Yorkshire (West Riding) and in Lord Kitchener Lodge No.3402 in the District of Cyprus, the candidate for Initiation is introduced wearing a white 'jump suit' in which he remains throughout the ceremony in the former lodge, changing whilst the lodge is being closed and then joining his new-found brethren at the Festive Board. This is a very old custom (Amphibious was founded in 1786, although the warrant was probably reissued to another group of people early in the 19th century), and there are other documented examples of candidates wearing similar attire in the 18th century.

Before the candidate is introduced – usually the month before – a ballot will have taken place. Depending on the type of ballot box used – whether it has two drawers or one – ballot balls of different colours will be used. Normally they are black and white – white to admit, black to reject – a method of voting that goes back to Roman times. As an interesting variation, Union Lodge No.129 at Kendal in the Province of Cumberland and Westmorland have balloting material which may be distinguished by shape (balls and cubes), rather than colours because they once had a blind Organist who obviously needed this facility.

The Ballot Box

Assuming the ballot proceeded in the candidate's favour, he will present himself for Initiation, having been told by his sponsors to come along in a dark suit, white shirt and black tie and that his socks should be black or of a sober colour. In other words he is dressed in the traditional English manner of dressing for a funeral. The English Constitution adheres to this practice for a reason. One sees pictures of American lodges with brethren wearing check shirts and Stetson hats and, even in Scotland, any formality in dress tends in many lodges to be confined to the office-bearers. The theme of mourning came into English Masonry in the years after World War 1, with the intention of showing respect for those who fell. This then is a modern symbolism, comparatively recently introduced.

The Candidate is Prepared

The candidate will be deprived of all money and metallic substances (keys etc), blindfolded, have his left shoe removed and replaced by a slipper and his right arm, left breast and knee made bare. From its cartoons of Masons, *Private Eye* seems to think we all dress like that for every meeting, but in fact this is the only time the candidate will be required to appear in precisely this manner.

The candidate comes into the lodge poor and penniless – just as he came into the world. He later learns a lesson about charity by recalling this fact. The lack of metallic substances is in recognition of the fact that we are commencing here to build a spiritual temple and, as at the building of King Solomon's physical Temple, *'the house, when it was in building, was built of stone made ready before it was brought thither: so that there was neither hammer nor axe nor any tool of iron heard in the house, while it was in building'* (1 Kings, Chapter 6 v.7)

The hoodwink or blindfold symbolises that we are coming from the profane world, which we now desire to leave temporarily, in order to gain knowledge. As the 18th century catechism says:

Q: Why was you hoodwink'd?
A: That my heart might conceal or conceive, before my eyes did discover.

Q: The second reason, Brother?
A: As I was in darkness at that time, I should keep all the world in darkness.

Julian Rees points out that there is nothing new in blindfolds; they were used for exactly the same purpose in the Ancient Mystery rituals of Egypt and Greece. We enter into a 'corridor' of darkness and when we have given satisfactory answers to certain questions and declared, in our Obligation, that we will live as Masons are expected to live and abide by the principles of Freemasonry, the hoodwink, or blindfold, is removed and darkness is dispersed.[2]

The slipper is thought to be derived from folklore, and particularly Scottish folklore. In Scotland it was (and perhaps still is in some places) the custom for the bridegroom to attend his wedding with his left shoe untied. Bernard Jones describes the preoccupation in Scotland for ensuring that the couple about to be married have no knots in their clothing:

The Clothing of an Initiate

'Unknotted garments and the unlatched shoe, or missing shoe, carried too much importance in ancient and medieval folklore for any other conclusion to be possible. In old Scottish days every knot in the clothing of the bride and bridegroom was carefully loosened before the wedding ceremony; afterwards, the couple separated, each with their attendants, to retie the knots, the whole company then walking round the church, carefully keeping the church walls always upon the right hand (that is, unconsciously following what their ancient forebears had thought to be the path of the sun). Knots were thought to mean danger, particularly in relation to the fruitfulness of the union of the young couple. Obviously, a later custom of the Scots bridegroom attending his wedding with the left shoe unlatched – a custom that is not yet entirely a matter of the past – is a rather less inconvenient survival of the older one, although probably all that the bridegroom knows about it now is that the unlatched shoe makes for "luck" and averts "danger".' [3]

Presumably the fact that the knots were retied after the ceremony is the origin of the euphemism 'tying the knot' in relation to getting married. There are, of course, other possible derivations. We think of Moses being told to *'Take off your sandals for the place you are standing on is holy'* (Exodus, Chapter 3 v.5). In mosques the shoes are removed before stepping on to the large, central carpet. Our lodges, as the First Degree Tracing Board points out, stand on holy ground also. However, this does not explain the Masonic procedure of removing just one shoe and then replacing it with a slipper, or as Jones points out from another 18th century catechism:

Q: What did you pay for freemasonry?
A: An old shoe, an old shoe of my mother's.[4]

In this, the *'mother'* is presumably the mother lodge, implying that lodges kept slippers, then as now, to issue to candidates.

The candidate's right arm being bare shows that he carries no weapon – either offensive or defensive. It also shows that he has come into the temple prepared to do some work. His breast being made bare some say (especially in Scotland) proves his sex, particularly when challenged by the Inner Guard with the point of a sharp instrument, but, more importantly, in exposing his heart in this manner, he symbolically displays his sincerity. The bare knee is thought to be a sign of humility. But note that it is the left knee and ask why this is. The left side of the body has always been considered the weaker. I am not sure whether it proves or disproves this thesis, but it is said that in the event of a sudden crisis, drivers of cars will always pull to the left and therefore countries like Britain and Cyprus where we drive on the left should (theoretically at least) have safer roads. Our candidate therefore takes his Obligation kneeling on his weaker side, counterbalanced by having his right hand on the Volume of the Sacred Law. It may also be noted that, throughout the ceremony, the candidate is instructed to step off with his left foot. This is a further illusion to the weakness of the left side and shows him trampling down the serpent of evil as he sets out on his journey.

Why did we adopt this mode of preparation anyway?

The first thing to note is that there is an element of mental *undressing* inherent in getting rid of the accoutrements we normally carry with us – wallets and cheque books, mobile phones, car keys – indeed all the trappings of the outside world. Having rid ourselves of these for the moment, because we have no need of them for now, we are ready to experience the spiritual enrichment of Freemasonry just as we began to experience life when we were born, bringing nothing with us into the world.

Indeed, so much importance is attached to the leaving of the profane world, albeit temporarily, that in Ancient and Accepted Scottish Rite, as practised in France under the GLNF (Grande Loge Nationale Française), the candidate is first placed in what is called a Chamber of Reflection (members of the English version of the Ancient and Accepted Rite, known commonly as the Rose Croix, will be familiar with such chambers), in which he will find things symbolic of this mortal and transitory life like a skull, a lighted candle and an hourglass. He will then be asked to answer four questions and afterwards write his last will and testament before the ceremony begins! The four questions enquire into what the candidate thinks to be man's duty to his creator, to himself, to his fellow-men and to his country. This is not a last will and testament made in the normal way, by disposing of property and leaving legacies. It is certainly not made in anticipation of his dying during the ceremony either! It is effectively a moral last will and testament which says: 'This is where I am at. I am now leaving the world of the profane in search of spiritual enlightenment. This is how I would like to be remembered and what I am seeking for the future.' Fairly obviously, the ways in which candidates handle this exercise vary considerably. When the will is written, the Inner Guard puts his sword through it and carries it in to the Master who will read it to the lodge.

Another and somewhat different version of this ceremony may be read in *War and Peace*. Reading that great novel is a mammoth task in itself, but the first few chapters of Book Five describe the hero, Pierre, being convinced that Freemasonry is for him and detail his reception into the brotherhood. The author, Leo Nikolayevich Tolstoy, was not a Mason. Freemasonry was banned in Russia by Czar Alexander I in 1822 and did not re-emerge until 1906, to be again banned by the Soviets in 1922. However, there was still interest in it among educated gentlemen (as there also was in Martinism) and the ceremony Tolstoy describes is thought to be genuine at the period which the novel is describing, which is around 1806. We will return to *War and Peace* at various points in the text to seek further guidance.

Getting back to our own ceremony, another thing the candidate will acquire (although he won't know it at the time) is a cable tow, which will be put round his neck, whilst he is in a state of darkness. The cable tow is a very ancient symbol. Regrettably, since the adjustments made to our Craft ritual after the Union of 1813, the old symbolic meaning of it within Masonry appears to be lost. Some Masonic scholars compare it with the noose or halter associated with captivity and slavery, explaining that the cable tow shackles the candidate to the outside world from which he has come in search of light. Indeed the ritual says: *'there was likewise this cable tow with a running noose about your neck'*. Given the analogy with birth we have followed, however, perhaps we could also compare the cable tow with the umbilical cord, cut when we emerge from the womb ready to go our own way into the world?

The Candidate seeks Admission

The candidate is now ready to come into the lodge and, after a final check, the Tyler will give three knocks on the door. He should do this at longer intervals between the knocks than he would simply do for something like a brother arriving late, to indicate that this is a candidate and he is now prepared. Some lodges get the Tyler to knock first and inform the Master that the candidate is now ready, upon which the Master will instruct the Inner Guard to *'let him be regularly announced'*.

The three distinct knocks, of course, have a special significance. We will look at the symbolism of the number three later, but this particular occurrence brings to mind the Christian invocation *'Ask and ye shall receive, seek and ye shall find, knock and it shall be opened unto you'*. Masonry in England was, at one time, exclusively Christian and this is one obvious remnant of that period. As Julian Rees points out, the de-Christianising process which took place in 1816 left us with a ritual containing much less spirituality than previously – effectively, as Rees puts it: *'the baby was thrown out with the bath water'*.[5]

The other thing is, as J. S. M. Ward says: *'the three separate knocks of an Entered Apprentice symbolise that in the uninitiated man, Body, Soul and Spirit are all at variance'*. We will return to this point later, but for now let's understand that the First Degree is about the body, the Second Degree is about the Soul, and the Third Degree is concerned with the Spirit.[6]

The candidate is, of course, entering at the West end of the lodge. Here we should notice another similarity with birth and with Christianity in that the baptismal fonts in most churches are found at the West end of the building. Having been vouched for at the door of the lodge, the Worshipful Master calls on the Deacons to go and collect the candidate who is first admitted in a state of darkness and led inside the porch by the Inner Guard and then tested as to whether he feels the sharp instrument (which is a dagger, known usually as a poignard) pressing against him. Having replied in the affirmative, the Inner Guard will hand him over to the Deacons, who then conduct him into the centre of the lodge at the West end.

At this point, the candidate has left the profane world and entered into the world of the initiated.

A Prayer of Dedication is said

This is quite a simple prayer, but symbolically it achieves two things. Firstly, it marks the inclusion of the candidate with the rest of the brethren, in that a prayer is being said, on his behalf, in the lodge and he is part of it. Secondly, it sets out the object of the exercise in asking that he be *'endued with the competency of Thy Divine wisdom that assisted by the secrets of our Masonic art, he may the better be enabled to unfold the mysteries of true godliness'*.

The American Bro H. L. Haywood says that the candidate is showing that he *'was prepared to voluntarily submit himself to a process whereby he became transformed from the natural state into a spiritual state. Initiation, therefore, meant the gearing of the consciousness of the candidate to a new and higher principle, the making of a new man in the sense of attaining a new method of life and a new outlook upon the universe.*

'Speaking of this process St Paul writes in his Epistle to the Ephesians: "And be renewed in the spirit of your mind; And that ye put on the new man, which after God is created in righteousness and true holiness". This process of "putting on the new man" spoken of by St Paul (Ephesians 4: vv.23-24) involves our comprehension of the esoteric or spiritual interpretation of an Immaculate Conception, or, in other words, the bringing to birth of the Divine Principle to function within the organism of the natural man.' [7]

It is interesting to pause here and think why we pray in lodge. We are not there to worship God; you go to church or whatever else your place of worship is to do that. But you don't go to Parliament to worship God either, yet each day the proceedings there start with prayers. For more or less the same purpose we invoke a blessing on our work.

Some of the language of our prayers may seem archaic. They are in part derived from the Old Charges, rules for the government of the Operative Craft of stonemasonry, dating back to the Middle Ages. The oldest one still in existence is called the Regius Poem and first appeared in 1390. That is where *So mote it be* comes from – 'mote' being an obsolete form of the verb 'may' or 'might'. The prayer in the First Degree, which we have just looked at, originally appeared in William Preston's *Illustrations of Masonry* in 1775.

It's worth noting that this prayer is not only about the First Degree. It is effectively asking God's blessing on this candidate throughout his spiritual journey and his career in Masonry. After the prayer has been said the candidate is asked in whom he puts his trust. His answer will demonstrate to the watching brethren

Praying Hands

that he is a believer in a Supreme Being. This has always been a prerequisite in English Masonry and in most other Constitutions as well. Anderson's Constitutions of 1723, based upon the Old Charges of the Craft of stonemasonry, state:

> 'A Mason is oblig'd, by his Tenure, to obey the moral Law and if he rightly understands the Art, he will never be a stupid Atheist, nor an irreligious Libertine. But though in ancient Times Masons were charg'd in every Country to be of the Religion of that Country or Nation, whatever it was, yet 'tis now thought more expedient only to oblige them to that Religion in which all Men agree, leaving their particular Opinions to themselves; that is, to be good Men and true, or Men of Honour and Honesty, by whatever Denomination or Persuasion they may be distinguish'd; whereby Masonry becomes the Centre of Union, and the Means of conciliating true Friendship among Persons that must have remain'd at a perpetual Distance.'

Obediences like the Grand Orient of France that do not require a belief in a Supreme Being are unrecognised by us. Bro Rev Harold Schieck puts this very succinctly in his article entitled *In whom do you put your trust?*

> 'Everything in Masonry has reference to God, implies God, speaks of God, and points and leads to God. Every degree, symbol, obligation, lecture, charge, finds its meaning and derives its majesty from God, the Great Architect and Master Builder of the Universe.

> 'While Masonry is religious, it is not, even in the remotest sense, a religion. Masonry has no programs. Principles unite men, political programs divide them. So we are taught to leave our opinions, creed, no confession of faith, no doctrinal statement, no theology. Masonry does not assert and does not teach that one religion is as good as another. It does not say that all religions are equal simply because men of all religions are Masons. It is precisely because we are not a religion, we can come together as men of faith. Masonry asks only if a man believes in God. If he were asked if he believed in Christ, or

Buddha, or Allah, that would be a theological test involving a particular interpretation of God. Belief in God is faith. Belief about God is theology.

'From its very beginning, Masonry has been consistent that religion and politics are not suitable subjects for consideration within the Lodge Room. Masonry believes in principles and that religion and politics should be left outside the door of the Lodge Room.' [8]

This is very sound reasoning, and I can honestly say that I have belonged to lodges with men who I got to know quite well over the years, having in many cases visited their homes and met their families as well, yet I had no idea (or interest in finding out) whether they attended a place of worship and I certainly did not know which way they voted.

Turning again to *War and Peace*, the hero, Pierre, meets a man wearing a ring with a skull on it, known in Russia at that time as an emblem of Freemasonry. The man is Joseph Alexeivich Bazdeev and he is a very senior Mason and also a Martinist. There is one problem with Pierre, which is that he is an atheist. Bazdeev tells him: *'No one can attain to truth by himself. Only by laying stone on stone with the co-operation of all, by the millions of generations from our forefather Adam to our own times, is that temple reared which is to be a worthy dwelling place of the Great God,'* and Pierre replies that he doesn't believe in God.

Pierre becomes convinced not only of the existence of God but that belief in Him and admission to Freemasonry is right for him at what is a critical time in his life. He joins. Receiving the assurance that the candidate does believe in a Supreme Being, the Master may now instruct the candidate to proceed, albeit blindfolded, around the lodge, guided by the Deacon.

The Perambulation round the lodge

The movement here, and everywhere else in the course of our ceremonies (with one notable exception), is in the direction of the Sun – in other words clockwise as should be all movement in lodge. Bernard Jones points out that it is actually a circumambulation (a walking round), as opposed to a perambulation, which is a walking through. Unfortunately perambulation has slipped into the lingua franca of English Masonry.[9]

Soon after the Deacon and the candidate have stepped off, or sometimes before they even move, the Master and Wardens will gavel and announce to the brethren that Mr So-and-so is about to pass before them to show he is properly prepared. They step off with the left foot symbolising the foot trampling the mythological serpent of evil, as we saw above.[10] During the perambulation, the candidate will knock and be admitted at the pedestals of the Junior and then the Senior Warden. This means that, in effect, he has sought admission three times. Why?

Anyone who has had the pleasure of witnessing the Greek Orthodox Easter (or *Pascha*) celebrations, which are always held at night, culminating at midnight, will have seen the priest exit the church, walk round it three times in procession, then knock on the door with the invocation *'Lift up your heads, O ye gates, that the King of Glory may come in!'*. This refers to the Risen Christ and is answered from within the church by *'Who is this King of Glory?'*, to which the priest rejoins *'The Lord God mighty in battle!'*. This is also done three times – in allusion to the Trinity – and similar things are done elsewhere in Christianity, probably giving rise to the origin of the fact that we give three knocks, three times – at the door of the lodge and then at each of the Wardens' pedestals.

The Master questions the Candidate

The three questions asked are intended to elicit from the candidate the fact that he is joining Masonry for the right reasons. Is he joining from some mercenary motive, is he genuine in his desire for knowledge and is he prepared to persevere through the Ceremony of Initiation?

Like the declaration of belief, after the prayer, and the perambulation to show correct preparation, this is a matter not of satisfying the Master who already knows that this is a genuine and properly prepared initiate, but of demonstrating these facts to the brethren of the lodge. Sometimes in our courts, judges used to ask questions, to our astonishment, like *'Who is Elvis Presley?'* or *'What is bingo?'* Now, it may well be that the judge concerned was so cocooned from the real world that he genuinely did not know what household names and everyday things were. It could also be that he was clarifying matters for members of the jury who may have been even more removed from that real world.

The Candidate moves from West to East

At the Master's command, the Senior Warden will direct the Junior Deacon to instruct the candidate to advance to the (Master's) pedestal in due form. Some distance away from that pedestal, the Deacon and the candidate will halt and then advance by three irregular steps. Symbolically this means that the candidate is taking three great and important steps towards light but, as in life, his steps will falter and be irregular as temptation and distraction lead him away from the true path. The steps are also thought by some to symbolise the three life phases of youth, manhood and old age. In the end he gets there and is in a position to signify his obedience and fealty to his Lodge, his Craft and to the principles of Freemasonry.

Ward points out that the candidate advances three steps with his feet forming a square each time and there is a fourth square on the Volume of the Sacred Law. This, he claims, shows symbolically that he seeks the god within. Perhaps I am alone in finding difficulty with this, but some symbolism is obviously intended. Another thing is that the posture of the candidate at the pedestal also comprises three squares, formed with the left arm, the left knee and the right foot – then there is again a fourth square on the Volume of the Sacred Law. It is possible that doing things in fours could allude to a number of things: the square itself, the unpronounceable name of the Hebrew God YHVH, and the Four Evangelists are examples. The Tetractys (four square base) of Pythagoras is also relevant, because it bears the column with a circle (or globe) on top that we see in the Second Degree Tracing Board. We will look at the significance of the number four when we consider the Cardinal Virtues later in this chapter.

St Paul's Lodge No.2277, Limassol, Cyprus

It is worth noting that, at one time, it was normal to have an altar for the purpose of resting the Three Great Lights and administering Obligations in the centre of the room, quite distinct from the Master's pedestal. This custom still persists in other obediences and in some places in the English Constitution as well; I have seen it in Yorkshire and also in one lodge – St Paul's No.2277 – in Cyprus, as illustrated below. The Master will leave his own

The First Degree 89

pedestal and descend into the body of the lodge to attend to anything necessary at this central altar.

The Obligation is taken

On arrival in the East, the candidate will be told what he is about to do. It will be explained that Masonry is free and requires a perfect freedom of inclination; by assenting to take the Obligation he is demonstrating again to the brethren that he has not arrived in this position as a result of any form of coercion. Having been assured that there is nothing in the Obligation inconsistent with his civil, moral or religious duties, he is also informed that its mysteries are reserved to worthy men alone and, for that reason, he must swear to keep the symbolic secrets from the eyes of the profane world. This is not as restrictive as it sounds. Any person of good character who believes in a god can join Freemasonry, if he really wants to know what it is all about. The curious but not really interested are of no consequence to us.

This is the last opportunity the candidate will get to withdraw from the proceedings. If he feels (and I've never seen it happen) that this Obligation is in some way inappropriate, he may leave at this point and nothing more will be said – we wish him well. However, after this point he is very much 'in' and the taking of the Obligation will make him a Freemason.

The Obligation will normally be taken kneeling, unless it would be inconsistent with the faith of the candidate for him to kneel and place his hand on the Scriptures. In such a case words such as *'As an Israelite, you will please be covered and stand in a posture of reverence'* are normally used and, whilst the symbolic act of kneeling to show humility and reverence for the Word of God and to display the earnestness of the candidate taking his Obligation, are replaced by him standing in a posture of reverence, there is no lessening of inherent sincerity and the candidate's religious traditions are not offended. Indeed, although again I've never seen it done, arrangements can be made to facilitate an affirmation being made by one whose faith precludes him from swearing an oath. The Society of Friends or Quakers, I am told, hold such beliefs.

The act of placing his hand (or in this Degree having his hand placed) on the Scriptures is also worth a comment. This gives rise to what is known as the 'due guard' (derived from the French 'dieu garde', meaning 'God keep') – in other words the position in which the hand was placed whilst taking the Obligation. This concept is much better known in Scotland, both as a preparatory step before giving the sign of the Degree but also as a means of covering the grip from the eyes of the profane. The due guard in England, so far as I know, is confined to only one lodge – All Souls Lodge No.170 at Weymouth in the Province of Dorset. There is though a remnant of the practice elsewhere in the English Constitution in the way we place our hands when voting to approve the minutes or the last meeting or on some other matter on which we must take a decision. Lodges working rituals other than Emulation sometimes make the sign by first extending the hand to the front (but without raising it above the shoulder because that would be offensive as resembling a Nazi salute) and this could be construed as a further remnant, but only in the First Degree. However Bro Rev Neville Barker Cryer takes a different stance and ascribes the placing of the hand when voting etc rather to the action of St Lawrence the Martyr when he stood before his accuser prior to his martyrdom, as will be familiar to members of the Allied Masonic Degrees.[11]

This seems a good place to consider at what point the Scriptures are open when we take our Obligations. There will be other points of view, but the generally accepted place is at Psalm 133, which reads as follows:

'Behold, how good and how pleasant it is for Brethren to dwell together in unity! It is like the precious ointment upon the head, that ran down upon the beard, even Aaron's beard; that went down to the skirts of his garments. As the dew of Hermon, and as the dew that descended upon the mountains of Zion; for there the Lord commanded the blessing, even life evermore.'

This is a well-known psalm, frequently sung at Masonic Church Services because it is so apt in describing the spirit of our meetings. Indeed, so well does this psalm express the fraternal spirit of Freemasonry that it crops up in other degrees – notably in the Degree of Grand High Priest in the Order of the Allied Masonic Degrees and in two places in the ritual of the Order of the Secret Monitor – to describe the excellence of the harmony of our lodges. The symbolism is clear. You (the candidate) have come among this great brotherhood, dwelling together in harmony, and now you are going to be required to pledge your loyalty and fidelity to it.

In the 18th century, in lodges of the Antients' Grand Lodge, the Scriptures were opened at the 2nd Epistle of St Peter, which describes the fact that the *'Stone the builders rejected has become the Head of the Corner'*. Familiar as this will be to Mark Masons, the stone St Peter is describing here is Christ. Some lodges today open their Volume of the Sacred Law in the First Degree at the 4th Chapter of the Book of Ruth which tells the story of Ruth and Boaz.

Referring again to the Old Charges as the source of some of our archaic language, in the Cooke MS (c.1425) we first encounter *'Hele'* and in the Edinburgh House Manuscript of 1696, where we come across *'Hele, conceal and never reveal'*. 'Hele' is another archaic English word meaning to hide or cover. God is referred to as The Great Architect of the Universe. Although this phrase was first coined in modern times by the Swiss Protestant reformer John Calvin in the 16th century, as we have already seen it was also one of the titles of the Egyptian God, Thoth. Elsewhere in the ceremony phrases like *'To God, our neighbours and ourselves'* and *'Ancient as having subsisted from Time Immemorial'* are said to come from William Smith's *Mason's Pocket Companion*, published in Dublin in 1751.

Although the Obligation is straightforward as a promise to keep the secrets from the prying eyes of the profane world, in a way not dissimilar from the manner in which Operative masons swore to protect their trade secrets centuries ago, there was until comparatively recently the addition of a physical penalty of a blood-curdling kind which, in my view, added nothing to the import of the ceremony and caused us, as a fraternity, no end of trouble. Whilst there are records of dire punishments meted out in the name of criminal justice to 15th and 16th century felons, involving tongues being cut out and bodies being buried in sand until the tide had washed over them three times etc, such penal clauses were never incorporated in trade oaths – had any group of tradesmen inflicted death on one of their number it would have been a hanging matter! Similarly, had the Society of Freemasons ever punished a perjured individual in that way, the full majesty of the law would have been invoked; one cannot go round committing murder because someone has broken the rules of the society!

Moreover we know for a fact that, in the early days, no such penal sanctions were included! Bernard Jones quotes numerous examples of oaths, but for this purpose one will suffice and it comes from the Grand Lodge MS. No.2 (date about 1650) which contains the following oath of secrecy:

> *'I, A.B., do in the presence of Almighty God and my Fellows and Brethren here present promise and declare that I will not at any time hereafter by any act or circumstance whatsoever directly or indirectly publish, discover or reveal or make known any of the secrets, privileges or counsels of the fraternity or fellowship of Freemasonry which at any time hereafter shall be made known to me. So help me God and the holy contents of this Book.'* [12]

The penalties seem to arrive in about 1730 and the brother or brethren who caused them to be introduced into Freemasonry was misguided to say the least. They were discovered and reproduced, bringing Freemasonry into contempt, not because of the inherent severity (after all, they were never carried out) but because the gullible were willing to accept that, because of some imagined privileged position, Freemasons could get away with wilful murder!

In the 18th century such extravagant language might have been the norm, but, one would have thought, by the middle of the 19th century the Craft should have dispensed with them. The revision of the ritual in 1816 (see above) would have been an excellent opportunity for this. Sadly Freemasons do not like change and, much as these penalties served no useful or symbolic purpose, they were retained under the familiar dictum of 'That's the way we've always done it'. In 1964 Bro Bishop Herbert proposed some amendments in the form of a 'Permissive Alternative' version of the Obligation whereby it could be pointed out that the penalties were merely symbolic of the fact that a Mason revealing his secrets would be held in contempt by his fellows.

Unfortunately this did not go far enough, because in the 1980s there was a lot of anti-Masonic feeling generated by people who, frankly, didn't know what they were talking about, but it did do some harm. It is as well to pass over that period because we have survived it, but those penalties were the thing that our critics homed in on every time. Mud sticks and it has to be said that we helped it to stick by not ridding ourselves of an 18th century hangover that never did us any good.

One interesting point in the concluding paragraph of the Obligation is the phrase *'without evasion, equivocation or mental reservation of any kind'*. These words also appear in the Coronation Oath sworn by British Sovereigns as follows:

> *'And I do solemnly, in the presence of God, profess, testify and declare, that I do make this declaration and every part thereof ...., without any evasion, equivocation or mental reservation whatsoever.'*

The Candidate is restored to Light

I suppose the idea of restoring light to the candidate is not so much bringing him into the light of the room in which he now finds himself among his newly acquired brethren, as bringing him into the light of Freemasonry and therefore into the light of knowledge. The darkness in which he existed previously should remind him of the darkness in which he has spent his entire life up to this time. This is the true symbolism at this point and the act of taking off the hoodwink is often accompanied with a loud noise like the clapping of hands and sometimes preceded by the Master reciting a text of Scripture from Genesis, Chapter 1: *'And the Spirit of the Lord moved over the face of the waters; and God said "Let there be light" and there was light.'*

The Greater and Lesser Lights are revealed

The first thing that is done after the restoration to light is that the Master points out what are described as the three Great, though emblematical, Lights in Freemasonry. He will go on to explain their purposes in that the Sacred Writings are to govern our faith, the Square to regulate our actions and the Compasses to keep us in due bounds with all mankind, particularly our brethren in Freemasonry.

At this point the candidate is unlikely to notice that both points of the compasses are concealed by the square. Symbolically, the Compasses and Square united represent the union of Heaven and Earth. The progressive uncovering of the Compasses revealing nothing in the First Degree, one point in the Second Degree, and both points in the Third, symbolises the gradual acquisition of knowledge, bringing us more and more towards the light.

The Lesser Lights are the Sun, the Moon and the Master of the Lodge. In pointing these out, the Master will usually ask the Wardens to stand and then point out that the Lesser Lights are situated in the East, South and West and what they are are meant to represent. This implies that the Master is representing the Sun, the Junior Warden is representing the Moon and the Senior Warden is representing the Master – and, of course, this cannot be right. Why should the Senior Warden represent the Master? A lot of confusion has been caused by this and various lodges have tried to get round the problem by a variety of devices. In some Masonic Provinces in the English Midlands when the Lesser Lights are being pointed out the Junior Deacon, for the candidate's benefit, points to the Junior Warden (Sun), Senior Warden (Moon) and the Master.

The situation is very confusing and one is led to think that something has been taken away (perhaps in the 'standardization' of the ritual in the early 19th century) that would have provided a key to it all. We say at the Opening of the Lodge when describing the positions and duties of the various officers, that the Master is placed in the East because *'As the Sun rises in the East to open and enliven the day, so the Worshipful Master is placed in the East to open his lodge and employ and instruct the brethren'*. In my Scottish Lodge we say: *'As the Sun rises in the East, so rises the Right Worshipful Master in the East'* (at which point the brethren stand).

Perhaps it would be a good idea to go back to basics and look at what we are really trying to say. We have three things which not only constitute the Three Lesser Lights but at one time were regarded as the Three GREAT Lights of a Masonic lodge. So the meaning has to be crucial, but, following the words of the ritual alone, it has become totally confused! If we take out the words *'They are situated in the East, West and South'* and concentrate on the fact that the Lights represent the Sun, Moon and the Master of the Lodge, we can think of the Junior Warden representing the SUN at its meridian, the Senior Warden closing the lodge at a time when the MOON is risen or rising, and the MASTER representing himself. This makes much more sense.

The Candidate learns the Secrets

In order to obtain the secrets of the degree the candidate is instructed to advance one pace. This, he is told, is the First Regular Step in Freemasonry. It is pointed out that all *'Squares, Levels and Perpendiculars are true and proper signs to know a Mason by'*. What is the meaning of this statement? We have already seen the importance of squares when we considered the way in which the candidate approaches the pedestal and kneels there. At this point the Master will say *'You are therefore expected to stand perfectly erect, your feet formed in a square, your body being thus considered the emblem of your mind and your feet of the rectitude of your actions'*. The Level, being an emblem of equality, shows that we are all equal when we come into Masonry. The Perpendicular, like the Plumb Rule, is an emblem of uprightness and shows that we are expected to be upright and honest in our dealings. If you like, this is an advance 'peek' at the Working Tools of the Second Degree.

What then is the purpose of secrets? Don't we get enough 'stick' about this? We are called a secret society; how can we be? Don't secret societies meet in secret places and nobody knows when? Anybody can discern the whereabouts of his local Masonic Hall from the telephone directory or the internet. In Scotland lodges advertise their meetings in the newspapers – 'Lodge So-and-so Third Degree, all welcome'. If you respond to such an advertisement, be prepared to prove yourself!

Isn't membership of secret societies something people never reveal? All my family and friends know I'm a Mason and I don't mind who else knows either. Are not the activities of secret societies covert and never revealed? There is more about the ritual, history and symbolism of Freemasonry on the internet these days than there is about most other things, so that one falls as well. It has to be said also that some Masons, when trying very hard to make a good impression on non-Masons and particularly on the media, proceed to hang themselves with remarks like *'We're not a secret society, we're a society with secrets'*. Unfortunately to the profane world that means exactly the same thing!

Our proceedings are private, but anyone of good character can join – if they're interested. We are an ancient society claiming a line of descent from the ancient craft of stonemasonry. When apprentice masons learnt their trade they were taught trade secrets. It still happens today. They are taught so much until they are ready to learn more advanced things. Similarly, we say in our First Degree Charge (see below): *'by never attempting to extort or otherwise unduly obtain the secrets of a superior degree'*.

The booklet supplied on admission to the Freedom of the City of London which is entitled *Good Advice to Apprentices; or The Covenants of the City Indenture (Familiarly Explained and Enforced By Scripture.)* from a copy dated 1863, quotes as follows:

' *"His secrets keep"* – that is he shall conceal the particular secrets of his art, trade, or science, without divulging or making any one privy to them to the detriment of his Master, whose interest may very much depend on a peculiar management and knowledge of his business. To behave thus is to serve faithfully; and fidelity is the glory and perfection of a servant, as his want of it is his greatest discredit and reproach.'[13]

When I left school a lot of my friends were 'serving their time' as apprentices to one trade or another. During the course of that apprenticeship, which usually lasted for five years then, they would gradually hone their skills by learning different aspects of their trade. There would be things they would not learn about until later in their apprenticeship. An apprentice motor mechanic, for example, might start by learning to check levels and getting to know the uses of certain tools. He would not jump straight in and start stripping down gearboxes. So some things would be learnt at the start, but others would be kept from the apprentice until time and circumstance entitled him to a participation in those secrets. That method of training young men and women happens less frequently now, but the principles of learning any job still apply.

As far as the protection of his master's secrets goes, that certainly still applies. If I got a job collecting trolleys from the car park of a major supermarket, they wouldn't thank me for telling one of their rivals which prices they had reduced that day!

We can bear this out further by looking at an ordinance of the Aberdeen Guild of Tailors dated 18 February 1678 which reads: *'It is striclie* (sic) *statute and ordained that whatever entering freeman of the Craft, or any other freeman thereof, shall anyways divulge to the Magistrate or any Burgess of Guild, directly or indirectly, any of the Craft's secrets, especially concerning their procedure when entering freeman of the trade ... shall never carry public charge among the said trade as deacon, master or box-master until they give all satisfaction for the said misdemeanour'*.[14]

The Wardens test the Candidate

Just as the Wardens tested the candidate shortly after his entrance to prove to the brethren in the lodge that he was properly prepared, so they now test his familiarity with the knowledge of the secrets that have just been imparted to him. He will, of course, be prompted by the Junior Deacon because most of what he has been told will, understandably, have gone over his head.

The Candidate receives his apron

We covered aprons in the earlier chapter on The Symbolism of the Lodge Room, but it should be emphasised here that the apron he receives will be pure white, without adornment, and in some places the flap will be turned up. This is a very old custom, harking back to Operative days and certainly to 18th century Speculative days as well. From an Operative point of view, given that the Entered Apprentice was the one who did the 'rough' work, chipping away at an ashlar to *'render it fit for the hands of the more expert workman'*, he would have a need to protect himself and his clothing by covering his chest. In the Speculative sense, the overall shape will be that of a triangle on top of a rectangle, and the symbolism implied here is that the flap is raised because the Divine Wisdom has yet to penetrate the gross matter of the body.

It is interesting to note that some old aprons had a buttonhole at the top of the flap, to allow the wearer to affix it to his waistcoat. We may also note that, in all three Degrees, the Master delegates the duty of investing the candidate with his apron to the Senior Warden, rather than doing it himself. This is said to be because the Principal Officers of the Lodge (Master, Senior and Junior Wardens) represent the body (Junior Warden), soul (Senior Warden) and spirit (Master). The soul registers the spiritual advance of the candidate and therefore the officer representing the soul is called on to mark the progress made in the science.[15]

I also tend to the belief – although because it is such an old custom, it is impossible to prove it one way or the other – that this is the reason that some lodges do not cut the sign in the Opening of any Degree until the Senior Warden has gavelled. The majority probably (and certainly those working Emulation Ritual) do it before the Master gavels, but, in the former case, it is as if we are implying that the soul has received the message from the spirit. The other thing about the Entered Apprentice apron (and also the Fellowcraft's) is that it is tied with strings, rather than a snake belt, as all aprons once were. The old custom appears to have been to tie these strings at the front, and this is said to be the origin of the tassels that adorn our aprons nowadays.[16]

The Charity address in the North East Corner

The candidate will be conducted by the Junior Deacon to the North East corner of the lodge and told to place his left foot across the lodge and his right foot down it, and to pay attention to the Worshipful Master or the brother who is about to deliver the address. In many lodges nowadays this address is being done by quite junior brethren, which is a good thing because it serves as an excellent 'test-piece' and it also confirms that those junior brethren are getting the message about the central importance of charity in Masonry. The feet formed in this position are, of course, symbolic of the Square; Ward is of the opinion that they are forming an angle clamp binding together the candidate's former life in the North with the light he seeks in the future from the East.

The candidate has been placed in the North East part of the lodge, just as foundation stones are laid at the North East corners of buildings. There is good reason for this: in the north-east they are in the Sun, which gives the builders light to work by. In a lot of lodges, particularly those working Emulation, the Ashlars are placed on the Warden's pedestals, but still in a lot of places they are on the floor, the Rough Ashlar in the North East and the Perfect Ashlar in the South East. In such cases, this means that the candidate will place his feet in a square at two sides of the Rough Ashlar in the First Degree and the Perfect Ashlar in the Second.

After this beautiful address has been given, the Worshipful Master will draw the candidate's attention to the Warrant of the Lodge, which symbolises the fact that the lodge which the candidate has now joined is recognised by the sovereign body in the country concerned – in the case of England and Wales, the United Grand Lodge of England – and is, as we say in some rituals, *'empowered to make Masons and receive fees'*. He will also receive our Book of Constitutions and a copy of the By-laws of that particular lodge, together with some sound advice on their uses.

By now the realisation is probably dawning on the candidate that he is 'in', and again, in some rituals, he will be asked if he intends to become a subscribing member of this, his Mother Lodge, to which he will almost certainly reply in the affirmative and the Secretary will be instructed to take a note of that intention. The term 'Mother Lodge' is used less in England than in Scotland, but is still known and taken to refer to the lodge in which a Mason was initiated.

The Working Tools are presented

The symbolism of the 24-inch gauge, the common gavel and the chisel is explained in the address given when the working tools of the First Degree are presented. As with all working tool addresses, the Operative uses of the tools are detailed first: *'The 24-inch gauge is to measure our work, the gavel to knock off all superfluous knobs and excrescences and the chisel to further smooth and prepare the stone to render it fit for the hands of the more expert workman'.*

Most rituals go on to explain that *'as we are not all Operative masons'* etc. I actually prefer *'as we are not* met *as Operative masons'* because some of us may well use these tools in our daily working lives or for DIY purposes. When we come into lodge, we are not doing those things; we are met as Free and Accepted or Speculative Masons and so apply these tools to our morals.

And so we are taught that the 24-inch gauge represents the 24 hours of the day. We are admonished to use them partly in prayer to Almighty God. It could certainly be argued that Masons should pray, even though prayer is a habit very easy to get out of. We have acknowledged a belief in God – otherwise we would not be Masons – and therefore prayer is surely an integral part of our duty to Him.

We will also spend part of our time in labour and refreshment – that is inevitable. But the final use of our time to which we are exhorted is *'to help a friend or brother in time of need without detriment to ourselves or connections'*. This refers to the practical application of the Masonic charity to which we have just had our attention drawn. The words *'without detriment to ourselves or connections'* are no more than common sense; we must always put our families first. In the First Degree Tracing Board Lecture we hear *'a Mason's charity should know no bounds, save those of prudence'*. Much as we might want to sort out hunger in the Third World single-handed, none of us can afford to do it, so we prudently support efforts by Freemasonry and other charities to attain that end, to an extent that we can afford.

The common gavel and chisel are the actual implements with which we work on the Rough Ashlar of our minds, symbolically chipping away at our imperfections and hopefully becoming better people in the process.

The Charge is delivered

The Charge given in the First Degree cannot be said to be laden with symbolism because it is not intended to be. It is an explanation of the principles by which a Mason should live and an exhortation to the candidate to do so. If properly done, this address will remain with a brother for the rest of his life. I often think that there is more emphasis on the brother delivering the Charge than on the candidate, because it is seen as a 'if you can do this, you can do anything' ritual test-piece. We do really need to appreciate that it is not the fact that Fred Bloggs got to the end of the Charge with only one or two prompts that counts! It is the fact that Fred understood it, the way in which he delivered it, and the impression it made on the candidate.

One interesting aspect of the Charge is that it exhorts us to adhere to *'the ancient landmarks of the Order'*. It is difficult to adhere to anything, when you're not sure what it is. The landmarks are basically those tenets of Masonry without which whatever was going on would not be Masonry. Examples are the need for a belief in a Supreme Being and having the Volume of the Sacred Law open at meetings. I am not going to attempt a list because Grand Lodge never has and any foreign Grand Lodge that has done so has met with criticism from all quarters for including things which have not been applied since Time Immemorial, which, of course, in Masonic terms is the year of the establishment of the Premier Grand Lodge of England in 1717.

The Tracing Board is explained

Or is it? I believe the First Degree Tracing Board Lecture to be firstly a crucially important ritual document, secondly by far the best explanation not only of the symbols of the First Degree but of the lodge temple in general, and thirdly a beautiful piece of prose, even though many complain of the standard of English in our ritual. I had the privilege of delivering it when my son was initiated into Mosaic Lodge No.5028 in the Province of Worcestershire and it is always a joy to relearn it. Sadly, though, it is a big chunk and many would not even attempt it. Time is also a factor, particularly if there is other business to transact on a night of Initiation. However, we would do well to encourage our newer brethren to at least read it.

A young man recently joined our lodge and was presented with a copy of the Emulation First Degree Ritual, as is our custom. When I

The First Degree Tracing Board

saw him a week later he asked me what he would be expected to learn and did it include all seven sections of the First Degree Lecture contained in the book? I told him all he needed to learn were the questions and answers before Passing to the Second Degree, but that it would be a very good idea to read the Lecture and also the address on the Tracing Board on which it is based. Enthusiasm like that, particularly in one whose first language is not English, is most welcome and I wish him a long and happy career in Freemasonry.

I have referred to the Lecture on the First Degree Tracing Board throughout this book, but to summarise the symbolism at this point:

The Lecture begins by referring to the fact that symbols date back to the Ancient Egyptians and probably to periods of antiquity before that. The idea of many fraternal societies including our own has been the maintenance of a set of symbols which is esoteric, the meaning being known to those to whom they have been communicated and nobody else. We next look at the form of the lodge and consider that it is described in this vast extent firstly to show the universality of the science of Freemasonry, but also to point out to us that our charity should also be boundless, limited only by prudence in knowing what we can afford to give.

It is then pointed out that our lodges stand on holy ground. When Masonic temples are opened for business they are ceremonially consecrated in solemn form. The ground on which they stand – the Lecture says – is holy because it commemorates Abraham's willingness to sacrifice his own son, Isaac, at God's command; David's trust in and prayers to the Lord to stay a pestilence; and Solomon's dedication of the Temple at Jerusalem. Of course, not all lodges meet in Masonic Halls or temples. Many meet in hotels, some in golf clubs, schools and other public buildings and in the 18th century nearly all of them met in inns and taverns. Nevertheless, wherever it is, when a lodge is open in due form the ground upon which it stands is at least notionally and symbolically holy.

For this reason it is necessary that lodges are laid out from East to West to symbolise the Tabernacle of Moses and the Temple of Solomon. This is also the case with most churches, although we are not claiming that status for our lodges – we do not need to because we are not a religion. Another reason why lodges are laid out from East to West is because learning began in the east and spread its influence westward.

I always find the wording of this passage irritating where it says *'the third last and grand reason, which is too lengthy to be entered upon now is explained in the course of our lectures which I hope you will have many opportunities of hearing'*. The fact is that it is unlikely that the candidate will have *any* opportunities of hearing the lectures, unless he goes to one of the excellent demonstrations given by the Emulation Lodge of Improvement or some other ritual organization. The delivery of the lectures requires a degree of ritual expertise, not always found in lodges, and time and circumstances severely restrict many ordinary lodges from providing the resources to deliver even a couple of sections of one lecture during the course of the working year. Not only that; the reason is simply that east to west is the direction in which God instructed Moses, Aholiab and Bezaleel to lay out the original Tabernacle in the wilderness. Surely a form of words could be devised to express that succinctly?

Next we look at the pillars which appear on the Tracing Board itself, representing Wisdom, Strength and Beauty, in the persons of Solomon King of Israel, Hiram King of Tyre and Hiram Abif. Solomon, of course, did not have the original command from God to build the Temple. His father, King David, received that, but because of his backsliding, David was not allowed the build the Temple in his lifetime and that task fell to his son. Hence the 'wisdom' attributed to Solomon is the possession of the management-skills to see the project through. Hiram King of Tyre was the 'quartermaster'. He provided the timber and other raw materials and also the men, and transported them from Lebanon down to the seaport of Joppa. For this reason, the quality of 'strength' is assigned to Hiram King of Tyre.

Hiram Abif is an intriguing character. He was an architect and an artist, as well as bit of a jack-of-all-trades, who seems to have been master of them all as well. He is described in the Bible as 'a cunning man' – the word 'cunning' meaning clever and resourceful in this context. In 2 Chronicles, Chapter 2 v.14 he is described thus: *'The son of a woman of the daughters of Dan, and his father was a man of Tyre, skilful to work in gold, and in silver, in brass, in iron, in stone, and in timber, in purple, in blue, and in fine linen, and in crimson; also to grave any manner of graving, and to find out every device which shall be put to him, with thy cunning men, and with the cunning men of my lord David thy father'*.

In fact we could be forgiven for wondering if there is anything behind the use of the term 'cunning man' on the part of the translators of the King James Bible in the early 17th century. Cunning men (and women) were part of the British folk magic scene until the 19th century. They were good magicians (as opposed to witches) and often protected against witchcraft by their spells. The term 'white witch' is supposed to have come into the language as an alternative name for cunning man/woman. Whilst witches were usually put to death, the activities of cunning men were usually overlooked and even though to claim possession of magical powers was illegal under the canon law of the Roman Catholic Church and was equally frowned on by Puritans after the Reformation, little was done about it and even some priests are known to have indulged in 'cunning' activities. Another alternative name was, of course, 'wizard' and if we think back to fairy tales and such things, wizards (as opposed to witches) are usually good guys – Merlin being the obvious example. The term is not altogether dead. There are still a number of inns in England called 'The Cunning Man'.

Beauty is therefore attributed as the quality appropriate to Hiram Abif, and the paragraph concludes by pointing out that that these three qualities are here symbolised by pillars of the Ionic (Wisdom), Doric (Strength) and Corinthian (Beauty) Orders of Architecture. Looking at the ceiling of the lodge as depicted on the Tracing Board, Jacob's Ladder is then considered and we are told that its principle 'rounds' represent the Christian Theological Virtues of Faith, Hope and Charity. Harry Carr was of the opinion that, on boards where seven steps were shown, the other four were likely to be the Four Cardinal Virtues of Temperance, Fortitude, Prudence and Justice.[17]

Some early boards – notably those painted by Josiah Bowring – portray three female figures standing on rungs of the ladder, symbolising the three Theological Virtues of Faith, Hope and Charity. On the First Degree Tracing Board used by the Lodge of Brotherly Love No.329 at Yeovil, in the Province of Somerset, the figures are holding a symbolic item each – a cross for Faith, an anchor for Hope and a heart for Charity.

Other boards merely have the letters 'F', 'H' and 'C' on the rungs. Some also have a key suspended (see the chapter on Symbols no longer used).[18]

We go on to find that the ladder reaches to the heavens and rests on the Volume of the Sacred Law. This is an exhortation to study the book of our faith in order to prepare ourselves for a better place. We hope by the practice of Faith, Hope and Charity to eventually arrive at *'an Ethereal Mansion, veiled from mortal eyes by the starry firmament here depicted by seven stars, which have an allusion to as many regularly made Masons, without whom no lodge is perfect, neither can any candidate be legally initiated into the Order'.*

To my mind, the symbol of Seven Stars is one of those symbols in Masonry which has a meaning stated in our lectures and which we all accept, yet has also deeper esoteric meaning. In the Book of Revelation Chapter 1 v.20 Jesus reveals to St John, the author of the book:

'The mystery of the seven stars which thou sawest in my right hand, and the seven golden candlesticks. The seven stars are the angels of the seven churches: and the seven candlesticks which thou sawest are the seven churches.'

The symbolism behind the Ornaments – Mosaic Pavement, Blazing Star, Indented or Tesselated Border; Furniture – Volume of the

POINT WITHIN A CIRCLE

Sacred Law, Square and Compasses; and Jewels – Moveable: Square, Level and Plumb Rule and Immoveable: Tracing Board and Rough and Perfect Ashlars is then explained. This we have already covered in the chapter on The Symbolism of the Lodge Room.

We then come to the point within a circle, which is a complicated concept that a lot of experienced people, even if they are aware of it, still do not understand. The idea is based on the Divine or Golden Proportion, recently referred to in the novels of Dan Brown, and represented by a constant of Φ – the Greek letter Phi, which has a value of approximately 1.618. Tremendous importance is attached to this constant as the basis of many things of historical, natural and scientific significance. Kepler describes it as *'one of the two great treasures of geometry'* (the other being Pythagoras' Theorem or the 47th Proposition of the Book of Euclid). Both Noah's Ark and the Ark of the Covenant were 'Golden Rectangles', based on the Golden Proportion.

Quite simply, it is about dividing a rectangle into a square and a smaller rectangle. What is the purpose of doing this? This is the basis for understanding by means of logarithms (remember those things we learnt about before we had calculators?) the spiral patterns of nature. Leonardo da Vinci illustrates it in his drawing of the Vitruvian Man whose extended limbs fit exactly into both a circle and a square. Many things in nature and architecture are based on this Golden Proportion. The Parthenon in Athens is a perfect golden rectangle. The spiral of a human DNA molecule is also based on this concept.[19]

Leonardo da Vinci's Vitruvian Man

There is a plethora of literature you can read and a host of good websites you can visit which deal with Phi, how it interacts with the Fibonacci sequence of numbers etc., but what has this got to do with Freemasonry? We are told in the Tracing Board Lecture that *'in all regular, well-formed, constituted lodges there is a point within a circle round which the brethren cannot err. This circle is bounded between north and south by two grand parallel lines, the one representing Moses and the other King Solomon.*'

Fine, but the lines used to represent St John the Baptist, '*the forerunner of Christ*' and St John the Evangelist, '*the beloved apostle of Our Lord, who finished with his learning what the former had begun with his zeal*'. These two saints were, of course, the patrons of Freemasonry and of Operative stonemasonry before that. Indeed in the 18th century, lodges used to have two Installations a year, the first on 24 June (St John the Baptist's day) and another on the feast of St John the Evangelist (27 December).

Early in the 19th century, when the Craft was de-Christianised, the two lines were renamed in honour of Moses and King Solomon so as to be acceptable to '*that religion in which all men agree*'.

We learn that '*On the upper part of this circle rests the Volume of the Sacred Law, supporting Jacob's Ladder* (see above) *which reaches to the heavens; and were we as conversant in that Holy Book, and as adherent to the doctrines therein contained as those parallels were, it would bring us to Him who would not deceive us, neither will He suffer deception. In going round this circle we must necessarily touch on both those parallel lines and likewise on the Sacred Volume; and while a Mason keeps himself thus circumscribed, he cannot err.*'

The Two Saints John

That passage seems straightforward enough, but this is another example – like the Seven Stars – of a deeper symbolism. If we think of the circle as God's world in which we have to run out the course of our lives, man is at the centre with his conduct regulated by the two parallels and with the Volume of the Sacred Law to bring him to God. Dipping in to the Third Degree for a moment, we remember that the centre is described as '*that being a point from which a Master Mason cannot (materially) err*'.

Next, the Lewis is explained. We have already looked at this in the chapter on the Symbolism of the Lodge Room. As Don Falconer points out in his paper on the Lewis:

'*The lewis is a device that has been used by stonemasons and erectors for many centuries. It provides an anchorage in a stone,* which enables lifting tackle to be attached to assist in the raising and lowering of stones that are too heavy or too awkward to be man-handled into position during transportation and erection. The first time that a speculative craft freemason learns about the lewis is usually as an entered apprentice, during the lecture on the tracing board, when he is told that lewis denotes strength and signifies the son of a mason. The use of the word in speculative craft freemasonry seems to have arisen as a result of the old friendship between France and Scotland, which came to be known as the "Auld Alliance".

'One of the earliest initiatives that resulted from this friendship was the involvement of the Travelling Masons of France in the design and construction of the Abbey of Kilwinning, which was founded about 1150. The French operative freemasons introduced the device into Scotland as a lever. The Scottish operative freemasons were soon calling the device a lewis, which at first sight appears to be an adaptation of the French word. Nevertheless, the intimate association between the operative freemasons and the clergy in those days must not be overlooked. The clergy regularly spoke in Latin, which at least the Master Masons must have understood and spoken, so that the word lewis is more likely to have been an adaptation of the Latin word leuis which means to levitate.

'It is of interest to note that by 1676 the Compagnonage, the brotherhood of masons who comprised the Compagnons du Tour or Travelling Masons of France, had changed their name for the lifting anchorage to louve meaning a she wolf, which is the feminine of loup meaning a wolf. It is said to be in allusion to the vice-like grip of a she-wolf's jaws when angry. From that date onwards the Compagnonage also referred to the son of a mason as a louveteau meaning a wolf cub and to the daughter of a mason as a louveine. These expressions seem to have originated from a play on words, most probably having in mind a requirement in ancient Egypt for the candidate in the Mysteries of Isis to wear the mask of a wolf, in deference to the wolf-headed god Upuaut, which signifies "he who opens the way", which is a most appropriate symbolism for a candidate in freemasonry.

'The Romans introduced the lewis into Britain for the construction of Hadrian's Wall around AD200, when it was erected to prevent the incursions from Scotland into England. An astute observer can still find mortices in many of the more massive stones in the ruins of Hadrian's Wall. Later, when Oswey was king of Northumberland, the Saxons used the lewis when they constructed the abbey at Whitby, which was founded by St Hilda in 657 to accommodate the monks and nuns. Whitby Abbey was the chief seat of learning in the north of England for several centuries. Thereafter the device was used widely in England, although it was not known as a lewis until the name was introduced from Scotland by Dr James Anderson.

'Thus the lewis symbolically comprehends the teachings of all the working tools of an apprentice freemason, reminding us that knowledge, grounded on accuracy, aided by labour and sustained by perseverance will, in the end, overcome all difficulties, raise ignorance from despair and promote happiness in the paths of science. Furthermore the lewis is a most appropriate symbol of strength.'

Falconer concludes by quoting the Harris Manuscript, giving an Operative definition of the term lewis:

'Harris MS No.1:

' "You shall not make any Mold, Square or Rule for any that is but a Lewis; a Lewis is such a one as hath served an Apprenticeship to a Mason but is not admitted afterwards according to this manner and Custom of making Masons." ' [20]

The Lecture on the Tracing Board finishes with a mention of four tassels *'pendant to the corners of the lodge'* which symbolise Temperance, Fortitude, Prudence and Justice. Though the key number in this Degree is three, as discussed below, four is also important in relation to these tassels and also, as we saw, to the steps taken to the pedestal. We might like to consider why this is. These are, of course, the Four Cardinal Virtues and they are well known outside Masonry. In Christian terms they are considered of prime importance and are often associated with the three

Theological Virtues of Faith, Hope and Charity. They are called cardinal (from the Latin word *cardo*, meaning a hinge) virtues because they are hinges on which all moral (from another Latin word *mores* – fixed values) virtues depend. We are taught that they should govern our actions, order our passions, and guide our conduct according to faith and reason. Other than having pure religious connotations, they also occur in popular literature. James Joyce uses the Four Cardinal Virtues as a sub-theme in *Dubliners*, as does F. Scott Fitzgerald in *The Great Gatsby*.

To us, the virtues themselves are symbolic of the Four Original Forms in Freemasonry. These are of very early origin and are first heard of in 1724. They are the Guttural, Pectoral, Manual and Pedal (or Pedestal) referring to parts of the body – the throat, heart, hand and foot. These forms are referred to in the 6th section of the First Lecture (Emulation Book of Lectures or Emulation First Degree Ritual). The guttural relates to the penalty of the Obligation, the pectoral to the safe deposit of secrets in a Freemason's breast, the manual to the placing of the hand during the Obligation and the pedal or pedestal to the position of the feet. On reading this section today the connection of the Four Forms with the Four Cardinal Virtues may seem a little tenuous, but think of a further (non-Masonic) symbolism: Temperance is represented by the throat in that it is the conduit through which we take food and drink, in which we should be temperate to avoid gluttony and drunkenness, and also the outlet for our speech which should also be temperate, avoiding extremes. Then there is Fortitude, associated with the breast, implying the need for us to be of firm heart and strong-willed. Prudence relates to the hand as we read in St Matthew's Gospel, Chapter 6 vv.1-4:

> '1. *Take heed that ye do not your alms before men, to be seen of them: otherwise ye have no reward of your Father which is in heaven.*
> 2. *Therefore when thou doest thine alms, do not sound a trumpet before thee, as the hypocrites do in the synagogues and in the streets, that they may have glory of men. Verily I say unto you, They have their reward.*
> 3. *But when thou doest alms, let not thy left hand know what thy right hand doeth:*
> 4. *That thine alms may be in secret: and thy Father which seeth in secret himself shall reward thee openly.*'

The meaning of verse 3 particularly concerns us because it relates to hands and we also remember, in connection with the giving of alms, the words of this Lecture *'a Mason's charity should know no bounds, save those of prudence'*. Finally, what have the feet got to do with Justice? This is probably the most tenuous connection; perhaps we should think of the words of the Extended Version of the Second Degree Working Tools: *'To walk justly and uprightly before God and man, turning neither to the right nor left from the paths of virtue'*.

Four was considered a sacred number by many of the Ancients. We have already looked at the four squares formed when the candidate is advancing to the pedestal to take his Obligation. In the system of Pythagoras, four was called the perfect or sacred number. Ancient civilizations tended to have four-letter names for their gods: the ancient Syrians called their god Adad; the Egyptians, Amum; the Romans, Deus; all four letter names. We mentioned above that the ancient Hebrews also had a four letter word (in the original Hebrew writing) called the Tetragrammaton; Royal Arch and Rose Croix Masons will know of this symbol. The name itself was considered so sacrosanct that it was forbidden for a Jew to pronounce it.

The final sentence of the First Tracing Board Lecture says that *'the characteristics of a good Freemason are virtue, honour and mercy, and may they ever be found in a Freemason's breast'*. A noble sentiment, but this is the only place I can think of where these characteristics are mentioned. They are expanded upon in the 7th section of the First Lecture, which is well worth reading.

The Ancient Hebrew Tetragrammaton or Yod-He-Vau-He

The Lodge is closed

The Closing consists of a check that we are still properly tyled and then a reminder by the Senior Warden of his position and duty. The phrase *'After seeing that every brother has had his due'* may be more readily understood by Mark Masons, to whom the payment of wages has a significance. In the Craft we are concerned that every brother has had what is his due in the lodge – the right to speak and be heard, if he so wishes, and to be given proper consideration as a member of the lodge. However, that is most certainly not the origin of the statement and we will consider it more fully in the chapter on the Second Degree. Bro Rev Neville Barker Cryer points out that, in some lodges in the north of England, the Senior Warden answers to the effect that the wages have been paid. Now, we know from the Second Degree Tracing Board that Entered Apprentices did not receive wages, but a weekly allowance of corn, wine and oil, so that would be the 'due' in this sense.[21]

The Lodge will then be closed by the Senior Warden at the Worshipful Master's command and with solemn prayer by the Chaplain.

The Symbolism of Three

The key number in the First Degree is Three, as we have seen: three working tools; three principal officers (the Master and his Wardens who rule the lodge); three Masonic Principles – brotherly love, relief and truth; three steps to the pedestal; three risings and so forth. We will conclude this chapter by looking at other aspects of the symbolism of this number. The number three has associations with synthesis, reunion, resolution, creativity, versatility, omniscience, birth and growth. The number is very positive in symbolism, mythology and religious thought. 'Third time lucky' is a very old saying. When we wish to accord especial praise or congratulation to somebody, we give them three cheers.[22]

Religious triads are very common: Thrice Great Hermes, the Holy Trinity of Christianity, the Hindu Trinity of Brahma, Vishnu and Shiva. The number three was sacred to the Egyptian triad of Osiris, Isis and Horus. The hierophant in Egyptian mysteries took an oath of secrecy with both hands on the sacred delta (i.e. the equilateral triangle) referring even then to the triple essence of the deity. For this reason, in the Lecture on Numbers given in the Zelator Grade of the Societas Rosicruciana in Anglia, the number three is called majestic.

In folklore, Genii grant three wishes. Fairy tales involve people having to undertake three tasks or solve three riddles. In mythology there are Three Graces, Three Fates, Three Furies.[23]

In Christianity there are three Theological Virtues – Faith, Hope and Charity; there were three Magi who attended on the Infant Jesus; Peter denied Christ three times; there were three crosses at Golgotha; the Resurrection took place after three days; Jesus then made three appearances to his disciples after rising from the dead. Three is also the first number that has a beginning, a middle and an end. It is the basic family unit and also represents body, soul and spirit. For this reason the number is sacred to many civilizations from the Maori to the Norse.[24]

Three is known as a masculine number, associated with water on its own and with the triangle of three sides. In alchemy it is the number of the basic substances sulphur, salt and quicksilver (mercury). In philosophy the triad or triple step is pivotal as in Hegel's dialectical progress of thesis, antithesis and synthesis.[25] Two more connotations are added in the ritual of the Royal Order of Scotland – that there are three terms in a syllogism and three sides to an equilateral triangle. The equilateral triangle, as we have already seen, was established in the symbology of the Ancient Egyptians and remains crucially important in Freemasonry today.[26]

Katharine Thomson tells us that Mozart in creating *The Magic Flute* drew on the special significance of the number three in Freemasonry. *'Most of the songs are in three-part harmony ... Many songs are in triple time; threefold repetitions are frequent, and major triads are of particular importance ... In Mozart's music certain keys are associated with Freemasonry, notably Eb major ... [with] the key signature of three flats.'*[27]

Other Mozart specialists argue that *The Magic Flute* is clearly a Masonic opera. They note the three chords repeated three times, the three attendants of the Queen of the Night, the three boys, the three doors, the three trials, and so on. We will look at music – and Mozart – again in the chapter on the Second Degree when we come to consider the Seven Liberal Arts and Sciences. Remember, however, that Mozart was an Austrian Freemason, used to a Scottish Rite ritual and I should warn my English brethren that if they read the libretto of *The Magic Flute*, similarities will not immediately be apparent until they look at the inherent symbolism. Members of the Ancient and Accepted Rite or Rose Croix will probably see a lot more in it than Craft Masons.

From Labour to Refreshment

The candidate's first Festive Board will be an experience to say the least. I have placed my description of it at the end of the chapter on the First Degree because a) it had to go somewhere, and b) there is no Festive Board like your first. We have already seen that fraternal societies with shared meals at the end of their meetings are anything but a modern innovation. Indeed the word 'Compagnonage' in reference to the Continental Operative stonemasons of the Middle Ages, and also the word 'Companion' that we use in connection with the Royal Arch Degree, are in part derived from the French for 'eating bread together'.

The candidate will probably be aware that his new lodge has a meal after the meeting is over. This may be in the Masonic Hall or if that doesn't have the facilities, perhaps in a local hotel or similar establishment. He may have been in the dining room before if he has attended what is called a Ladies' Festival in the south of England and a Ladies' Evening in the north or some similar function. He cannot – unless he is very observant – be expected to realise that, unlike in the temple, both Wardens are seated in the West. This is done because both Wardens at one time, as we have already seen, did sit in the West and we maintain that ancient tradition at our Festive Boards. Realistically also, if we tried to lay out the dining room like the temple, it would give us considerable problems.

The candidate will probably enjoy a very good meal – far better than he could hope to get in a lot of well-known restaurant chains and, having satisfied his appetite, will then find out about the after proceedings. There will be toasts to our leaders at Grand and Metropolitan, Provincial or District levels and one to the Worshipful Master so we can all congratulate him on an excellent ceremony. Depending on local tradition, what is known as 'fire' or 'honours' may be accorded to the toast which will consist of movements imitative of the First Degree sign, totalling 21 and representative of a 21-gun salute. Quite often the candidate gets his leg pulled at this juncture by his new brethren making the movements so quickly that he cannot possibly be expected to follow them, until a kind brother explains what is going on – all harmless fun!

There are many local variations on this practice. In Dorset, for example, it is customary to make the sign just once whilst singing:

Prosper the art, prosper the art
Join in the chorus, prosper the art.

Then again singing:

Prosper the man, prosper the man
Join in the chorus, prosper the man.

At this point even the person being toasted will stand while the sign is made again and the brethren sing:

Prosper the lodges, prosper the lodges
Join in the chorus, prosper the lodges.

I have also seen a variation of this delightful custom performed in Nottinghamshire.

There may also be toasts to the Masonic Charities, absent and seafaring brethren and the visitors, but on a night of Initiation the most important toast will be that to the candidate himself. The toast will normally be proposed by the candidate's proposer or seconder and will usually be accompanied by the singing of the Entered Apprentices' Song. Local customs vary, but there is one practice we should refer to because of its symbolic content. That is the forming of the Chain of Union after the song has been sung. This custom is still quite prevalent in Yorkshire and I am reproducing the wording in full.

The brethren form the chain with outstretched arms and gently sway from side to side. A brother, usually a Past Master, will then explain the purpose:

'Brother initiate, the circle we have now formed is known to us as the Initiate's Chain and should remind us of our united friendship and loyalty to each other, of which it is a symbol.

'It is with outstretched arms that we receive you into the loving circle of our hearts, and so into this your Mother Lodge, also the wider circle of Masonry Universal.

'You will observe that each brother's arms cross the breasts of his neighbours, to remind us that a Mason's charity should not cease with his brethren but should extend into the popular world. This Chain is without beginning or end, symbolising that Masonry encircles the earth.

'It reaches from the past, represented by the Immediate Past Master across the present, represented by the Worshipful Master into the future, represented by you Brother Initiate.

'It is a double-linked chain, so that should it please the GAOTU to call a brother to Higher Service in the GL Above, the Chain is not broken, only weakened and then strengthened by the inclusion of another.

'The swaying movement of the brethren symbolises the Chain being tested and proved and so, whatever trials and difficulties we may be called upon to face in this life, may this Chain which is forged by brotherly love, relief and truth be equal to all occasions, remaining firm and unbroken.'

Clearly this is both a superb piece of ritual and very noble sentiment that sums up for the candidate the strength and quality of the fraternity he has joined.

---

1   Bernard Jones – *Freemasons' Guide and Compendium*
2   Julian Rees – *Through Ritual to Enlightenment*
3   Jones, op. cit.
4   Ibid.
5   Rees, op. cit.
6   J. S. M. Ward – *The EA Handbook*
7   H. L. Haywood – *The Builder, May 1923*
8   Harold Schieck – *In whom do you put your trust?* (MasonicWorld.com)
9   Jones, op. cit.
10   Ward, op. cit.
11   Neville Barker Cryer – *Craft and Royal Arch Legends (Cornerstone Society 2000)*
12   Jones, op. cit.
13   Henderson and Pahl – *Understanding Freemasonry (Pietre-Stones)*
14   R. F. Gould – *AQC 11 1898*
15   Eric Place – *The Most Ancient Garment in the World*
16   Harry Carr – *The Freemason at Work*
17   Carr, op. cit.
18   T. O. Haunch – *Tracing Boards, Their Development & Their Designers*
19   Harvey Lovewell – *Geometry and Freemasonry*
20   Don Falconer – *The Lewis (Pietre-Stones)*
21   Neville Barker Cryer – *Tell me more about the Mark Degree*
22   *The Complete Dictionary of Symbols*
23   J. C. Cooper – *Traditional Symbols*
24   Cooper, op. cit.
25   Udo Becker – *Continuum Encyclopaedia of Symbols*
26   Falconer, op. cit.
27   Katharine Thomson – *The Masonic Thread in Mozart*

The Second Degree

Queen Bee, build your palace,
Put your family to work
And teach them to make honey – Russian Proverb

The Degree of a Fellowcraft or the Ceremony of Passing takes us into the intellectual age and the Middle Chamber, representing the soul or psyche – Jung's 'personal unconscious'. At one time a Fellowcraft was qualified to be Master of a lodge and even Grand Master. Indeed some Masonic historians claim that at one time there was only one Degree which was later split into two, giving us the Entered Apprentice and Fellowcraft stages. W. L. Wimshurst claimed that that is precisely what the first two Degrees were – preparatory stages before the Third Degree, which is the real Initiation. In Ireland, as late as 1858, the first two Degrees were 'invariably' being conferred on the same night, with the 'Charity test' being done in the Second Degree.[1]

All three Degrees are about gaining wisdom, but the second is particularly so because it stresses the advantages of acquiring knowledge, appreciating the natural world around us and thinking about the Liberal Arts and Sciences, with the emphasis being on geometry. In other words, those of Bro John Acaster of the Manchester Association for Masonic Research, it is time to *'open our minds'*.[2]

At the end of the Charge after Initiation, we are, of course, exhorted to *'make a daily advancement in Masonic knowledge'*, but what form should this advancement take? We would all do well to take that exhortation seriously, but what we do about it will obviously depend on our interests and our talents, as well, of course, as the time available.

One of the Scripture readings in the Exaltation Ceremony in Royal Arch Masonry is taken from Proverbs, Chapter 2 and says:

> 'So that thou incline thine ear unto wisdom, And apply thy heart to understanding;
> Yea, if thou criest after knowledge and liftest up thy voice for understanding;
> If thou seekest her as silver, and searchest for her as hidden treasure;
> Then shalt thou understand the fear of the Lord, and find the knowledge of God.
> For the Lord giveth wisdom; out of His mouth cometh knowledge and understanding;
> He layeth up sound wisdom for the righteous; he is a buckler to them that walk uprightly.'

Perhaps another way of looking at it is that it is not simply a matter of having the Second Degree, with all its stress on improving our intellectual powers, conferred on us, learning the ritual and then delivering it, possibly for many years. The key thing about acquiring wisdom is surely understanding what one acquires. The Fellowcraft Degree, according to Jacques Huyghebaert, is not about hewing and rendering the stone. That has already been done by the Entered Apprentice. It is about verifying and placing the stones according to the plan. This theme is very much developed in the Mark Degree, which is often referred to as an extension of the Fellowcraft Ceremony.[3]

The word 'Fellowcraft' seems to have come to us from James Anderson's Constitutions of 1723, being derived from the same Scottish source as Entered Apprentice. However, fellows of various institutions are well known and in many cases this is the highest accolade available. Some institutions have introduced the grade of Companion to provide a higher grade for those who have given exceptional service.

Let's examine this degree, as we did with the First, by means of a synopsis of events, looking at the symbolism at each of the 16 different stages.

1 The Questions before Passing
2 The Lodge is opened in the Second Degree
3 The Candidate is prepared
4 The Candidate seeks admission
5 A Prayer of Dedication is said

6   The Perambulation round the Lodge
7   The Candidate is presented
8   The Candidate moves from West to East
9   The Obligation is taken
10 The Candidate learns the Secrets
11 The Wardens test the Candidate
12 The Candidate receives his apron
13 The Address in the South East corner
14 The Working Tools are presented
15 The Tracing Board is explained
16 The Lodge is closed in the Second Degree

The Questions before Passing

The objective of testing the candidate before passing him is to assess his readiness in terms of knowledge of the previous Degree. Well, it should be. However, as with the delivery of the First Degree Charge, the acid test in reality to the Past Masters and brethren looking on and listening is: How well does he remember the words he has been given to learn? Is he going to be a competent ritualist? Do we have a future Worshipful Master here?

In some places it is even customary to finish the questions and when the Master says *'These are the usual questions; I will put others if any brother wishes me to do so'*, one of the Wardens will stand and ask for the candidate to recite his First Degree Obligation. This might be seen by some as an advantage in that those who cannot learn ritual will be identified early on, but is understanding not more important?

The questions concern the mode of preparation, the nature of Freemasonry and the qualifications of its members but there is one final question: *'How do you demonstrate the proof of your being a Mason to others?'* to which the answer is: *'By signs, tokens and the perfect points of my entrance'*. This, perhaps, does require a little explanation.

In the First Section of the First Lecture in the Emulation Book of Lectures, there is the following catechism:

Q: Will you give me the points of entrance?
A: If you give me the first I will give you the second.

Q: I hele?
A: I conceal.

Q: What is it that you wish to conceal?
A: All secrets and mysteries of, or belonging to, Free and Accepted Masons in Masonry.

Q: This being open Lodge, what at other times you wish to conceal you may now safely reveal?
A: Of, at, and on.

Q: Of, at, and on what?
A: Of my own free will and accord, at the door of the Lodge, on the point of a sharp implement presented to my naked left breast.

As Michael Lawrence points out in *The Perfect Points of my Entrance*:

'There are three distinct possibilities that one could consider the phrase refers to when demonstrating he is a Mason, i) his Entrance as a Candidate, ii) his Entrance into Freemasonry, iii) his Entrance into a lodge at work. My first point of reference is from the Entered Apprentice Lecture, First Section, which as you read seems to point to all three:

'Of my own free will and accord, indicating his entrance into Masonry. At the door of the Lodge, indicating his entrance into a Lodge at work. On the point of a sharp implement presented to my naked left breast, indicating his willingness to undergo such trials and approbations to prove his membership or entrance into Freemasonry.

'Mackey states when referring to this subject that: "...in the earliest lectures of the 18th century these were called Principle Points...... They are called so because they refer to four important points of the initiation. The Guttural refers to entrance upon penal responsibilities; the Pectoral to the entrance into the Lodge; the Manual to the entrance on the Covenant; and the Pedal to the entrance on the instructions in the North-east."

'Interestingly enough, the first reference we have of Guttural, Pectoral, Manual and Pedal is from an exposure of 1725 entitled "The Grand Mystery of Free-Masons Discovered." Here we find no mention of point of entrance, but merely as Freemasons signs. Up until 1750, the points of entrance were no more than secret signs or tokens, but undefined. After this date we then find the sudden introduction and association of the Cardinal Virtues imposed on the four signs, and the whole seem to merge as the points of entrance.

'The Sixth Section of the Entered Apprentice Lecture refers to them as the "original forms" and we now learn that:

' "Guttural, the throat, alludes to the penalty of my obligation, wherein I have sworn that, as a man of honour and an Entered Apprentice Freemason, I would rather have my T.C.A. than improperly disclose the secrets of Freemasonry. Pectoral, the breast, wherein are deposited those secrets, safe and secure from the popular world who are not freemasons. Manual, the right-hand on the Volume of Sacred Law, in token of my assent to the Obligation of a Freemason. Pedal, the feet in the form of a S, in the North-east part of the Lodge, denoting a just and upright Mason.

' "Q: They have a further allusion?
' "A: To the four cardinal virtues; namely, Temperance, Fortitude, Prudence, and Justice."

'The importance of these virtues must never be overlooked, and each initiate is reminded of them in the Charge "Let Prudence direct you, Temperance chasten you, Fortitude support you, and Justice be the guide of all your actions." However, they do not really associate themselves with the Points of Entrance.

Having satisfactorily answered the test questions, the candidate will be entrusted and then retire for preparation.

It is obviously necessary to do all this in the First Degree, so that the candidate has the information he needs and then the lodge can be opened in the Second Degree, so that he can be passed.

The Lodge is opened in the Second Degree

There are two important symbolic points about the Opening of the Lodge in the Second Degree. Firstly, we come across the initial reference to the Square, which is defined here as *'an angle of ninety degrees or the fourth part of a circle'*. This harks back to what we looked at in the First Degree about the formation of the square and the point within the circle. Secondly, in the prayer said whilst Opening, we ask God to assist us in our undertakings; *'that the rays of heaven may shed their (benign) influence over us, to enlighten us in the paths of virtue and science'*. In a way this is a connecting link between the First and Second Degrees in that moral truth and virtue is what the First Degree is about, whilst the Second Degree is concerned with the 'intellectual faculty' and the paths of heavenly science.

The Candidate is prepared

Despite exhaustive searching, I have been unable to discern a rationale behind the mode of preparation for the Second Degree. One can only assume that the left arm is being displayed for the same purpose as the right arm was displayed in the First Degree, and that the right knee is bare because this is the knee he will bend to take his Obligation. We could, of course, argue that at this stage the candidate has made progress in Masonry and therefore the emphasis can switch from the weaker, left side to the stronger right.

The Candidate seeks admission

This time, of course, the candidate is not hoodwinked and he will be looking to be admitted with a lot more confidence. He will have displayed his proficiency in the First Degree and is now eager to learn more. The Tyler will give the knocks of an Entered Apprentice which symbolise the fact that body, soul and spirit are separated. The candidate comes properly prepared and with everything necessary that will 'recommend' him to be passed. The word 'recommend' is important because it contrasts starkly with what is said in the Third Degree. Here he has worked well as an Entered Apprentice and he hopes, by dint of that, to be considered for promotion.

A Prayer of Dedication is said

This is quite a simple prayer, doing no more than ask that we continue to direct the candidate along the Masonic path and strive, through obedience to the principles laid down in the Volume of the Sacred Law, to continue our labours to the glory of God.

The Perambulation round the Lodge

The candidate is conducted round the lodge, as in the First Degree, although this time he will be able to see where he is going. It will on this occasion be necessary to demonstrate to the watching brethren that not only is the candidate prepared to receive his Second Degree, but that he is proficient in what he learnt in the First Degree. This he will now demonstrate with the assistance of the Wardens and the Deacons by passing round the lodge twice.

The Candidate is presented

Having now proved himself to be proficient in the knowledge of the First Degree, the candidate will be placed in the charge of the Senior Warden who informs the Master that he is properly prepared and ready to receive the Fellowcraft Degree.

The Candidate moves from West to East

The ascent of the winding staircase is at first a bit baffling, principally because whereas all other movements both in the ceremonies and around the lodge generally are done in a clockwise direction, as we have already seen, the notional staircase, however, is a 'widdershins' or anticlockwise movement. Most Second Degree Tracing Boards show it as this. What is also contradictory is that if we read the Second Degree Tracing Board Lecture, we find that the Fellowcrafts, when they went to receive their wages, *'arrived there by a porchway or entrance on the south side'*. When the candidate arrives at it he starts in the North East, at roughly the same place he stood in for the Charity address in the First Degree. In some lodges the instruction from the Deacon is the same: *'left foot across the lodge, right foot down the lodge'* etc. In a way this is logical because he starts from the point he left off at in the last Degree, advancing again to the East for further light.

The late Bro Harry Carr set little store by what he called 'the clockwise fetish' and advised us not to set any particular store by

The Second Degree   123

this exceptional anticlockwise movement. He suggested that the idea of moving clockwise arose from the movement of the Sun and also from the early days of Freemasonry when the lodge board was drawn on the floor, which was also the origin of the practice of 'Squaring' the lodge. If you think about it, though, were the steps to be started from the middle of the floor (as they are in some lodges) they would be in a clockwise direction.[5]

The five steps taken towards the pedestal symbolise the Five Noble Orders of Architecture and the five senses, which we will consider later.

The Obligation is taken

The Obligation is again a promise to maintain the secrets of the Degree. It also contains a promise to maintain the principles of the former Degree and to answer signs and obey summonses. We have already seen that this time the candidate will kneel on his right knee. Obviously we also note that his left arm is supported in the angle of a square, more or less forcing his arm (although he doesn't know it yet) into the position of Joshua's hailing sign.

As we did in the First Degree, let's look at where the Bible is open in the Second. Amos, Chapter7 vv.7-8 says this:

'Thus he shewed me; and, behold, the Lord stood upon a wall made by a plumb line, with a plumb-line in his hand.

'And the Lord said unto me, Amos, what seest thou? And I said, A plumb line. Then said the Lord, Behold, I will set a plumb-line in the midst of my people Israel; I will not again pass by them anymore.'

This portrays a vision in which the Lord appeared to Amos to set new rules for the future. It prophesies what will happen if life is not 'perpendicular'. No prophet can any longer intercede for the Hebrews. It is up to them. The vertical wall, supposed to be built in true perpendicular by the aid of a plumb line, is now tested and found to be out of plumb. God will set a new plumb line (possibly a Messiah) in the midst of the people of Israel, and they must align their lives with the new plumb line, or be condemned. God will no longer pass by them in forgiveness, simply because they are Israel, as he has in the past.

Bernard Jones has this to say of the penalty contained in the Obligation:

'It was common in ancient days for the parties to a contract to profess to subject themselves, in the event of their violating their engagements, to such a death as had befallen a victim sacrificed by them in making the contract. Thus, among the ancient Hebrews, the contracting parties killed and cut in twain a heifer and then walked between its two portions. We learn of this in the Book of Jeremiah where, speaking of the men that have transgressed His covenant, and had not performed the words of the covenant which they had made before Him when they cut the calf in twain and passed between the parts thereof, the Lord said, "I will even give them into the hand of their enemies, and into the hand of them that seek their life: and their dead bodies shall be for meat unto the fowls of the heaven, and to the beasts of the earth." (XXXIV, 20).

'In the days of King Edgar, according to Gould, a thief was punished by mutilation, his body, in which there was still life, being "cast to the beasts of prey and the fowls of heaven". A murderer in old German days was punished by having his "flesh and body" thrown to the beasts in the forest, the birds in the air and the fishes in the sea.' [6]

The Candidate learns the Secrets

It is not immediately apparent why the story of Joshua's longest day is introduced into the Degree at this point. It has nothing to do with the building of the Temple, nor does it appear to be connected with the intellectual development which is the objective of this Degree. It is referred to as a sign of prayer. Some rituals say 'perseverance', others say 'prayer and perseverance'.

There are other instances in the Bible of people holding up their hands in this manner. In Exodus, Chapter 17, Moses held up his hand during a battle against the Amalekites and whilst it was up, Israel prevailed, but if he lowered it the advantage went to the other side. Later we will see that King Solomon also held up his hands as he dedicated the Temple. Joshua's act in his battle against the Amorites is backed up by other contemporary evidence.

In the Book of Joshua, Chapter 10, it says this:

> *12. Then spake Joshua to the LORD in the day when the LORD delivered up the Amorites before the children of Israel, and he said in the sight of Israel, Sun, stand thou still upon Gibeon; and thou, Moon, in the valley of Ajalon.*
> *13. And the sun stood still, and the moon stayed, until the people had avenged themselves upon their enemies. Is not this written in the book of Jasher?* * *So the sun stood still in the midst of heaven, and hasted not to go down about a whole day.*
> *14. And there was no day like that before it or after it, that the LORD hearkened unto the voice of a man: for the LORD fought for Israel.'*

* As an aside, this reference to the Book of Jasher is the only incidence I know of the Bible referring to another work. The Book of Jasher was written by Jasher, son of Caleb, one of Moses' lieutenants, who later judged Israel at Shiloh. Jasher covers biblical history from the creation down to Jasher's own day and his book is sometimes referred to as 'The Lost Book of Jasher'.

But, back to Joshua: with God, of course, all things are possible. Indeed the previous verse tells us that God had struck the Amorites with hailstones to such an extent that more Amorites had been killed by hailstones than by the swords of the Israelites. But did the Earth, *'constantly revolving on its axis in its orbit round the sun'*, really stop doing so for a period of time?

There are other legends – Chinese, Greek and Indian – of gods or great heroes stopping the Sun, but this is something more than that. For one thing it is reiterated in the Bible in the Book of the Prophet Habakkuk, Chapter 3 v.11: *'The sun and moon stood still in their habitation: at the light of thine arrows they went, and at the shining of thy glittering spear.'*

And there is much more than that. Chinese history records a king called Yao declaring that in his reign the Sun stood so long above the horizon that it was feared the world would have been set on fire. Yao is known to have been a contemporary of Joshua the son of Nun. The (heathen) Latin poet Ovid tells us that a day was once lost, and that the Earth was in great danger from the intense heat of an unusual Sun. The Greek historian Herodotus recounts that the priests of Egypt showed him their temple records, and that there he read a strange account of a day that was twice the natural length. South American Indians and Aborigines have records of this happening. Science also confirms that one full day is missing from astronomical calculations at this time.

Probably one more question needs to be asked, and that is what is the correct way to hold the hand – palm to the front or palm edgeways? Some offer the explanation that palm to the front was the way it was done in the Antients' Grand Lodge and the other method was that used by the Moderns. I could subscribe to that because lodges in Liverpool that work Bottomley Ritual, believed to be descended from the ritual of the many Antients' lodges that formerly existed in Lancashire, hold the hand to the front. Harry Carr notes that this is also the manner of making the sign in Bristol – a one-off (with strong Irish influence) but none the less a very ancient ritual.

Both ways are obviously correct, according to the traditions of one's lodge, but illustrations of Israelites praying in those days (although we cannot know for certain) do tend to show them holding up both hands with the palms to the front, as King Solomon did when he dedicated the Temple. This can also be seen with the figure of the man contained in the Arms of Grand Lodge (see above).

All well and good, but we still haven't found out what relevance this sign has to the Second Degree. As we have seen, the fact that Joshua held up his hand to stay the movements of the Sun and Moon is not connected with the building of the Temple or, apparently, with the development of our intellectual faculties. Masonic scholars, commentators and symbologists are strangely reticent on the reasons for the inclusion of this sign – even J. S. M. Ward! In Scotland things are slightly different. The 'Joshua sign' is part of the 'due guard' (see above) of the Second Degree, referring to the position of the hands when taking the Obligation of the Degree. The left hand is held in that position because it is holding a wand. That doesn't really help us in the English Constitution, so I am going to make a suggestion which you may like to consider.

If we think of the sign under its alternative name found in some rituals of the 'Sign of Perseverance', it could suggest that perseverance and application are going to be necessary in the fulfilment of our goal of improving our minds as part of our Masonic development. Bro Kipling, as usual, sums it up nicely in his poem *If*:

> *If you can fill the unforgiving minute*
> *With sixty seconds' worth of distance run...*

Could it then be that as Joshua – the last ruler of Israel truly approved of by God – held up his hand to hold the Sun and Moon, asking for help to grant perseverance in overthrowing the enemies of his Lord, so we are asking for the tenacity and strength of purpose to make it as Freemasons? Could this be related to what we saw when considering the winding staircase – the road is a difficult one?

The Wardens test the Candidate

Quite simply, this is another way of demonstrating to the brethren present that the candidate understands what he has been taught in both degrees.

The Candidate receives his apron

In much the same manner as in the First Degree, the Master again delegates the Senior Warden to invest the candidate with his apron – this time that of a Fellowcraft – which he does *'to mark the progress you have made in the science'*. We looked at the Fellowcraft's apron in the chapter on the Symbolism of the Lodge Room, but it is worth adding here that in addition to the meaning given there, the two rosettes also symbolise the dual nature of man (body and soul) and, in this context, are said also to refer to the Two Great Pillars, which are central to the Second Degree Tracing Board.

There then follows an exhortation by the Master which sums up the purpose of the degree and highlights the intellectual side of things. Why is it necessary to do this, as a step along the road to Masonic Light? At this point the candidate is told: *'You are expected to make the liberal arts and sciences your future study, that you may the better be enabled to discharge your duties as a Mason and estimate the wonderful works of the Almighty.'* Estimate, in this context, of course means to esteem or appreciate, rather than the usual meaning of the word in this day and age.

If the Second Degree Tracing Board Lecture is delivered, the candidate will learn that the Seven Liberal Arts and Sciences are grammar, rhetoric, logic, arithmetic, geometry, music and astronomy. These arts and sciences have been around since the dawn of time – Plato (c.427-347BC) taught them and he refers to them in his *Republic* – and it is ironic that astronomy should be placed last in the list because it was probably the first thing the ancients became interested in. Not only will they have noted the movements of the Sun, Moon and stars in connection with the harvesting of crops, tides and so on but will have venerated them as objects of worship.

Fine! But why is the candidate being urged to study these things? We may be assured that those doing the urging probably don't know either. A quick answer may be that geometry is pre-eminent among these arts and sciences and what we are concerned with in Masonry is the building of a temple for which we use *sacred* geometry composed of all seven of them. Looking at it another way, Masonry was born in an age when people were interested in architecture. Well-heeled young men went on the Grand Tour to see fine buildings on the Continent of Europe.

The Baptistry, Florence – exterior

The ritual says (in the Third Degree) that we are led to *'contemplate the intellectual faculty and to trace it from its development, through the paths of heavenly science even to the Throne of God Himself. The secrets of nature and the principles of intellectual truth were thus unveiled to your view.'*

In the 18th century a liberal education was considered very advantageous, if not essential, for any young man of means. This was, after all, the period known as both the 'Enlightenment' and the 'Age of Reason' and having finished their schooling, largely based on the Classics which will have included something of the Seven Liberal Arts and Sciences, they would take the Grand Tour

The Baptistry, Florence – interior

of major locations in Europe, starting with Paris and then going on to Italy, visiting Florence, Pisa, Rome and finally Naples. And there was great interest on the Continent then, and had been for some time. Despite the disapproval of some sections of the Church, there had been a revival of concern about ancient knowledge dating from pre-Christian times. Dante mentions the Seven Liberal Arts and Sciences in both his *Commedia* of 1304 and his *Convivia* of 1306, and the scientific system of the much-persecuted Cathars in France was founded on the doctrine of correspondences: grammar corresponded to the Moon, dialectic (logic) to Mercury, rhetoric to Venus, music to Mars, geometry to Jupiter, astronomy to Saturn, and arithmetic or illumined reason to the Sun. Accordingly, to the seven planetary spheres – the first seven of Dante's nine heavens – corresponded the Seven Liberal Arts respectively.[7]

The overall experience of the Grand Tour on the education of an intelligent young man of the 18th century was almost bound to stimulate an interest in architecture and from that geometry, said to be the fount of all other arts and sciences. The word 'geometry' is derived from two Greek words signifying measurement of the Earth.

The aim of a liberal education in those days was that a person acquired general knowledge and developed his general intellectual capabilities. The liberal curriculum offered by universities then was divided into the Trivium (grammar, rhetoric and logic) and the Quadrivium (arithmetic, geometry, music and astronomy). They had, of course, been in those groupings since Plato's time, if not before that. The Second Degree is concerned with developing the intellect and therefore this liberal education was and is very relevant. Harking back to my earlier point, such studies will not help you to learn ritual parrot fashion, or to select a good team of officers, but they may help you to understand Freemasonry.

So it is easy to see why the concept of a liberal education would have been adopted in Masonry in the first place, and why William Preston in his system of lectures devised later in the 18th century developed that theme – because that is what the young men of that age were being encouraged to study. But there is, as usual, more to it than that. There is good reason why Masonry in particular should be interested in these arts and sciences, by which we improve our minds. They come into Masonry very early for reasons we have already seen. In fact we even find them referred to in the Old Charges of Operative stonemasons. In the Regius Poem (c.1390) we read:

> *'Many years after the good scholar Euclyde taught the craft of Geometry wonderfully wide. So he did at that time introduce many other divers crafts Through the grace of Christ in Heaven. He established the Seven Sciences.'*

Back still further, some of the stone carvings on that fascinating building, Chartres Cathedral, are said to be representations of the seven arts and sciences. The Cooke MS (c.1425) is even more explicit on the necessity of these arts and sciences within the Mason Craft:

> *'Thanked be God our glorious Father and Founder and Former of Heaven and of Earth, and of all things that in them is, that He would vouchsafe of His glorious Godhead to make so many things of divers virtue for mankind. For He made all worldly things to be obedient and subject to man; for all things that be comestible of wholesome nature, He ordained it for man's sustenance. And also He hath given to man wits and cunning of divers Sciences and Crafts, by which we may work in this world to get our living to make divers things to God's pleasure, and also for our ease and profit. Which things if I should rehearse them, it were too long to tell and to write: wherefore I will leave.*

Chartres Cathedral

> *'But I shall show and tell some: that is to say, how and in what wise the Science of Geometry first began, and who were the founders thereof, and of other Crafts more, as it is noted in the Bible and in other stories.*

'How and in what manner this worthy Science of Geometry first began, I will tell you, as I said before. You shall understand that there be Seven Liberal Sciences, by which seven Sciences all Sciences and Crafts in the world were first found. And in especial, for it is the cause of all, that is to say the Science of Geometry – of all others that are.

'Which Seven Sciences be called thus – As for the first, that is called the Foundation of Science: his name is Grammar; he teacheth a man rightfully to speak and to write truly.

'The second is Rhetoric, and he teacheth a man to speak formably and fair.

'The third is Dialectic, and that Science teacheth a man to discern the truth from the false, and most commonly it is called the Art of Sophistry.

'The fourth is called Arithmetic, which teacheth a man the Craft of numbers, for to reckon and to make counts of all manner of things.

'The fifth is Geometry, which teacheth a man all the metes and measures, ponderations or weights, of all manner of Crafts.

'The sixth is Music, that teacheth a man the Craft of song, in notes of voice and organ, trump[et] and harp, and of all others pertaining to them.

'The seventh is Astronomy, that teacheth man to know the course of the sun, and of the moon, and of all other stars and planets of heaven.

'Our intent is principally to treat of the first foundation of the worthy Science of Geometry, and who were the founders thereof. As I said before, there be Seven Liberal Sciences – that is to say, seven Sciences or Crafts that be free in themselves – which seven live only by one, that is Geometry. And Geometry is as much to say, "the measure of the earth". Et sic dicitur: a *'geo', graece, quod est 'terra', latine, et 'metron' quod est 'mensura': unde Geometria – i.e. 'mensura terrae vel terrarum'. That is to say, in English, that Geometry is as I said derived from 'geo', that is in Greek 'earth', and 'metron' that is to say, 'measure'. And thus is this name Geometry compounded, and is translated, "the measure of the earth".*

'Marvel ye not that I said that all Sciences live only by the Science of Geometry. For there is no artificial nor hand craft that is wrought by man's hand, but it is wrought by Geometry. And a notable cause: for if a man work with his hands, he worketh with some manner of tool: and there is no instrument of material things in this world, but it comes from the nature of earth, and to earth it will turn again. And there is no instrument, that is to say, a tool to work with, but it hath some proportion, either more or less and proportion is measure, and the tool or the instrument earth, and Geometry is defined as "the measure of the earth". Wherefore I may say that men live all by Geometry, for all men here in this world live by the labour of their hands.'

Architecture (and therefore geometry) is mentioned in Anderson's Constitutions of 1723 where the author talks of the Palladianism (a system of architecture invented by Andrea Palladio, an Italian architect of the 16th century and based on the Ionic, Doric and Corinthian styles) which was a prominent feature of early Georgian architecture and had also been prevalent in the work of Inigo Jones (1573-1652), who had studied architecture in Italy and followed many of the ideas of the Roman architect, Vitruvius. The Philo Musicae (basically a Masonic music and architectural society) founded in 1725 sets out in its first minute book a dissertation on the Seven Liberal Arts and Sciences and in particular geometry and music, which it terms twin sisters. Albert Einstein once claimed that Bro Mozart's music had always existed as part of the fabric of the Universe, just waiting for someone of Mozart's genius to bring it out. But we can go back a lot further than that to see that the ancients were very conscious of the connection between the two. Our old friend Pythagoras is said to have first noted this on listening to a blacksmith hammering on his anvil. When you think about it, if we

Albert Einstein

are listening to somebody sawing or hammering at a constant rhythm are we not sometimes tempted to put words to it and make a little song out of it to amuse ourselves? Pythagoras, of course, saw harmony in many things, and this discovery stimulated him to further exertions in discovering the musical octave and the diatonic scale (doh-ray-me-fah-soh-lah-te-doh).

The connection between music and architecture/geometry hinges on the fact that both are governed by rules of proportion and symmetry that bring about perfect harmony. But, again, there is more to it than that because the correlation between music and mathematics (in terms of value of notes etc) is well known. And then, looking at the link between astronomy and geometry, as man observed the movement of the heavenly bodies forming regular shapes and plotting various courses, so he would link this into another form of proportion and symmetry used to erect temples and other buildings. Astronomy then probably had a lot to do with astrology, but when erecting temples our ancestors would be concerned with the position of the Sun and the measuring tools they used were the compasses, the plumb line and the gnomon. A gnomon is a scientific instrument that can be used for finding the declination of the Sun through the year, among other things. The term is also used for the part of a sundial that casts the shadow. Anaximander (c.610–546BC) is credited with introducing this Babylonian instrument to the Greeks, although the Chinese had it long before that.

So we can see that all Seven Liberal Arts and Sciences tie in together, and although astronomy is the most ancient, geometry is pre-eminent. To give an idea how important these studies were to our early Speculative forebears, at one time in the Old King's Arms Lodge in London an active study of architecture and related subjects was undertaken. There were readings from Palladio's work (see above) and lectures and discussions on everything from optics to welding – forge welding had been practised since the Middle Ages. Between 1733 and 1741 that lodge had many evenings devoted purely to the study of architecture. This was the age of the learned society and studying this sort of thing in one's spare time would be considered fashionable.[8]

The Address in the South East corner

In some lodges the candidate will hear the address with his right foot across the lodge and his left foot down the lodge, so that his feet are on either side of the Perfect Ashlar placed in the South East corner. In the previous Degree, when he stood in the North East corner his feet were the other way round – his left across the lodge and his right down it on either side of the Rough Ashlar. This, he is told, is to mark (or symbolise) the progress he has made in the science, as he was told when he received his apron. This may seem strange because he seems to have gone from the Rough Ashlar (defined as a stone, rough and unhewn as taken from the quarry) to the Perfect Ashlar (a stone of true die or square fitted only to be tried by the Square and Compasses) in the course of just two Degrees! Surely he is only now, as he is told immediately after the Obligation, at the *'midway'* of Freemasonry. We all know he has the very important step of the Third Degree yet to take and he is therefore very far from having 'arrived'. However, given as we have already seen that the Craft started off, some say, with only one Degree and then split into two so that the Fellowcraft was the second and final stage from which one could become Master of a lodge, a Grand Officer or even Grand Master, then we really would in those days have arrived at the Perfect Ashlar.

Some would say that there is a third structure – the broached thurnel or the broaching turner which is appropriate to the Third Degree. It has also been termed or spelt as the broached dornal and the broked mall. As you can see from the illustration, it is a cube with a point on it and could be used for penetration.[9] I don't know whether it is appropriate as a possible 'third stone' because nobody really knows where it fits in the big picture. The Royal Order of Scotland has its own symbolic interpretation, but from the Craft point of view this term, like the perpend (as opposed to perfect) ashlar which was an oblong stone used as a header, seems to have fallen into disuse. Both terms seem to have dropped out of use early on in English Speculative Masonry and are only now encountered in reference books.[10]

The Broached Thurnel or Broaching Turner

We will see later that the Third Degree was a later development and, even when it came in, it was not necessarily available to every brother. I strongly suspect that what we say about being in the midway of Freemasonry, when explaining the position of the Square and Compasses in the Second Degree, is either a post-1813 innovation, following the Union of the Antients' and Moderns' Grand Lodges, or at best a product of William Preston's lectures in the late 18th century.

The Working Tools are presented

It is the only degree in which the Working Tools – the Square, Level and Plumb Rule – are actually tools that a working mason would use. Why choose these tools in particular?

A good clue to this appears in the 5th section of the Second Lecture of the Emulation Book of Lectures. Here we learn that the skilled rulers or overseers were *'men of science'* and skilled craftsmen who presided over lodges consisting of seven Entered Apprentices and five Fellowcrafts. There was, of course, a higher grade, equivalent to an architect, which we only encounter in the Third Degree and who would use tools appropriate to an architect. For the purposes of the rulers or overseers, though, the Square, Level and Plumb Rule are just what they would use to measure and test the work. The work, don't forget, has already been done. The Entered Apprentice has hewn the rough ashlar to make the perfect ashlar. As we say in the Long Explanation of the Working Tools of the Second Degree: *'The square is to try and adjust rectangular corners of buildings and to assist in bringing rude matter into due form, the level is to lay levels and prove horizontals and the plumb rule is to try and adjust uprights, whilst fixing them on their proper bases.'* Use of these tools to check that the stone was fit for its intended purpose is what their work would have consisted of.

The Second Degree Working Tools

The Tracing Board is explained

The Second Degree Tracing Board is quite often delivered in lodges, either after the Second Degree Ceremony has been worked or as a standalone item on a night when there is not much other work on. It is often convenient to do it immediately after the candidate has been passed because the Second Degree ceremony is marginally shorter than the other two and the explanation of the board will frequently be given – often by a Past Master – at the end of the ceremony.

Much of the lecture is narrative, describing the dimensions of the two great pillars at the porchway or entrance and explaining the symbolism inherent in them. The pillars, we are told, were seventeen cubits and a half each in height, twelve cubits in circumference and four in diameter. Don't let's get into the old argument about how long a cubit was or what kind of cubit we are talking about. For biblical purposes it was about 18in or, if you must, 45cm. This means that the pillars were around 26.25ft high, 18ft round and had a diameter of 6ft. I have to say these are not the proportions portrayed on most Tracing Boards!

We also learn that the pillars were *formed hollow the better to serve as archives to Masonry, for therein were deposited the constitutional rolls*. It is now generally accepted that this statement is fanciful; firstly because there was no Masonry, as we know it, in those days, and secondly because those pillars were more likely to be imitative of the two pillars erected by either Seth or Enoch on which were inscribed all the knowledge of the arts and sciences at that period (see above). I have a small quibble with this which we'll look at in a moment.

The Lecture goes on to say that the pillars were made of molten brass. It's a fine point, but this would not be likely to be brass as we know it; neither would any of the other references to brass in the Bible. Brass is today an alloy of copper and zinc, but something called 'brass' has been known since prehistoric times, even before zinc itself was discovered. It was produced by melting copper together with calamine, a zinc ore. In the German village of Breinigerberg an ancient Roman settlement was discovered where a calamine ore mine existed. During the melting process, the zinc is extracted from the calamine and mixes with the copper. Pure zinc, on the other hand, has too low a boiling point to have been produced by ancient metalworking techniques, even if they had discovered it. The many references to 'brass' appearing throughout the Bible are thought to signify another bronze alloy, or copper, rather than the strict modern definition of 'brass'.[11]

At this point, Hiram Abif is introduced for the first time, as the Superintendent of the casting. In the Third Degree the candidate is told that at the building of the Temple, Hiram was *'as you are no doubt well aware, the principal architect'*. It is hard to see how the candidate can be *'well aware'* since this is the only reference to him other than the mention of his name alone, later in this lecture. (Hiram is, of course, mentioned in the First Degree Tracing Board Lecture as well, but it is unlikely that the candidate will have heard that at this point.)

What the Bible says about Hiram at this point is: *'He was a widow's son of the tribe of Naphtali, and his father was a man of Tyre, a worker in brass: and he was filled with wisdom, and understanding, and cunning to work all works in brass. And he came to King Solomon, and wrought all his work'* (1. Kings, Chapter 7).

Next we come to the two chapiters made by Hiram. So, back to the First Book of Kings, Chapter 7:

'16. *And he made two chapiters of molten brass, to set upon the tops of the pillars: the height of the one chapiter was five cubits, and the height of the other chapiter was five cubits:*
17. *And nets of checker work, and wreaths of chain work, for the chapiters which were upon the top of the pillars; seven for the*

one chapiter, and seven for the other chapiter.
18. And he made the pillars, and two rows round about upon the one network, to cover the chapiters that were upon the top, with pomegranates: and so did he for the other chapiter.
19. And the chapiters that were upon the top of the pillars were of lily work in the porch, four cubits.
20. And the chapiters upon the two pillars had pomegranates also above, over against the belly which was by the network: and the pomegranates were two hundred in rows round about upon the other chapiter.
21. And he set up the pillars in the porch of the temple: and he set up the right pillar, and called the name thereof Jachin: and he set up the left pillar, and he called the name thereof Boaz.
22. And upon the top of the pillars was lily work: so was the work of the pillars finished.'

Hiram, the architect, was a Phoenician and some would claim also a Dionysian Artificer, although there is no evidence for this, but I suppose it is possible. In any event, Phoenicians were known to have been influenced by Egyptian architectural styles, and it may well have been that the pomegranates were simply a rosette type of ornamentation and that the lilywork was lotus work, the lotus being a popular and symbolic plant in Egypt at that time. Notwithstanding that, we have our own symbolism as stated in this Lecture: the network denoting unity, the lilywork peace, and the pomegranates unity. I cannot be sure why our ritual compilers ignored the chainwork, especially given our penchant for chains of union etc, but we can perhaps assume that the symbolism of unity had already been covered (but see the Chain of Union in the chapter on the First Degree). The Bible actually says that there were bowls on top of the chapiters, yet we persist in having representations of the celestial and terrestrial globes delineating, in the latter case, maps of America and Australia 3000 years before Columbus and Captain Cook!

The ritual explains that these pillars were set up to remind the Israelites of their escape from Egypt. I said above that it is also believed they were set up to symbolise the two pillars erected by Seth, the grandson of Adam, one of brick and the other of stone, containing all the knowledge of the arts and sciences which had been amassed up to his time. My quarrel with this is that the

Jewish Historian Josephus claimed that Seth's pillars were still to be seen in his day (he was born about AD37) in the land of Siriad. The idea was that Adam had prophesied the destruction of the Earth at one time by fire and at another by water, so that if the brick pillar was destroyed by water, the stone pillar would remain and vice versa. Why then, given the fact that the pillars still existed, would Solomon need to symbolise them in his Temple? There is no mention of Seth's pillars in the Bible, but there is no mention of Solomon's pillars symbolising anything else either.[12]

Incidentally, the Ritual of the Royal Order of Scotland claims the pillars were built by Enoch who was five generations after Seth. The inclusion of the story of the Ephraimites and everything surrounding it is an adaptation of a biblical account to fit in with the ritual. You can read the actual story in the Book of Judges. The full account is in Chapter 12, vv.1-15, but the verses that concern us are verses 4 to 6:

> '4. Then Jephthah gathered together all the men of Gilead, and fought with Ephraim: and the men of Gilead smote Ephraim, because they said, Ye Gileadites are fugitives of Ephraim among the Ephraimites, and among the Manassites.
> 5. And the Gileadites took the passages of Jordan before the Ephraimites: and it was so, that when those Ephraimites which were escaped said, Let me go over; that the men of Gilead said unto him, art thou an Ephraimite? If he say Nay;
> 6. Then said they unto him, Say now Shibboleth: and he said Sibboleth: for he could not frame to pronounce it right. Then they took him, and slew him at the passages of Jordan: and there fell at that time of the Ephraimites forty and two thousand.'

The dictionary defines a Shibboleth as *A custom, phrase or use of language that distinguishes members of a particular social class, profession etc from other people.*

I suppose a good example would be that if someone out of the blue, in the office or in the pub, said 'I'm just going to restore myself to my personal comforts,' then we would know he was probably a Mason, but non-Masons present would not. The word 'Shibboleth' is derived from the Hebrew word for an ear of grain, which explains why it is symbolised by an ear of corn. The fall of water could refer to the passages of the River Jordan and the fate of the Ephraimites when they tried to cross it. It could also be saying that if you have grain, you have bread, and bread and water are all you need for sustenance so that it symbolises the concept of 'plenty'.

Then we have a story as to how the Craftsmen went to receive their wages. It is generally acknowledged that this is entirely fictitious. There is, as we will see, a record in the Bible of a winding staircase and indeed of a middle chamber. However, it is extremely unlikely that two wardens would stand at the foot and the head of the stairs and test every man coming to be paid – there were something like 83,000 of them! However, we will play along with this fiction because it is part of our ritual and therefore part of the overall scheme of things.

Having satisfied the Junior Warden, the workmen ascended the winding staircase and we are told that it came in sections of three, five and seven steps. Consider that for a moment. When we see a ladder or a staircase on a First Degree Tracing Board it is straight – a straight path leading to God. In this instance, however, the stairs wind because the intellectual path is a more difficult one. We have looked at the symbolism of three in the chapter on the First Degree, we will look at the symbolism of five in a moment, and we will think about the symbolism of seven in connection with the Third Degree. For our purposes here we are told that three symbolise the Three Grand Masters who ruled the Temple construction project, just as our Worshipful Master rules his lodge with the assistance of his two wardens.

The Tower of the Five Orders at the Bodleian Library, Oxford

We are then informed that five hold a lodge in allusion to the Five Noble Orders of Architecture – Tuscan, Doric, Ionic, Corinthian and Composite. The magnificent Tower of the Five Orders at the Bodleian Library in Oxford exemplifies these styles.

The Bodleian website has this to say:

'By the time of Bodley's death in 1612, further expansion to the library was being planned. The Schools Quadrangle (sometimes referred to as the "Old Schools Quadrangle", or the "Old Library") was built between 1613 and 1619. Its tower

The Second Degree   141

forms the main entrance to the library, and is known as the Tower of the Five Orders. The Tower is so named because it is ornamented, in ascending order, with the columns of each of the five orders of classical architecture: Doric, Tuscan, Ionic, Corinthian and Composite. The astronomer Thomas Hornsby observed the transit of Venus from this tower in 1769.'[13]

The ritual gets the first two orders a different way round and the reason for this is explained in the 4th section of the Second Lecture in the Emulation Book of Lectures. The Tuscan is placed first in the list because it was the simplest, but the Tuscans were an Italian colony of the Dorians and will therefore have adapted their Order of Architecture from the Doric – so the Doric pre-dates the Tuscan.

The Dispensary, Ormskirk, Lancashire

An example of simple, Doric columns may be seen in the town of Ormskirk at a building called The Dispensary, which has long ceased to have any medical function. I include it because the stone for the frontage was provided by the First Earl of Lathom (when Baron Skelmersdale), a former Provincial Grand Master of West Lancashire to whom also the Chapter House at Liverpool Cathedral was dedicated and endowed by the Freemasons of that Province. The columns may be deemed to be of the Doric Order because they have no bases.

Arguably the finest example of a display of the different Orders of Architecture (or three of them anyway) may be found in the city of Bath. John Wood the elder, almost certainly a Freemason and definitely an antiquarian with a strong interest in things Roman and things Druid – especially Stonehenge and Stanton Drew – wanted to build a circular structure in the city but was frustrated in his efforts at least twice. Eventually he got the chance to build the King's Circus and this he built in the shape of a key (some, who don't know the Masonic significance of the Key, say that it is in the shape of a question mark), the top of which is circular and entered by three roads. The first road is the 'barrel' of the key and there are two others into the circle itself. The effect of this is to form another Masonic symbol – the triangle – within the circle.

Royal Crescent, Bath

Wood's circular structure was inspired partly by the Roman Colosseum, but his ideas also came from Stonehenge, Stanton Drew and King Solomon's Temple. It is always difficult to get into the mind of an architect who is inspired by various themes, as anyone who has visited Barcelona and seen the work of Antoni Gaudi will appreciate. That is why the cathedral of the Sagrada Familia (or Holy Family) can never be completed – because it was all in Gaudi's head!

The diameter of the Circus circle is supposed to equate to 60 cubits (equivalent to 317ft or 97m), the height and width of King Solomon's Temple and also of Stonehenge.

The subject of Wood's Circus is covered in an excellent book by Kirsten Elliott and Neill Menneer which points out that *'Another striking example* [of Masonic symbolism] *is Wood's use of the three classic orders of architecture: Doric, Ionic and Corinthian. At ground floor level is a circle of columns in plain, strong style which some modern purists insist is not Doric but Tuscan, but which to Wood was certainly Doric. At the second level are Ionic columns, slim and graceful with scroll volutes at the top. Above these are columns in the more elaborate Corinthian style, topped with acanthus leaves.*

The Second Degree   143

Crowning the whole edifice is a ring of acorns. Here John Wood has returned to the Druids.'[14]

They go on to point out that there are over five hundred carvings above the Doric pillars (i.e. between the ground and the first floor levels), some of which are Masonic – notably compasses and beehives. Wood did not get to build the Circus. The foundation stone was laid in 1754, but he died in that year and the work was completed by his son, John Wood the younger.[15]

The Second Degree is very much the degree of the middle chamber. One author has suggested that, like the testing of the workmen, the middle chamber is fictitious. This is not correct – in 1 Kings, Chapter 6 v.8 the middle chamber and the winding staircase are clearly identified:

'The door for the middle chamber was in the right side of the house: and they went up with winding stairs into the middle chamber, and out of the middle into the third.'

The Circus, Bath

The Lodge is closed in the Second Degree

The symbolic reference in the closing of the lodge is to the sacred symbol, situated in the centre of the building which alludes to the Grand Geometrician of the Universe. This is the letter 'G', which may be suspended from the ceiling or displayed in a similar form in a central position. It has been said that this stands for God – the Great Architect and Grand Geometrician of the Universe. But it is only in Germanic languages that 'G' is the initial letter of the word. In biblical Hebrew, Greek and Latin this does not apply.

144   A Guide to Masonic Symbolism

It has also been suggested that the 'G' is for geometry, the foundation of all the other arts and sciences. Indeed, in this Degree we refer to God as the Grand *Geometrician* of the Universe as if to stress the crucial importance of geometry.

By far the best interpretation, to my mind anyway, is that the letter 'G' is symbolising the Greek letter Gamma, to which it is broadly equivalent. Gamma, in Greek, is written Γ and this is, of course, the Square! We have already looked at its symbolism, but at this stage we can content ourselves by observing that here, in this Degree of Fellowcraft, the candidate qualifies himself to work with the Square on levels and perpendiculars. He is not yet ready to use the Compasses, which are the instrument of the Master Mason, but he has arrived at that stage which was once as far as he would have needed to go before becoming Master of his lodge, or even Grand Master.

The Symbolism of Five

As three was the crucial number in the First Degree, so five predominates in the Second. We will also look the five-sided Pentagram or Pentangle which has great symbolic significance in Freemasonry. Five is considered a circular number because it comprises the four cardinal points plus the centre. The rose and lily are both highly symbolic in Masonry and elsewhere and they are five-petalled flowers. We have five digits on each hand and foot.[16]

To the ancients five was the number of Venus and also of Apollo (the God of Light) who had five qualities: omnipotence, omniscience, omnipresence, eternity and unity.

In Christianity we have the parable of the five loaves and two fishes feeding 5000 (Matthew, Chapter 15 vv.32-39). We also have the five wounds of Christ. In both Christianity and Judaism there are five books of the Law of Moses. In Hebrew tradition the number five symbolises radical intelligence – a good reason for its being so crucial in a Degree which is about improving the intellect. Islam has five pillars of piety. The ancient Chinese considered five as the harmonic union of Yin and Yang and recognised five colours, five tones, five smells, five planets and five metals. In Alchemy five represented the quintessence, the fifth element which was life-giving and life-sustaining with the other four elements of earth, water, fire and air. As such it was a famous talisman.[17]

In Masonry we have, of course, five Orders of Architecture, five points of fellowship and it takes five to hold a lodge (the Master, two Wardens and two Fellowcrafts). The five senses – touch, taste, smell, sight and hearing – once played an important role in the Second Degree and are mentioned by Browne in his *Master Key* of 1802. Other orders attach further meanings. The Royal Order of Scotland talks of five distinctions of time. The Societas Rosicruciana in Anglia regards five as the number of health and safety.

The Pentagram or Pentangle

The origin of the Pentagram, Pentangle or Pentalpha is thought to have been in Mesopotamia four thousand years ago as an astronomical plot of the movements of the planet Venus (Ishatar). Pythagoras adopted it as an emblem of health and harmony, symbolising the Hieros Gamos or the marriage of Heaven and Earth combining the number two (which was considered terrestrial and feminine) with the number three (thought to be celestial and masculine). So as such, the number five symbolises the microcosm of the human body and mind. It is also acknowledged as a symbol of wisdom and has always been considered to have magical properties. It also features in popular literature, specifically in the Arthurian legend of *Sir Gawain and the Green Knight*.

The Pentagram is, of course, the jewel of our Grand Master, consisting of three triangles representing the three Grand Masters of King Solomon's Temple. It is simply a five-pointed star drawn with five straight lines and yet its use is widespread throughout many countries and cultures. It appears (as a pentagram, rather than a star) on the flags of Morocco and Ethiopia. It is the symbol of the Baha'i faith.

We looked in the previous chapter at the rather complex concept of the Golden Proportion, which has a value of approximately 1.618. In Mesopotamia the Pentagram was frequently found engraved on various artefacts and was thought also to be some sort of royal seal. That age-old symbol – the rose – contains many Pentagrams. The geometric proportions of the Pentagram are those of the Golden Proportion.

'In symbolic language, it is: Three things working through two things to yield one thing. As a symbol it becomes a means of reawakening, forming a symbolic bridge between heaven

(circle) and earth (square). It is a means through which we can examine the relationship between nature-man-creator. It is the only value in the universe that relates to One by creating four elements that pass through four, three, and two.' [18]

---

1   Bernard Jones – *Freemasons' Guide and Compendium*
2   John Acaster – *The Central Importance of the Second Degree*
3   Jacques Huyghebaert – *Some Reflections regarding the number Five*
4   Michael Lawrence – *The Perfect Points of my Entrance*
5   Harry Carr – *The Freemason at Work*
6   Jones, op. cit.
7   Thomas D. Worrel – *The Spiritual Vision of the Seven Liberal Arts*
8   Jones, op. cit.
9   Frederick Smyth – *A Reference Book for Freemasons*
10 Don Falconer – *The Jewels of the Lodge*
11 Wikipedia – *Brass*
12 Flavius Josephus – *Jewish Antiquities* (Whiston Translation)
13 Bodleian Library website
14 Kirsten Elliott and Neill Menneer – *Bath*
15 Bath Museum website
16 *The Complete Dictionary of Symbols*
17 J. C. Cooper – *Traditional Symbols*
18 Udo Becker – *Continuum Encyclopaedia of Symbols*

The Third Degree

*I saw a dead man's finer part
Shining within each faithful heart
Of those bereft. Then said I 'This must be
His immortality.'*
THOMAS HARDY (1840-1928) *HIS IMMORTALITY*

The Master Mason (or Holy of Holies) is about the spiritual being, Jung's 'collective unconscious', one step closer to the Divine. This is what W. L. Wimshurst called *'the real initiation'*. The First Degree is concerned with the body and the Second Degree with the soul. Here we unite both of these with the spirit.

The Third Degree has not always been with us. Early in the 18th century the Craft was a two-degree or bi-gradal system and only became tri-gradal from about 1730 onwards. The exposure *Masonry Dissected* produced by Samuel Prichard in 1730 is the first concrete proof we have of a Third Degree being worked, although R. F. Gould was of the opinion that it was being conferred as early as 1724.[1]

Even then it was by no means universal and, as we have seen, many 18th century Masons contented themselves with the two Degrees that were necessary to become Master of a lodge, a Grand Officer, or even Grand Master.

Bernard Jones says: *'Masonic students do not conceal their belief that the amazing popularity of a so-called "exposure" published in 1730 played no small part in the gradual standardising of lodge work and ritual. This was Prichard's* Masonry Dissected, *which, unreliable as all such irregular prints must necessarily be, yet gave the public of the day some idea of the masonic ritual, and nowadays is valuable to the historian chiefly because by its use of such terms as Enter'd Prentice, Fellow Craft, and Masters' Part. It indicates that speculative masonry in 1730 or before was acquainted with the Hiramic legend. Prichard's book of twenty-two pages was the publishing best-seller of its day; it ran through three editions in eleven days, was reprinted in two newspapers, separately published in Scotland, Ireland, in the Continental cities, and in America, and passed through an immense number of editions – on an average one every three years in England alone – through a period of about a century.'* [2]

This is no doubt correct, but I can't help thinking that the biggest market for Prichard's book was probably the Masons themselves, who were unable to buy a printed ritual and probably found learning difficult without one. Even today some lodges refuse to have anything written down, relying instead on verbal transmission of everything. I should stress that these will now be very few, but I do know of at least one.

We'll consider the legend of Hiram Abif later, but note here what Albert Pike says about the genesis of the Third Degree: *'Hiram Abif was probably never heard of in a lodge until after 1717, and the substitute for the master's word certainly was not until several years later. The legend of the Third Degree was introduced by the new comers into Masonry, who brought into it all that is really symbolic and philosophical in the three degrees.'* [3] Bernard Jones tends to disagree with this: *'Dated 1726 is the Graham MS. which is believed to have been copied from an earlier document and undoubtedly supports the idea that the Third Degree legend in some form or other was known in the seventeenth century.'*

Jones goes on: *'The three-degree system is thought to have been working in Paris in 1731, in Kirkcudbright, Scotland in 1735; in Sweden in 1737; but it must not be thought that wherever it went it was welcomed. There were many English lodges in which it was not eagerly adopted, while in some Scottish lodges it met open hostility, as is made clear elsewhere in these pages.'* [4]

So, when the Third came in, it seems to have been a bit of an 'exclusive club' to which many Masons would never attain. Indeed in Scotland, where the Third does not appear much, if at all, before the formation of the Grand Lodge of Scotland in 1736, it was practised at first only in isolated instances and some lodges contented themselves to go through the 18th century without working it at all.[5]

In 1971, Bro Rev Canon Richard Tydeman gave a Prestonian Lecture entitled *Masters and Master Masons – A Theory of the Third Degree* which posed the question as to whether the original function of the Third Degree was to install a brother as Master of his lodge. This Bro Tydeman supports firstly with the confusion of the terms Master and Master Mason during the early 18th century, the fact that the working tools are those of an architect (the master of the work), rather than those of a manual labourer, and the fact that in the Third Degree alone the Tracing Board is facing the Master rather than the brethren in the lodge. There were also other arguments, and whilst not everyone agreed or agrees with this theory, many did. I have returned to it in the chapter on the Installation.[6]

There is much speculation as to whether the Degree developed into its present form with the purpose of acquiring substituted secrets to facilitate the creation of the Royal Arch where the genuine secrets could be fully recovered. In other constitutions this does not happen, particularly where the Royal Arch, if it exists, is not part of the usual progression.

Once again, let's go through the ceremony as it is now practised in England and look at the symbolism at the different stages. A synopsis may be given as follows. Let's follow this as we did in the preceding two Degrees:

1 The Questions before Raising
2 The Lodge is opened in the Third Degree
3 The Candidate is prepared
4 The Candidate seeks admission
5 A Prayer of Dedication is said
6 The Perambulations round the Lodge
7 The Candidate is presented
8 The Candidate moves from West to East
9 The Obligation is taken
10 The Exhortation
11 The Raising
12 The Charge
13 The Candidate learns the Secrets
14 The Candidate retires and re-enters
15 The Candidate is invested
16 The Traditional History
14 The Tracing Board is explained
15 The Working Tools are presented
16 The Lodge is closed in the Third Degree

The Questions before Raising

These summarise what the Fellowcraft has learnt to date, laying particular stress on the fact that his study in the Second Degree has been *'The hidden mysteries of nature and science'*. The catechism goes on to consider wages, which we have already looked at in connection with the Second Degree, and finishes up by reminding us of the two great pillars and their significance.

The First Artificer in Metals

Going on to the entrusting of the candidate, the choice of the word TC is a curious one. He was indeed the first artificer in metals or as it says in Genesis, Chapter 4 v.22: *'an instructor of every artificer in brass and iron'*. He was the son of Lamech (who was also the father of Noah) and his step-brothers were Jabal the father of those that dwell in tents and keep cattle and sheep, and Jubal, the inventor of music. As the first artificer, TC would be the prototype of Hiram Abif who was *'a man cunning to work in gold, and in silver, and in brass, and in iron'* (2 Chronicles, Chapter 2 v.7). But TC should not be seen as a good guy in the context of the Third Degree. Josephus says that he had great strength, exceeding all others, and was adept in martial performances and that *'he procured what tended to the pleasures of the body by that method'*. In other words, he was more interested in worldly gain that in things spiritual and hence the import of his name is 'worldly possessions'.

Philo of Alexandria says of Tubalcain: *'He was a hammer-beater and forger of brass and iron for the soul of that man who is intent on corporeal pleasures or external things is beaten by a hammer, like a piece of iron on an anvil, being drawn out according to the long and thin-drawn extensions of the appetites. Accordingly, you may see men fond of their bodies at every time, and in every place laying lines and nets to catch those objects that they desire; and others, who are lovers of money or covetous of glory, letting loose their desire and eagerness for those things to the furthest boundaries of earth and sea, and dragging in from all quarters by their unlimited desires, as if by so many nets, whatever can gratify them, till the excessive tension, being broken by its great violence, drags back those who are dragging at it, and throws them down headlong. All these men are causes of war, on account of*

which they are said to be workers in brass and iron, by means of which metals wars are carried on.'[7]

Now, it is interesting that we refer at this point to someone who puts personal gain before virtue and truth. In relating the legend of Hiram we are about to consider this again when referring to the three ruffians who murdered him. J. S. M. Ward points out that the word used originally may have been Tymboxein, a word derived from the Greek meaning 'buried' or 'entombed'. However, I believe the word TC is perfectly apposite, when you think about it, given that by entering upon the Third Degree we are placing things spiritual above worldly possessions.[8]

The Lodge is opened in the Third Degree

One of the first puzzles of the Third Degree may be found in the Opening. Up to now we have been told that we came into the lodge in the West and are proceeding towards the East in search of light in the form of knowledge. Yet when the Worshipful Master asks the Senior Warden *'Whither directing your course'*, the answer comes back 'The West'. The Junior Warden is then asked what inducement he has to move in that direction and says: *'To seek for that which was lost which by your instruction and our own industry we hope to find'*.

If the source of all knowledge and light is in the East, why is it that the Third Degree supplies an *'Inducement to leave the East and go to the West'*? Several reasons could be suggested as to why, on this occasion, we head westward, rather than eastward in search of light. For one thing the holiest part of King Solomon's Temple was situated in the West and this is where Hiram is laid to rest. Secondly, as a Christian reference, the Three Wise Men, or Magi came from the East, directing their course to follow a star westward. Thirdly, after the destruction of the Temple and the captivity of the Jews in Babylon, they returned after seventy years by permission of King Cyrus to Jerusalem, travelling from East to West. These matters pertain to the Royal Arch and are also extensively covered in the workings of the Rectified Scottish Rite in Continental Europe, but they are beyond the scope of this book.

Then we come to the curious question *'Where do you hope to find them?'* and the equally baffling answer *'with the centre'*, not in, at or on the centre. We have seen in reference to the First Degree Tracing Board that the centre of the circle, bordered by two grand parallel lines is the symbol of God. William Preston's version of the answer *'by working towards the centre'* makes more sense. Although we are going to the West in search of the Genuine Scts, we are relying on God, the Centre, to aid us and in working through the Third Degree we are moving towards the knowledge of ourselves and by that the knowledge of God.[9]

Then, of course, when we finally open the lodge we cut the sign without recovering (a necessary measure that so many – some quite senior – people appear to be unaware of). It is necessary because, at that stage, we have not found the substituted secrets and therefore are only proceeding on our journey westwards. The lack of recovery at this point, and this point alone, symbolises that fact.

The Candidate is prepared

Here again the preparation is an extension of what has gone before, emphasising the candidness of the candidate – now both his feet are slipshod, both sides of his breast are visible and both arms are bare.

The Candidate seeks admission

Getting quite used to it now, the candidate is led to the door of the temple and the Tyler gives the knocks of a Fellowcraft. These signify that body and soul are united but the spirit is still at variance, so the candidate seeks further light and hopes he is entitled to take the final step. He is received on the points of the Compasses, highly significant in this Degree because now he is said to be passing from the Square to the Compasses or from the tools of a craftsman to the equipment of an architect or master builder. This is borne out by the fact that he is said to come with *'the united aid of the S&C'*.

The first thing he will obviously notice is that the lodge is in near darkness with just one light at the Master's pedestal. Why does this light remain lit? Well, for one thing, it would be very difficult if it didn't, but there is also a symbolic reason. The fact that the Master's light is on indicates that the lodge is open and that the Master is present and it must never be extinguished. Harry Carr reproduces a letter written in 1839 by the then Grand Secretary, William White. White was being asked for clarification of an earlier decision taken after the Union when the Lodge of Reconciliation (later to evolve into the Emulation Lodge of Improvement) made a recommendation to this effect. He replied in the terms I have stated, adding that the Master's light alone should illumine the lodge during the Third Degree, but went further by saying that the recommendations of the Lodge of Reconciliation had been adopted by Grand Lodge and, not only should the light be kept on, but it should not be covered in any way by a lanthorn or anything else. Lanthorn is an archaic word for lantern and what was probably being implied was a metal sleeve with a star cut into it which is placed over the Master's light so that the amount of light it gives out is reduced.

A Prayer of Dedication is said

The prayer lays great emphasis on the trial element of the Third Degree, asking that the candidate be endued with fortitude and so on. Although the ceremony is not that much of an ordeal, it is more a question of trying to convey the real import of the ceremony of Raising, because it symbolises the battle against evil in our lives and our constant striving to live by Masonic principles.

The Perambulations round the Lodge

Now there are three of them and they serve the same purpose as the perambulations in the previous two Degrees, except that this time the candidate is displaying his proficiency as both a Mason and a Craftsman.

The Candidate is presented

Now the Senior Warden, who in some obediences (and I believe should in ours as well) would have coached and carefully tested the Fellowcraft in his knowledge of the two preceding Degrees, presents the 'finished product' on the basis that he should be 'entitled' to take this last and greatest step.

The Candidate moves from West to East

Many Masons simply accept this strange series of seven steps as something 'which is there' and never seek to look for a meaning behind it. The first three steps are *'as if stepping over an open grave'*, and the last four are in some rituals called *'bold or marching steps'*. It may never occur to many – even Christian – Masons that what we are describing is the form of the Cross. We start off at the head, step to the right limb, then the left and with the first of the marching steps arrive at the foot of the cross, to commence boldly and in confidence our approach to the pedestal. The seven steps also symbolise the Seven Liberal Arts and Sciences. Notice that the number of steps increases – three in the Entered Apprentice Degree, five in the Fellowcraft Degree and now seven.

The Obligation is taken

As with the previous Degrees, let's look at where the Scriptures are normally open in the Third Degree. It is at Ecclesiastes, Chapter 12 vv.1-7. A clergyman, who was also a Freemason, once described the Book of Ecclesiastes to me as a 'collection of wisecracks'. Certainly, from our point of view, the symbolism behind the words is worth examining.

> 'Remember now thy Creator in the days of thy youth, while the evil days come not, nor the years draw nigh, when thou shalt say, I have no pleasure in them;'

This is a commentary on the halcyon days of our youth when our passions and prejudices have probably yet to develop. We may have ups and downs when we are young but, if we are in a secure environment, there tends to be an aura of goodness and a feeling that life isn't too bad. We may also, because we haven't been let down by life yet, feel that we have the potential to achieve great things.

> 'While the sun, or the light, or the moon, or the stars, be not darkened, nor the clouds return after the rain;'

Continuing on the same theme, but adding that, of course, in youth we can normally expect to enjoy good health. These two verses remind us to search for God, the source of our being and the arbiter of our destiny, while we are young and to let Him guide us throughout our lives.

Then we have four verses describing the process of growing old.

> 'In the day when the keepers of the house shall tremble, and the strong men shall bow themselves, and the grinders cease because they are few, and those that look out of the windows be darkened.'

The house is the body and its keepers are the hands which we use to pick things up or protect ourselves. In old age these often tremble. I remember a very likeable Brother in Birkenhead, called

Bill Buckley, who tyled many lodges there but was almost bent double and had to carry the lodge equipment round in an old supermarket trolley. He was so well-thought of that, at the end, other brethren were actually doing the job for him, yet he was still appointed Tyler, year on year. His body was so bent that I could hardly believe it when I was told he had once stood six feet four and had been a Sergeant in the Liverpool Scottish Regiment.

The *grinders* are, fairly obviously, the teeth and *those that look out of the windows* are the eyes as advancing years impair their effectiveness.

'And the doors shall be shut in the streets, when the sound of the grinding is low, and he shall rise up at the voice of the bird, and all the daughters of music shall be brought low;'

This refers firstly to deteriorating hearing, then to difficulty in digesting food, nervousness at the feeling of being vulnerable causing a quick reaction to a sudden noise or the like, and the reduction of the power of the voice when singing, or even speaking, in old age.

'Also when they shall be afraid of that which is high, and fears shall be in the way, and the almond tree shall flourish, and the grasshopper shall be a burden and desire shall fail; because man goeth to his long home, and the mourners go about the streets;'

Old people are often afraid of heights because of loss of balance and equally nervous about going out into busy streets, particularly in the dark. This has in part accounted for the increasing popularity of daylight lodges in recent years. The hair (almond tree) goes grey, or white, or falls out. The sexual organs (grasshopper) diminish and become burdensome, and the desire that stimulates them reduces.

'Or ever the silver cord be loosed, or the golden bowl be broken, or the pitcher be broken at the fountain, or the wheel broken at the cistern.'

I have always believed this verse to refer to prostate cancer, although others might put different interpretations on it. To have acquired this scourge in biblical times, without the advantage of so much research done and knowledge acquired since, must have been horrendous. Possibly also the pitcher (of water) refers to the tendency of old people to be more emotional and easily moved to tears.

> 'Then shall the dust return to the earth as it was and the spirit shall return unto God who gave it.'

And finally, we die.

So effectively, it's a sermon encouraging us to seek God while He may be found. You may wonder why it is particularly relevant to the Third Degree. The Third Degree is about death, but we are not actually dying in the physical sense. Surely, then, all the more reason why we should be reminded of the need to seek God, because one day we will die and stand before the dreaded judgement seat. In some lodges, this passage of Scripture is recited later in the ceremony, after the candidate has been lowered into the 'grave', which hopefully bears out my point. The Obligation itself follows the basic pattern of the other two Degrees. We reiterate the promise to maintain the secrets and to be diligent in attending to the duties of Masonry by attending, as summonsed, all meetings within the length of our cable-tow.

We then lay specific emphasis on our duty to be loyal to and to assist our brethren, making a clear and unequivocal exception in that we cannot protect a brother who has violated the laws of God or the ordinances of the realm. The particular clause in the Obligation in which we swear to most strictly respect the chastity of those *'nearest and dearest'* to a Brother Master Mason *'in the persons of his wife, his sister and his child'*, symbolises the fact that we regard our Masonic affiliations as special. In the 18th century – an age when all women were considered 'fair game' – moral standards were different from today and we can find a good example in the *London Journal* of James Boswell, a Freemason and biographer of Dr Samuel Johnson, written in 1762-3:

> *'Thursday 31 March. .... At night I strolled into the Park and took the first whore I met, whom I without many words copulated with free from danger, being safely sheathed. She was ugly and lean and her breath smelt of spirits. I never asked her name. When it was done, she slunk off...*

'Friday 1 April. This being Good Friday, I endeavoured to excite in my mind a devout and solemn frame' [10]

From this we can see that the morals of that age saw nothing inconsistent in indulging in lewd sexual behaviour in the evening and then waking up the following morning in an attitude of piety. The key thing, however, is that this Obligation meant to say, in an age when such behaviour was the norm, whatever you get up to with women is your business, but you don't do it with female relatives of your brother Masons.

The Exhortation

The candidate is now Obligated and about to face a trial of his fortitude and fidelity. Before beginning this the Master delivers what is called a 'retrospect' of the degrees in Freemasonry through which he has already passed. That done, the legend of the death of Hiram Abif is repeated for the candidate's benefit and he is told that he is about to symbolically represent Hiram for the purpose of being raised.

The Raising

The first two attempts to raise the candidate are unsuccessful. Why? Because ordinary grips are tried and these fail because the flesh has decomposed. The final attempt is by using a stronger grip, variously known as the 'Lion's Paw' and the 'Eagle's Claw'.

The fact that this is done points to an earlier age when the Third Degree had not only the themes of Death and Resurrection but also the theme of Decay. How long had the body laid very indecently interred? How long did it take the Fellowcrafts to find the body of their Master? This theme is no longer prevalent in the Third Degree. Some scholars say that the first slip shows that science cannot find a soul, the second that logic cannot find a soul, and the successful third attempt proves that faith in the immortality of the soul is the only course. The third and successful attempt is based on the FPOF, in which the Master is assisted by his two Wardens.

The Charge

In the Charge given after the candidate has been raised we encounter a number of symbols. Breaking the passage down, we learn that the *'light of a Master Mason is darkness visible'*, symbolic of the fact that we are finally penetrating the mysteries of life and death and *'serving only to express that gloom which rests on the practice of futurity'* in the sense that we are being shown that death is no more than a portal through which all must pass to enter a higher life.

It often puzzles me that we do not insist in our candidates having, as well as a belief in a Supreme Being, also a belief in an after-life, because it is difficult to imagine what a brother who did not believe that there was something coming after we die would make of much of our Masonic teaching.

The word 'gloom' is interesting. It is referring to the semi-darkness in which the Third Degree is conferred, but it is one of those words whose meaning has changed over the years. The Bottomley Ritual used in the Liverpool area refers to the candidate being invested with his apron *'in mystery and in gloom'*. Today the word 'gloom' generally means sadness and misery, but, of course, the Third Degree is neither a sad nor a miserable event. It is used in this sense in allusion to the reduced lighting in the temple during the Third Degree. I should, of course, point out that these words could only be used in lodges where the lighting is not fully restored until after the candidate has been invested.

We go on to hear that *'it is that mysterious veil which the eye of human reason cannot penetrate, unless assisted by that light which is from above'* – that light, of course, being the Volume of the Sacred Law which, as the rule and guide of our faith, prepares us for the things which are to come. It is then pointed out to the candidate that he stands on the brink of a grave *'into which you have just figuratively descended and which, when this transitory life shall have passed away will again receive you into its cold bosom'*. This harks back to my earlier point about the death here being only symbolic, real death being none the less inevitable.

We are exhorted to think on this inevitable destiny and encouraged to guide our reflections to that most interesting of all human studies – the knowledge of yourself. Pythagoras, who would not have been at home with the Compasses because he never dealt with circles, none the less displayed a motto at his school at Croton – *Man know thyself*. So, what is meant in this context by 'self'? Plotinus, the metaphysicist and neo-platonist who lived in the 3rd century AD said: *'Now I seek to lead back the self within me to the All self'*. Those were his dying words and are sometimes reported as the *'Divine'* within me. Carl Jung, in *Seven Sermons to the Dead*, speaks of the self as a deeper centre of consciousness.[11]

Knowledge of oneself is regarded in Islam as the key to the knowledge of God. We are being charged to let reason dominate and suppress our emotions of lust and anger and purify our hearts, on the basis that these corrupt emotions will perish with our bodies, whereas the soul is immortal. Now, in the Third Degree as it says in the Holy Koran: *'We have stripped the veil from off thee and thy sight today is keen'*. This process of self-knowledge leading to knowledge of God was also known to the Greeks, as *Theosis*, and it is reassuring to see that Freemasonry is not really at variance with the major faiths and philosophies of the world.

Towards the end of the Charge, the ritual speaks of *'Lift(ing) our eyes to that bright Morning Star, whose rising brings peace and salvation to the faithful and obedient of the human race'*. This is generally agreed to be a Christian reference and some lodges where the membership is predominantly of other faiths, have amended their rituals accordingly. King David Lodge No.7256 in West Lancashire have substituted the words *'Lift our eyes to Him who brings peace and tranquillity to the faithful'* etc. The Morning Star also symbolises the dawning of a new day and so, whatever faith you follow, you can appreciate that being raised to the Sublime Degree of a Master Mason means that your spiritual outlook should be more optimistic because you can now see death as nothing more than a transition to a better life beyond the grave.

The Candidate learns the Secrets

After the Charge the candidate is wheeled round from his previous position in the North East to the South East. Nobody really knows why this is done, but Harry Carr has suggested that it is a summary of his movements through the three Degrees. In the First Degree he was placed in the North East corner to hear the Charity address. In the Second he was addressed in the South East corner to mark the progress he had made in the science. This makes sense when you consider that, having retired and returned and been invested with his apron, the next place he will go is the centre to hear the Traditional History completed.

The Candidate retires and re-enters

The candidate restores himself to his personal comforts and re-enters the lodge. In the other two Degrees getting his apron is the last thing he does before hearing about the tools with which he is now expected to work and then hearing a charge and perhaps a lecture on the Tracing Board. In this instance there is much more to do. He is conducted to the Senior Warden who symbolises the soul in the Second Degree and, as Ward says, *'even after death, man's spiritual advancement is registered by the soul'*.

The Candidate is invested

There have been many interpretations of the Master Mason's apron. The colour has been associated with the feminine principle and particularly with the Virgin Mary, with Cambridge University, with the Parliamentary cause in the English Civil War and, as we saw earlier, with the former colour of the Order of the Garter. There are several interesting features to it. The tassels – and this is the first apron on which we acquire tassels – are as we have already seen said to have evolved from apron strings. Please note that there are seven tassels; the significance of the number seven, both in Freemasonry and elsewhere, is discussed at the end of this chapter. J. S. M. Ward, who was not unknown for seeing symbolism where others did not, thought that the rosette, or rose, represented the Vesica Pisces – an ancient hieroglyphical device used among early Christians as a symbol for Christ and signifying literally the airbladder of a fish. This was a very popular symbol formed by the intersection of two circles based on the part in the centre which forms a fish-shaped oval rather like a rugby ball. It was frequently used in the design of churches from St John Lateran, and the old St Peter's at Rome, to the Abbey Church at Bath, which is one of the latest Gothic buildings of any consequence in England. The seals of all colleges, abbeys and other religious communities, as well as of ecclesiastical persons, were invariably made of this shape.[12]

Ward also saw the two triangles, one formed by the apron flap and the other from the triangle formed by the three rosettes, as intersecting each other, indicating the union of the spirit with man's nature and of the conjunction of the creative and the destructive aspects. If you find these concepts difficult to follow, you will not be alone.

The Traditional History

Like the Tracing Board which is discussed next, the Traditional History in the Third Degree is another post-Union innovation. It was first delivered in The Grand Stewards' Lodge and later at the

Emulation Lodge of Improvement. Prior to the Union, Browne's *Master Key* of 1802 was referred to, with his 'hieroglyphs' being used to explain the symbols. The legend of Hiram Abif (or Abiv), of course, appeared before that time. It is important to stress the crucial nature of the Hiramic legend in the Third Degree. Clearly, without it the ceremony does not exist, but why did our forebears create it in this peculiar manner?

The loss of Hiram's life is symbolically the temporary triumph of evil over good. The raising of Hiram reverses that and good prevails in the end. In factual terms, Hiram Abif was a real person, as we have already seen. He did not die in the manner depicted in the Third Degree, but probably returned to his native city of Tyre when the Temple was completed and may well have died of old age.

Hiram's death has been equated to other violent deaths in the Egyptian Mysteries and in Christianity, but in Masonry we are not claiming that an ordinary human being was raised from the dead by other humans because that is impossible. What we are showing is that evil used violence to suppress good. They were bound to win at first; it was three on to one and they were armed, whilst Hiram was not. But in the end their efforts came to nothing; they did not obtain the secrets of a master mason, because of Hiram's fidelity, and they ended up suffering a violent death by decapitation for their wickedness.

We can all probably point to a period in our lives when, whilst we may not have suffered violence, we may have experienced rejection because of the actions of others motivated by the hope of personal gain, or perhaps just a propensity to make trouble wherever they go. There are always those who will believe lies and misrepresentations, and as the saying goes, 'Mud sticks'. Bro Kipling sums it up in his wonderful poem *'If'*:

'If you can bear to hear the truth you've spoken,
Twisted by knaves to make a trap for fools.'

Like Hiram, who lay *'very indecently interred'*, or in other words, dumped under the rubbish, we may for a while be excluded and ostracised. Time is the great healer and eventually those with unworthy motives, though they may well prosper for a while, will trip themselves up. Hopefully (though I'm sure not always, at least not in this world) honesty and worthiness will in the end prevail.

We need to say a word about the Sprig of Acacia that was placed over the temporary grave of Hiram. If you have ever tried to go back to a place and identify a natural feature you previously saw, you will know it's nigh on impossible. Marking this place of temporary, albeit indecent, interment is therefore logical, but why Acacia? For a start, it has sometimes been wrongly referred to as *Cassia* – this is an entirely different plant with little symbolism attached to it, but even the venerable Dr Oliver referred to it as such. The Acacia is an evergreen tree growing widely in the Holy Land. It was the Shittim Wood of the Ark of the Covenant (we have seen elsewhere that timber was not that plentiful in Palestine and so perhaps there wasn't much choice; remember cedar wood had to be imported from Lebanon for King Solomon's Temple). The fact that the Acacia was evergreen symbolises the immortality of the soul, and it was quite common then to place a sprig of it over the grave of a friend or relative. It is also a symbol of innocence, so perhaps the Craftsmen who planted it were demonstrating that it was they, the innocent ones, and not the murderers who had planted it. A further symbolism of the Crown of Thorns being made from Acacia thorns will have been dropped at the de- Christianisation of the Craft after 1813.[13]

The fact that Acacia is finally acknowledged as a symbol of Initiation takes us back to the words of W. L. Wimshurst quoted earlier – that the Third Degree is the *'real initiation'*. The final triumph of good is symbolised by Hiram's being raised from the level to the perpendicular and then being decently interred in *'such a sepulture as became his rank and exalted talents'*. They could not bring him back to life, so this was the next best thing. Incidentally, Harry Carr pointed out that the word 'sepulture', rather than 'sepulchre', was put into the ritual after 1813 as a verb to signify burying him. In other words – because, of the two words, only sepulture has this meaning – 'having a funeral for him'.[14]

Nobody knows precisely where the legend of Hiram Abif came from or from what earlier, similar story it could have been adapted to fit into the Masonic context. Perhaps it wasn't adapted from anything. It is possible that our founding fathers in the 18th century, anxious to have a higher Degree that would be a bit exclusive and removed from connection with Operative masonry, followed by a higher Order in which the genuine secrets could be recovered, put the legend together just as an author would write a short story. Either way, the lesson we are being symbolically taught, as we approach the centre and the source of true light, is that good will triumph in the end.

The Tracing Board is explained

There are many aspects to the Third Degree Tracing Board and I have tried to give explanations by quoting not the Emulation version, which most of us are familiar with, but that used in Royal Cumberland Lodge No.41 in Bath (RC). I do this with their kind permission because it is the most comprehensive version I have ever come across and gives the best explanation of the symbols I have ever found:

The Third Degree Tracing Board

'*The coffin lies before you and you are not informed how soon you may become its tenant. The Skull and Bones are present to*

your view, and you know not how speedily your flesh may be consumed in the grave, and nothing left but those striking emblems of mortality.

'*The Sprig of Acacia is placed at the head of the coffin to remind you of the uncertainty of life, and is at the present day borne before Eastern Monarchs to teach them the same lesson, and that no evil deeds can escape the all seeing eye of God. If you think that the dispensations of providence may be subverted by human foresight, you will find yourself miserably mistaken; even your own conscience will bring to light the hidden things of darkness. Then let us learn from the sprig of acacia to practise all Masonic virtues, that on our departure from this frail life, we may be welcomed with this joyful salutation, "Well done, ye good and faithful servants, enter ye into the joy of your Lord."*

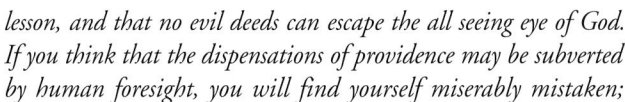

'*The Emblems of Mortality allude to the untimely death of our Grand Master Hiram Abif, and cry out with a voice almost more than mortal "Prepare to meet thy God". Infancy or youth, manhood or old age, all must pass to the embrace of corruption. They teach us that we should possess fortitude like him and that we should rather part with our lives than improperly divulge the secrets of our Order. They emblematically signify that state to which we are all hastening when having put off this mortal coil, the grave will receive us into its cold embrace and mingle us with our parent dust. Therefore we are warned to take heed to our steps in this our sublunary journey, try our actions by the Square and Compasses that we may live respected as Masons and when our sands are run teach us how to die.*

'*The Sprig of Acacia is an emblem of that immortal part of man which never dies, and when the cold winter of*

The Third Degree   165

death is passed away and the bright summer morn of the Resurrection appears, the Sun of Righteousness shall descend and send His Angels to collect our ransomed dust. Then if we are found worthy we shall be entrusted with his pass word by virtue of which we shall be enabled to enter his celestial Lodge above, where the supreme Great Architect of the Universe presides, and where we shall see the King in the beauty of Holiness and with Him enter an endless eternity.

'The Three Steps, usually delineated in a Masters carpet are emblematical of the three principal stages of human life, Youth, Manhood and Old Age. In youth as Entered Apprentices we are taught industriously to engage our minds in the pursuit and attainment of useful Knowledge. In manhood as Fellowcrafts we should apply the knowledge thus attained to the faithful and proper discharge of our respective duties, to God, our neighbour and ourselves, so that in Old Age, as Master Masons we may enjoy the happy reflections consequent on a well spent life and die in the hope of a glorious immortality.

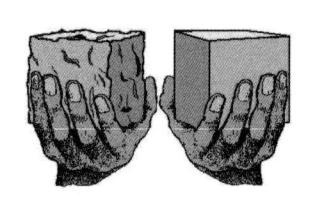

'The Mosaic Pavement alludes to that in the Holy place, on which the High Priest walked to enter the Holy of Holies, to offer up the yearly sacrifice for his own and the sins of his people; being chequered to remind him of the vicissitudes of human life. To purify himself and to implore the blessing of the Great Architect of the Universe by prayer and sacrifice in the Holy of Holies, to cleanse them from all their sins and iniquities. And while our feet tread the chequered pavement of this life of vicissitude, so ought we to purify our hearts from all malignant passions that our prayers may be acceptable to Him who sitteth on His eternal Throne of glory for ever and ever.

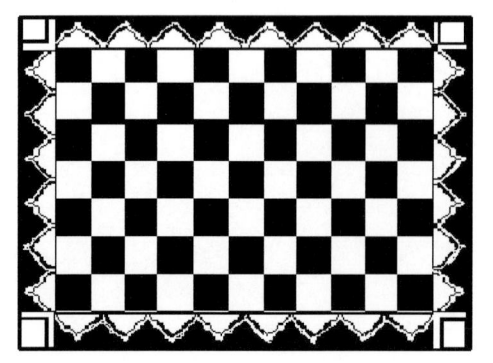

'The Porch with the Dormer alludes to a small window over the Holy of Holies, showing the glimmering light of the Sanctum Sanctorum on which rested the Divine Shekinah, and alludes to the light of a Master Mason which is darkness visible. Thereby indicating that glorious immortality which reason, even unassisted by revelation, enables us to discover even amidst the gloom that surrounds the prospect of futurity, yet aided by this feeble light, we are enabled to tread the King of Terrors under our feet and to look forward with confidence penetrating the gloom which surrounds futurity, casting our eyes on that refulgent Sun of our righteousness, whose rising brings glad tidings to all mankind, light to those who sit in darkness and walk in the valley of the shadow of death.'

It is worth noting, when talking about the Dormer, where it says in Emulation Ritual that the *'Porch was the entrance to the Sanctum Sanctorum, the Dormer (was) the window that gave light to the same'*, we are talking of the Dormer giving light to the Porch. Within the Sanctum Sanctorum or Holy of Holies the light of God shone so that no further illumination would be necessary.

'The colours that are wrought into the Party Coloured Veil are intended to represent the four elements. The earth from which the flax is produced may be considered as typified by the fine linen. The sea is represented by the purple colour, which derives its origin from the fish murex. The violet colour is emblematical of the air, the crimson of fire, and the whole represents the perfection of Masonry. Thus fine linen and violet colour represent Purity and Innocence. The purple, Awe and Reverence, and crimson Justice tempered with Mercy. And when the shades of age and imbecility shall have damped those energies which were once employed in the ardour of active virtue, our declining strength shall be cheered by the retrospect of what our benevolence effected while health and vigour remained, and the veil drawn aside opening to our view the bright prospect of that reward (point to the Ark of the Covenant) which is before us, and while we consider this life only as the beginning of our existence and look forward to the smiling world we are about to enter, we anticipate with inexpressible gratitude the cheering welcome we shall receive from Saints and Angels and the spirits of just men made perfect.'

It is not normal to refer to the four elements of earth, air, fire and water in Craft Masonry, although they do figure in the Royal Arch. The party-coloured veil appears on some Tracing Boards, notably that of Royal Cumberland itself. This pre-empts to a degree the Royal Arch and, in particular, the ceremony of Passing the Veils, which is still practised in many jurisdictions but not in England except – not very far from Bath – in Bristol.

In Exodus, Chapter 26 vv.31-34 it says: *'You shall make a veil woven of blue, purple, and scarlet thread, and fine woven linen. It shall be woven with an artistic design of cherubim. You shall hang it upon the four pillars of acacia wood overlaid with gold. Their hooks shall be of gold, upon four sockets of silver. And you shall hang the veil from the clasps. Then you shall bring the ark of the Testimony in there, behind the veil. The veil shall be a divider for you between the holy place and the Most Holy. You shall put the mercy seat upon the ark of the Testimony in the Most Holy.'*

The veil separated man from God and was called 'the curtain of the Testimony'. It could never be touched except by the high priest, and then only once a year to sprinkle blood on the mercy seat on the Day of Atonement.

The Ark of the Covenant is a symbol not now normally referred to in the English Craft. It is dealt with in the chapter on Symbols no longer used.

'Let me add, in conclusion, if you would enjoy such happy anticipations, when advanced in years and your bosom is becoming dead to the fascinations of life; you must circumscribe your thoughts and actions, by the instruction afforded by the emblems now lying before you. Even your reputation amongst mankind is dependent on the rectitude of your moral conduct.'

This is repeating what we looked at with reference to the passage from the Book of Ecclesiastes quoted above.

'If you wish for the commendation of the wise and good, and what is of still greater importance, the satisfactory testimony of your own conscience, you must be honest and true, faithful and sincere, and practise the virtues enjoined equally by Masonry and the Volume of the Sacred Law. You must keep within

compass, and act on the square with all mankind, for your Masonry is but a dead letter if you do not habitually perform its reiterated injunctions.

'*You may boast of its beauties, and you have just reason to do so, you may be an enthusiast in its forms and ceremonies, but unless you reduce it to practice, unless its incitements be made to bear on your moral conduct, you can enjoy no advantage over those who are still in darkness, and the benefits of masonry have been extended to you in vain.*

'*Circumscribe your actions then within the boundary line of your duty to God and men, and convince the World that the system of masonry, as practised by you, is something more than an empty name.*

'*Finally may the remembrance of the sprig of acacia which was placed on the grave of him who was truly the most excellent of Masons, and who parted with his life, rather than with his honour, stimulate his successors to emulate his glorious example. May the essence of virtue enshrine your moral conduct, and like the beautiful Rose of Sharon and the Lily of the Valley, intellectually exalt you. So that when death, the great leveller of all human greatness hath drawn its sable curtain around us, when the last arrow of our mortal enemy hath been despatched, and the bow of the mighty conqueror broken by the iron arm of time, when the Angel of the Lord hath decreed that time shall be no more, and when by this victory God hath subdued all things unto Himself, then may we hope to receive the reward of virtue by acquiring an inheritance in those Heavenly Mansions where every secret of Masonry shall be open, never again to be closed. Then may the Great Architect of the Universe the omnipotent Jehovah Himself, bid us enter His celestial Lodge where peace, order and harmony eternally shall reign.*'

The phrase '*Rose of Sharon and the Lily of the Valley*' is a Christian reference to the Saviour himself.

The 'sable curtain' is a curious reference. It was a metaphor used frequently in 18th century literature, particularly in poetry. For example, in *Night Thoughts* by Edward Young (1683-1765)

*'And like a sable curtain starr'd with gold,
Drawn o'er my labours past, shall close the scene'*

Young also uses it later in *The Consolation,* part of the same poem:

His grand pavilion sacred Fame reports the sable curtain drawn.'

Nathaniel Hawthorne uses the phrase in *Edward Randolph's Portrait*: *'snatched away the sable curtain that concealed the portrait'.*

Similarly the English author Henry Fielding refers in *Tom Jones* to *'an hour at which (as it was now midwinter) the dirty fingers of Night would have drawn her sable curtain over the universe, had not the moon forbid her'.*

The term was obviously in popular use in the 18th and 19th centuries, but has now ceased to be, so we can only presume it to be a reference to things beyond the grave, where *'the eye of human reason cannot penetrate'.*

Now for a word about the cipher on the Tracing Board. I am referring to the board designed in 1845 by John Harris for the Emulation Lodge of Improvement, because this is probably the most popular board in the English Constitution today. There are many others, some with more complex ciphers, but this is the one you're most likely to see. If we look at the top part:

The Third Degree Tracing Board – upper portion

Here we see a number of characters from the Masonic alphabet, familiar to Mark Masons. As you can see from the figures 3000, the characters are read from right to left, as Hebrew characters are. The figures, of course, refer, as it says in the Emulation Third Tracing Board Lecture, to *'the untimely death of our Master, HA. He was slain 3000 years after the creation of the world'.* This statement, of course, is another example of the licence we must grant to the framers of our ritual. The world was millions of years old before Hiram ever walked.

The three characters on the top line stand for HAB – Hiram Abif. Below and at either end of the plaque are two further characters which stand for TC – Tubalcain. Alongside the figure 3000 are the letters AL standing for Anno Lucis (the year of light).

So far, so good. Now let's look at the lower part:

Here we have two further characters from the Masonic alphabet, M and B, which stand for the substituted word in the Third Degree. Finally, there are three identical Hebrew characters each denoting the number five and referring to the three parties of five Fellowcrafts who went in search of Hiram.

The Third Degree Tracing Board – lower portion

The Working Tools are presented

The working tools of the degree are the Skirret, the Pencil and the Compasses. Royal Cumberland Lodge No.41 are, I believe, unique in having four tools – the last one being the trowel which is explained in the chapter on Symbols no longer used.

Concentrating on the first three, it is interesting to note that whereas, in the First Degree, we have tools of measuring and preparation, suitable for a person starting to learn his trade, then in the Second Degree we have the tools of a trained workman (or craftsman), now in the Third Degree we have the tools, or rather the equipment, of an architect. It is worth noting that the Greek word for mason is τεκτον *(Tekton)* and that the prefix 'arch' signifies a higher level – as in 'arch'bishop or 'archi'tect.

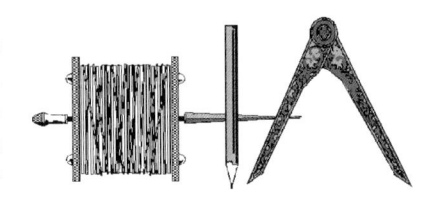

In the song popularised by Bro William Preston and produced in his *Illustrations of Masonry*, (and sung to the tune 'God save the Queen'), we have the words:

*'Hiram the Architect
Did all the Craft direct
How they should build.*

> *Solomon, great Israel's king*
> *Did mighty blessings bring*
> *And gave us cause to sing*
> *Hail royal art!'*

We are already familiar with the Compasses, but here we are given the Operative use of ascertaining and determining the limits and proportions of the several parts of the building and the Speculative counterpart of understanding the limits of good and evil.

The Pencil is, fairly obviously, a tool for writing and Speculatively for recording our words and actions. The Skirret was introduced only after the 1813 Union (probably by the Lodge of Reconciliation set up to produce the new ritual) replacing the plumb line. It is strange that they decided to replace a tool for checking uprights with something for marking out ground for foundations.

The symbol does not appear anywhere in Masonry before 1816 and still doesn't appear on our Grand Lodge certificates. The word itself is intriguing; it is said to be derived from the Old Norse 'Skyrta' giving rise to words like 'outskirts' or to 'skirt' around something. Indeed the Skirret is not really a mason's tool; it is more often associated with landscaping and so may have come to us from the Order of Free Gardeners or some similar source.

The Lodge is closed in the Third Degree

This bit of ritual is crucial because it shows us precisely where we are at, having completed the three Degrees of Craft Masonry. We came into Freemasonry seeking light. We have now united body, soul and spirit in that quest and hence the Third Degree knocks. We have not found the genuine secrets, which remain to be discovered in the Royal Arch, but we have learnt that, although death is merely a gateway to a better life, an honourable death is much to be preferred.

The phrase *'with gratitude to our Master we bend'* causes some confusion. Harry Carr thought that the Master in question could only be God and that this statement was a form of prayer. The prayers in the Third Degree are short anyway. In the Opening the prayer is no more than the request: *'May heaven aid our united endeavours'*. In the Closing, after saying *'with gratitude'* etc we go on to say *'all gratitude to the Most High'*. The two consecutive phrases are statements, rather than supplications. Carr's contemporary (and another fine scholar) Roy Wells disagreed; he thought the Master in question was King Solomon and we were bending with gratitude to him for giving us the substituted secrets. I tend to agree with Wells because, for one thing, the previous statement is *'I, as master of this lodge and thereby the humble representative of King Solomon'* etc, and we are then responding by expressing our gratitude to the King. Carr is, however, right when he says that the lodge Master should himself bow and say the words (though they never do) because the gratitude is not being expressed to him.[15]

Finally, in Closing the lodge, we are able to make our sign in full, with a recovery which we could not do in the Opening. That is because when we opened the lodge we were going in search of the genuine secrets which we had yet to obtain, so we could not give the recovery. At the end of our labours we still have not found the genuine secrets, but, because we are in possession of the substituted ones, a recovery is possible.

The Symbolism of Seven

As with the previous two Degrees, there is a key number and in this case it is seven. You may have noticed a slight inconsistency here. In the Second Degree we talk of Seven Liberal Arts and Sciences and now, in the Third, we have five points of fellowship. Remember we said above that the Third Degree was a later innovation and we have no record of it before the mid-1720s. There are two points to bear in mind. In the Second Degree Tracing Board the number seven is certainly referred to in the number of steps in one of the flights of the winding staircase – *'three, five and seven or more steps'*. The seven is in allusion to the number of years it took King Solomon to build his Temple and also to the Seven Liberal Arts and Sciences. There have always been Seven Liberal Arts and Sciences, so that was something the framers of our ritual could do nothing about.

But I believe the FPOF to be something different and that this may at one time have been part of the Second Degree. It is a convenient device for raising a candidate, but it is also a way of symbolically demonstrating the duties we owe to our brethren and so could have existed outwith the communication of the Hiramic legend.

In the ancient world, the number seven had great importance. It was considered the number of totality – symbolising the union of Heaven and Earth and the unity of body and soul to create perfection. The ancients knew seven planets, there were seven heavens (hence *in seventh heaven*) and seven ages of man. Then there were seven pillars of wisdom, seven colours of the rainbow, seven days of the week and seven wonders of the world. And, of course, there were the Seven Liberal Arts and Sciences.

Philo of Alexandria discovered that the seventh power of any number is both a square and a cube. The god, Apollo, had seven strings to his lyre. The ancients also found that the first seven digits added together make 28, the number of days in a lunar cycle. The major religions divide the week by seven, commemorating six days of creation plus the day of rest. Judaism in particular sees seven as the number of occult intelligence and has its seven-branch Menorah, seven great holy days and, of course, a temple, still central to their worship, that took seven years to build.

In Christianity the seventh ray of the sun is the one by which man ascends to the next world. There are seven sacraments and seven deadly sins. The Seven Gifts of the Holy Spirit, referred to in the 9th century hymn *Veni Creator*, as translated into *Come Holy Ghost* in the 1662 Book of Common Prayer:

'Thou the anointing Spirit art,
Who dost Thy sevenfold gifts impart.'

This is in itself a reference to the Seven Gifts as described by St Paul in Romans, Chapter 12 vv.6-8:

'6. We have different gifts, according to the grace given us. If a man's gift is prophesying, let him use it in proportion to his faith.
7. If it is in serving, let him serve; if it is in teaching, let him teach;
8. If it is encouraging, let him encourage; if it is contributing to the needs of others, let him give generously; if it is in leadership, let him govern diligently; if it is in showing mercy, let him do it cheerfully.'

The Book of Revelation is replete with references to the number seven: seven seals, seven angels with seven trumpets, beasts with seven heads and seven horns, seven spirits standing before the Throne of the Lamb etc ...[16]

Then in Masonry we say that seven or more make a perfect lodge (Master, two Wardens, two Fellowcrafts and two Entered Apprentices), we have the Seven Liberal Arts and Sciences again and the two occasions on which seven steps are referred to – in the third flight of the winding staircase of the Second Degree Tracing Board and in the advance to the pedestal in the Third Degree.

1 R. F. Gould – *AQC 11 1888*
2 Bernard Jones – *Freemasons' Guide and Compendium*
3 Albert Pike quoted in *AQC 11 1888*
4 Jones, op. cit.
5 Trevor Stewart – *AQC 119 2007*
6 Canon Richard Tydeman – *AQC 84 1971*
7 Flavius Josephus – *Jewish Antiquities* (Whiston Translation)
8 J. S. M. Ward – *The MM Book*
9 Harry Carr – *The Freemason at Work*
10 James Boswell – *The London Journal*
11 Ann Baring – *The Significance of Jung's Seven Sermons to the Dead*; presented to the Canonbury Masonic Research Centre, 22 November 2000
12 Ward, op. cit.
13 Carr, op. cit.
14 Ibid.
15 Ibid.
16 *The Complete Dictionary of Symbols*

The Installation

The rank is but the guinea's stamp; the man's the gowd for a' that.
ROBERT BURNS (1759-1796) – *A MAN'S A MAN FOR A' THAT*

Attaining the Chair of Master of his lodge marks the peak of a Mason's career, at least up to that point. He will have prepared for it long and hard. These days it is not impossible to get more than one bite of the cherry and to be Master more than once. I have been Master three times, albeit in three different lodges. It used to be the end of the road in days when further elevation to Provincial, District or Grand rank was a distinctly remote possibility, in the days before Past Grand and Provincial rank was introduced to celebrate Queen Victoria's Golden Jubilee in 1887, and when lodges were big enough to put a different brother in the Chair every year. Of course, many still are, but whatever the situation, one's year in office will require a lot of preparation. It is only natural that this preparation will be largely given over to learning ritual, planning the Installation meeting, who you are going to appoint as officers, who you are going to invite to see you go in the Chair and so on. Then there is the Ladies' Evening or Festival and all the myriad detail involved in that.

There used to be a toast to the Master Elect, accompanied by a rousing song, sung to the tune of '*The Red, White and Blue*' at St Michael's, Birkenhead Lodge No.4615 (sadly now no more):

'Then here's to the Master Elect,
Our Craft and our Lodge we'll respect,
Good luck to the year he reigns o'er us,
All hail to the Master Elect.'

It was probably sung and is maybe still being sung in other places and with variations, but I include it here to show that, symbolically, we are saying that the Master is 'king' for a year. But is this correct? If you read the various pieces of advice given to the Master before and after he attains the Chair, it is not kingship he is embarking on. True, he is the one who will decide what ceremony we are going to do month by month and, if he has a strong personality, he is likely to stamp that on the lodge for his year and possibly for time to come, although hopefully not too hard!

The term 'Reigning Master' is now discouraged in some places because the essence of a Master's function is not being 'the boss', it is imparting light and instruction, so that he is more of a teacher than a potentate. Let's then look at what the Installation is about and perhaps think how the Master can prepare himself for what he should really be doing.

The Preamble

In several ways the Installation ignores the Third Degree and concentrates on the fact that the Master Elect is a Craftsman:

> *'From time immemorial it has been an established custom amongst Freemasons for each lodge, once in every year at a stated period, to select from among those who are past Wardens, an experienced CRAFTSMAN, to preside over them in the capacity of Master.'*

When the new Master is being placed in the Chair he is informed that he is now a 'Master of Arts and Sciences'. This, of course, implies that he has mastered the Seven Liberal Arts and Sciences he learnt about in the Second Degree.

The first record of an Installation Ceremony is not until 1722, whereas the Time Immemorial referred to above in Masonic terms is 1717 – the date of the establishment of the Premier Grand Lodge in London, so from that alone we know that it was not always done. Added to that, the Grand Master in 1722, the Duke of Wharton, guided by Past Grand Master John Theophilus Desaguliers, established this Ceremony of Installation for the purpose of putting the Master in the Chair of a NEW lodge. Secondly, note that it says an experienced Craftsman to preside over them. Not a Master Mason. This is because there are no concrete records of the Third Degree being worked until 1730 and so a Fellowcraft could be Master of a lodge in the early days. In fact if you consider many academic and professional institutions even today, the grade of Fellow is the highest accolade to which one can attain. This is even confirmed later on in the ritual when we go on to say: *'Held in high estimation by his Brethren and Fellows'*.

Kenning's Definition of Installation was as follows:

'Installation is that ceremony by which the Grand Master, the Deputy and Pro (Assistant) Grand Masters and the Provincial Grand Masters and Masters of private lodges are placed in their seats of office. It seems to come from the Latin "In stallum" being the same ceremony by which knights and ecclesiastical office holders like deans, abbots, prebendaries and canons would be placed in their proper stalls. We generally apply it to the annual installation of the Worshipful Master in the royal chair of private lodge, which act can only be done "according to ancient usage" and which requires presentation to a board of installed masters.' [1]

This is not the case in some obediences. In the Ancient and Accepted Scottish Rite, as practised in Continental Europe, there is no such presentation and no inner working. It is largely a matter of the Master Elect being obligated and undertaking to rule his lodge wisely and well. He then goes on to obligate and invest his officers who will take an oath of allegiance to him.

The term 'Royal Chair' is seldom used now; it is usual to refer to the Master's Chair or the Chair of King Solomon. The first presentation is really to the lodge. It will be done in the Second Degree, for the reasons we've just looked at. Past Masters will be invited to occupy the Chairs of the Senior and Junior Wardens and the position of Inner Guard. It is essential that this is done as the lodge at this stage must be 'staffed' by Past Masters because the rest of the brethren will shortly be retiring. Another Past Master, possibly the lodge Director of Ceremonies or perhaps a friend or the proposer of the Master Elect, will present him to the Master in the Chair, who from then on effectively becomes the Installing Master, but the rest of the brethren look on and know that after they have left the lodge, that brother will be formally installed in the Chair which he will occupy on their return. However, as Kenning says above, the essence of Installation is the presentation to the Board of Installed Masters, and the Installing Master knows that after the brethren not qualified to participate have left the lodge, he must convene such a Board.

In the preamble to the Installation the Installing Master will explain what the ceremony is about and why we do it. The Master

178   A Guide to Masonic Symbolism

Elect will then be called on to take an 'external' obligation in the presence of all the brethren before those who have not yet attained the Chair of a lodge retire and he can be presented to an Installed Board, take the 'internal' obligation, learn the secrets of an Installed Master and receive the gavel – at which point, of course, the lodge formally comes under his direction. I sometimes, in lodges, see the Installing Master conclude the Installation Ceremony by saying *'The Lodge is now under your direction'*. This is clearly incorrect.

The 'external' obligation is a symbolic proof to all the brethren of the lodge that the Master Elect intends to discharge his duties to the best of his ability.

The Installed Board

The Board of Installed Masters will impose a further obligation on the Master Elect and he will then be placed in the Chair. Without giving too much away, the statement in relation to the Master's collar jewel – *'the square being the implement which forms the rood and proves the perfect mass is well applied by Master Masons to inculcate the purest principles of piety and virtue'* – is symbolically important and that is why it is included here. First of all, this is the first mention of Master Masons in the Installation and, some would no doubt think, tends to support Bro Tydeman's theory (see above in the chapter on the Third Degree) that the new Master Mason was actually the Master of the lodge as well when he received that jewel. Leaving that aside, I have always been baffled by the contention that the square *'forms the rood'*. Rood is, of course, an archaic word for 'cross', as in Holyrood House in Edinburgh.

I suppose it could be said that the standard Christian Cross is composed of squares, but we must surely be at a loss to understand why it should be included at this stage in an Installation Ceremony.

Holyrood House

The Readmission

This being satisfactorily concluded, the brethren of the lodge will be readmitted. They will come in groups (the size of the group tends to vary depending on the lodge, and the Emulation Ritual remains silent as to the number of brethren who should enter in each Degree. However, the Master Masons will greet their newly Installed Master in the Third Degree, the Fellowcrafts in the Second and finally the Entered Apprentices in the First. In each Degree the newly installed Master will be reminded of the Working Tools and their significances.

The Installing Master will then deliver up the Lodge Warrant. There are some ancient lodges, dating from Time Immemorial, that do not have warrants, but in most cases there will be one. The warrant is a charter from the United Grand Lodge of England, empowering the lodge to hold meetings. It is made legal by the affixing of the seal of Grand Lodge and will be signed by the Grand Master and Grand Secretary at the time of issue. The warrant is in the Master's personal keeping, and some lodges make him take it home after the meeting – particularly if they don't meet in a Masonic Hall or other secure environment. Most lodges have their warrant framed and hanging up in the Masonic Hall, but some still keep them in parchment scrolls, from which they should be taken out and displayed to the brethren so that they know the meeting is constitutional, for without the warrant that meeting cannot be held.

The Book of Constitutions and the Lodge By-laws will also be presented. Nobody seems to know where the By-laws came from, except that it makes sense to have a set of rules that reflects local conditions – *the Lodge shall meet at the Masonic Hall, Little Piddlecombe, on the third Friday etc.* Constitutions, however, have always been with us, at least since James Anderson produced the first edition of his Constitutions in 1723. Obviously every well-run society must have a rulebook.

The Investiture

This is a good place to look at the symbolism behind each officer invested, in terms of their relationship to the Master and his to them. There are some officers, of course, whose role is self-explanatory and their duties are not symbolic as such. What we are going to concentrate on here is what are sometimes called the seven 'Floor' officers, by which I mean the Worshipful Master, the Senior and Junior Wardens, the Senior and Junior Deacons, the Inner Guard and the Tyler. The Worshipful Master represents the creating spirit. He opens the lodge and is the divine spark, the spirit bringing light. This is why the Third Degree is thought of as the Master's Degree.

The Senior Warden, marking the setting Sun, represents the de-creative principle, the soul that enables the spirit to raise the body to divine things. We have seen that this is the reason he is delegated to invest the candidate with his apron in all three Degrees. He is the 'omega' to the Master's 'alpha' in the Opening and Closing of the lodge. In investing the Senior Warden, the Master presents him with three symbolic items: the level, the emblem of equality which he wears as a collar jewel, to point out the equal measures he is bound to pursue with the Master in the well-ruling and governing of the lodge; the gavel to assist him to preserve order; and the column by which he signifies that the lodge is at labour.

The Junior Warden is, of course, the meridian and represents the body and also the balance between life and death. The Junior Warden, when invested, also gets a gavel and column which he must lower when the lodge is opened and raise when it is closed or called off, as we have already seen. His collar jewel is the plumb rule, pointing out the *integrity* of the measures he is bound to pursue with the Master and Senior Warden in ruling the lodge. These three officers represent body, soul and spirit respectively and all three must co-operate to bring the candidate to light.[2]

The Senior Deacon is the conductor in the Second and Third Degrees, instructing the candidate as to the steps he must take and the signs he must give. He is the assistant conductor in the First Degree and also performs the function of a messenger between the Master and the Senior Warden.

Similarly, the Junior Deacon performs the conducting function in the First Degree, assisting the Senior Deacon in the Second and Third Degrees, and acting as the messenger between the Senior and Junior Wardens. The Inner Guard is the herald (in some Masonic Degrees that is what he is called). He announces the arrival of the candidate and communicates that he has passed the first test at the door of the lodge.

The Tyler represents the outside world from which the candidate is coming. He prepares him and announces his readiness, seeking admission on his behalf.

The Addresses

There is not much symbolism in any of these. They are largely pieces of advice to the Master, Wardens and finally the brethren about the ways in which they should conduct themselves, both in their respective offices and in life in general. The only thing that could be said is that in the Address to the Master the symbol of the Sun, whom the Master represents as we have already seen, is used to point out that, as the Sun brings light, so should the Master of a lodge communicate light and instruction.

The Extended Working

There are, of course, variations in the Ceremony of Installation as practised in different places, but there is one version which surely constitutes more than a variation, and that is the Extended Working of the Board of Installed Masters. This is thought to be derived from a ceremony worked, before the Union, in the Antients' Grand Lodge called the ceremony of Passing the Chair, or sometimes The Fourth Degree. The reason it was thought to be introduced was because being an installed master was an essential prerequisite to exaltation in the Royal Arch until 1838 (the Antients were, of course, very fond of the Royal Arch). The Ceremony of Passing the Chair (or Passed Master – note *Passed*, not Past) is still worked within the York Rite in the USA and on the Continent of Europe.

In England, the Extended Working of the Board of Installed Masters is still being worked in several places in the north of England and also in Bath and probably in many other places I've yet to visit. It contains many interesting features. Existing symbolism is referred to in the opening of the Installed Board which talks of the Rough and Perfect Ashlars. In addition to this there is reference to the Working Tools of an Installed Master – which are the Plan, the Plumb Line and the Trowel. The Plan is a plan of a building and the other two have uses which are the same elsewhere in Masonry.

After the Union, it was thought that this ceremony had been dropped, but some lodges continued to use it on a yearly basis to install their Masters. When this fact was discovered, attempts were made to suppress the ceremony, but after a lengthy series of debates in Grand Lodge in 1926 it was decided that lodges working the ceremony could continue to do so, provided they gave what I refer to as a 'health warning', which is a short statement pointing out that anyone not installed using this ceremony is no less an installed Master. I have to say that I have seen and enjoyed the Extended Working of the Board of Installed Masters many times and wish it was in more general use.

As an interesting aside, from the excellent history of St George's Lodge of Harmony No.32, in Liverpool, produced for their 250th Anniversary, we find that the 'Passed Master' ceremony was in use in their lodge not only before the Union but 17 years afterwards, and I quote: *'6th April 1830: Bro Deane took the chair and opened in the 3 Craft Degrees, when Bro Henry Ripley was duly installed as WM in the Chair and invested and saluted accordingly after which Bro Deane closed the Craft Lodge, Bro Ripley retired and a PM lodge was opened by Bro Lucas. Bro Ripley was then introduced, duly prepared and was admitted to the Degree of PM, which lodge being closed he again retired and a Conclave of Super Excellent Masons being opened, he was readmitted, passed thro' the Veils and duly raised to the Super Excellent Degree, the Conclave was then closed and a RA Chapter opened, upon which he with Bros E. G. Deane and Jno Molineaux Jnr were readmitted, duly prepared and exalted to the sublime Degree of H.R.A.M.'* [3]

Leaving aside obvious questions like what time it was before they got any dinner and what sort of state Bro Ripley's head was in at the end of all this, instances like this show the strength of lodge traditions in that here we see three ceremonies, officially no longer allowed after 1813, being worked and the Royal Arch still being conferred in a Craft Lodge!

By way of explanation, the ceremony of Passing the Veils is no longer worked in England as a preliminary to exaltation into a Royal Arch Chapter, except in Bristol where it was reintroduced early in the 20th century. It is still worked in Scotland and Ireland and within what is known as the York Rite, which exists in the USA and also in Greece and Cyprus. The Super Excellent Mason Degree referred to is effectively the Passing of the Veils and should not be confused with the Degree of Super Excellent Master which is practised in England as part of the Order of Royal and Select Masters (commonly known as the 'Cryptic'). H.R.A.M. stands for Holy Royal Arch Mason.

---

1. Kenning's Cyclopaedia of Masonry
2. J. S. M. Ward – *The EA Book*
3. St George's Lodge of Harmony No.32 – 250th Anniversary History

Symbols no longer used

After the Union of 1813, the ritual was modified and the design of Tracing Boards changed. A lot of symbols were consequently dropped. Some of them are retained in the Mark and other Degrees, but others are now absent from most of English Masonry, although still referred to in the USA. However, many of these symbols still appear on the Tracing Board of Royal Cumberland Lodge No.41 at Bath, in the Province of Somerset, and are referred to and explained in their beautiful Third Degree Lecture. I am again indebted to that lodge for permission to reproduce those explanations here. All italicised quotes are from Royal Cumberland's Lecture, unless otherwise stated.

18th Century Symbols on a handkerchief

It will also be seen from the illustration above that there was a plethora of symbols used in the 18th century of which the modern Mason has no knowledge. The picture appeared on a handkerchief displayed at the Quatuor Coronati Lodge in 1892. The handkerchief itself is not dated, but from the dress of the brethren depicted we are probably safe in assuming it to be from the 18th century. Several of the symbols relate to the Royal Arch, the Knights Templar and other Degrees and so are beyond the scope of this book.

Trowel

In Royal Cumberland Lodge the Trowel comes into the Third Degree as a fourth Working Tool. In practical terms it is explained thus: *'The Trowel is an instrument made use of for the*

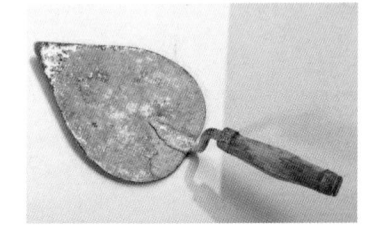

purpose of spreading the cement which unites the building into one common mass.' Speculatively: *'The Trowel instructs us metaphorically to make use of it for that most noble and glorious purpose of spreading the cement of brotherly love and affection, which ought to unite us into one sacred bond or society of friends among whom no contention should ever exist, save the honourable contention, or rather emulation, as to who can best work or best agree.'*

There is, of course, one continuing use of the Trowel in most lodges and that is as the jewel of the Charity Steward. When an address is given on its presentation, it follows very much on the lines of the passage above. Other than that, the Trowel is not referred to anywhere else in Emulation Ritual.

Ark of the Covenant

One could be forgiven for thinking that this symbol is in the wrong place, being described as a symbol no longer used. However, it no longer enjoys the prominence in our Craft ceremonies that it used to, and it is not referred to in the address on the certificate contained in Emulation Ritual nor in any alternative I can find. At the Union of the Grand Lodges on 27 December 1813 it was the focal point of everything, being placed in the centre of the room in which the Union took place. The Ark, of course, contained things which were acknowledged as Masonic symbols before the Union but now are not – the Pot of Manna, Aaron's Rod and the Tables of the Law. These are referred to below.

Bro G. W. Speth, writing in 1889, says: *'There is a link between the Jewish and Christian systems, and an important one, which I have to refer to. At the crucifixion the Veil of the Temple was rent, and He who died passed through. He passed through to that mystical chamber containing the symbolical coffin. This statement tells you the whole story. Here I might ask how it is that writers upon the "The Types" have overlooked the highest one of all. The Ark of the Covenant as a "Symbolical Coffin" was in itself the type of The Death and the Resurrection. The Tabernacle was made in imitation of the Universe, so Josephus tells us, and in this sense the Ark of the Covenant was a type or symbol to all mankind of the Death that awaits every man.'*[1]

The biblical Ark was a small chest measuring roughly two and a half cubits in length and a cubit and a half in breadth and depth. It was made of wood overlaid with gold, apart from the Mercy Seat with the two cherubim on it at the top – that was made of solid gold. It existed from the time of Moses until King Solomon's Temple was plundered by Nebuchadnezzar, King of Babylon. It then disappeared, never to be seen again, although many legends abound as to its whereabouts, and it continues to provide Hollywood with good storylines!

Beehive

The Beehive appears on a lot of old Masonic artefacts and tracing cloths/boards as a symbol of industry. On a pre-Union Tracing Board produced by John Browne (author of *Master Key* referred to elsewhere in this book), bees are used in three sets of five to represent the three lodges or classes of workmen, who went in search of Hiram Abif. The ritual used in explaining this symbol was as follows:

> *'The Bee Hive commends the right employment of time by practical industry; it teaches us that as we came into the world rational and intelligent beings, so should we also be industrious ones, and never stand idly by or gaze with listless indifference upon even the lowest of our fellow creatures, when in a state of distress, so long as it is in our power to help them, without being detrimental to ourselves, our families, or connections. The constant practice of these virtues is enjoined on all created beings, from the highest Seraph in Heaven to the lowest reptile that crawls in the dust.'*

In Christian art the beehive has been used to symbolise ordered communities (i.e. monasticism) and, by its connection with honey, eloquence – particularly in the words of Christ.

Shovel

This is a bit of a mystery. Harry Carr, in *The Freemason at Work*, quotes the Chester Gentleman-Mason of the 17th century – Randle Holme – who produced a work called *The Academie of Armoury* in around 1688. Holme lists the shovel, hand-hammer, chisel, pick and punch as being borne in Coats of Arms but, as

Carr points out, he does not confirm that they were used or mentioned in the ceremonies then worked. The hand-hammer could be the mallet and the chisel is definitely still in use; two of the others – the shovel and the pick – we are more familiar with in the Royal Arch. I cannot think what they would use a punch for![2]

Hourglass

The Tracing Board Lecture in the Mark Degree symbolises the Hourglass as reminding us *'By the quick passage of its sands of the transitory nature of human life'*. This rightly informs us that life is not a rehearsal and that, in the words of an anonymous Masonic poem:

'For each of us is given a bag of tools,
A measuring stick and a book of rules,
And each must make, ere life has flown,
A stumbling block or a stepping-stone.'

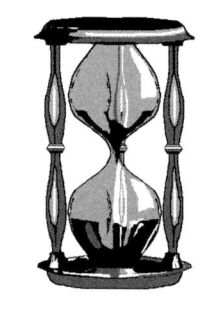

Another symbol – the Sundial – is sometimes found on 18th century Tracing Boards. This has broadly the same meaning as the Hourglass in showing that time is passing and that the best possible use should be made of it.

'The hour glass is an emblem of human life. Behold how swiftly the sand runs, and how rapidly our lives are drawing to a close. We cannot without astonishment, behold the little particles which are contained in this machine, pass away, almost imperceptibly and yet to our surprise, in a short space of an hour, all are exhausted. Thus wastes human life. At the end of man's short hour, death strikes the blow and hurries him off the stage to his long and darksome resting place, for there is no escape from the piercing arrows of death. The thick wall of the Palace of the King with the clay built cottage of the lowly pauper are equally pregnable to his darts, strength or weakness, health or sickness, riches or poverty, all in one undistinguishing perishable level, fall beneath his mighty arm. Wherever he levels his bow the aim is certain, the victim falls, the silken cord of life is cut in twain and the mourners weep about the streets. For the reunion of soul and body, when thus separated, exceeds all human powers, such hath been man in every age of the world, such is man in his most exalted moments and such is

each of us. Today, perhaps the sun of prosperity shines upon our persons and our families, health and strength invigorate our own persons and those of our beloved friends and we feel only for the sorrows of another's woe. But tomorrow aye, even before this night hath closed its sable curtain around us, some friendly heart may perchance sigh over our own breathless corpse. Alas my Brother!'

Scythe

This is related to the Hourglass in that it reminds us of the approach of death and the account of our lives and actions that we must render to our Creator.

Bro H. Meij says in *The Importance of the Scythe*:

'We learn in the (American) *Third Degree* lecture that the Scythe is an emblem of time, which cuts the brittle thread of life, and launches us into eternity. In classic Mythology, the scythe was associated with Saturn, the god of time, which in turn taught men to use the implement in agriculture. Many illustrations of time as a figure show an old man, usually bearded, having a hour glass in the one hand, and a scythe in the other.'[3]

'The scythe is often associated with destruction. However, upon deeper reflection, the scythe also cuts the old to make way for the new – and thus the cycle of life repeats itself. For example, in order to gather the harvest (grain, which feeds life) the giver (in this case the plant) must be killed. Until the fifteenth century, it was not the scythe, but the sickle that was portrayed in similar ways the scythe is today. This probably reflects the changing implements used in farming. It should be noted, that the 13th Major Arcana Card in the Tarot, Death, depicts a scythe not cutting down life, but the worldly illusions. This also corresponds with its meaning, which is not the end, but the beginning of a cycle. In this case, the scythe is a positive tool – one that opens the door to the realm of the true and invisible reality.'

In other words, the scythe or the Death Tarot card (if you attach any credibility to such things) does not denote an impending death, but rather the end of an era, of a relationship or a way of life.

'The Scythe is an emblem of time, which cuts the brittle thread of life and launches us into eternity. What havoc does the scythe of time make among the human race? If by chance we escape the numerous evils incidental to childhood and youth, and arrive in perfect health and strength, at the years of vigorous manhood, yet decrepit old age will soon follow, and we must be cut down by the all devouring scythe of time and be gathered into the land where our fathers have gone before us.'

Rope & Anchor

The Mark Degree Tracing Board also refers to this symbol as follows:

'The rope and anchor, as here depicted, are emblems of a firmly grounded hope arising from a well spent life, and of that spiritual rope and anchor by which we shall be safely moored to a peaceful haven where the wicked cease from troubling and the weary are at rest, and where we may hope to be welcomed by that joyful salutation "Well done, good and faithful servant, enter into the joy of thy Lord".'

The anchor has long associations with safe havens, particularly in the Christian sense. Sure and Stedfast Lodge No.9326, meeting at Liverpool in the Province of West Lancashire, has strong connections with the Boys' Brigade and the BB anchor forms part of their lodge crest. That lodge has the delightful addition of a closing hymn:

*'Will your anchor hold through the storms of life,
When the clouds unfurl their wings of strife?
When the strong tides lift, and the cables strain
Will your anchor drift, or firm remain?*

*'We have an anchor that keeps the soul
Steadfast and sure while the billows roll;
Fastened to a rock which cannot move,
Grounded firm and deep in the Saviour's love!*

*'Will your eyes behold through the morning light
The city of gold and the harbour bright?
Will you anchor safe by the heavenly shore,
When life's storms are past for evermore?*

*'We have an anchor that keeps the soul
Steadfast and sure while the billows roll;
Fastened to a rock which cannot move,
Grounded firm and deep in the Saviour's love!'*

The Anchor alone sometimes appears on old First Degree Tracing Boards, along with the Cross and the Cup. This was a representation of the three Christian virtues of Faith (the Cross), Hope (the Anchor) and Charity (the Cup). There might also be a representation of a woman and children as an additional allusion to charity, representing the widows and orphans supported by Masonic Charity. Clearly this harks back to an age when the Craft was exclusively Christian, and this combination of symbols disappeared after the Union of 1813.

Sword pointing to a heart

This is intended as a symbol of justice. Royal Cumberland: *'The Sword pointing to a Naked Heart demonstrates that justice will sooner or later overtake all evil doers. Although our thoughts, words and actions, may be hidden from the eyes of men, yet that All-seeing Eye, whom Sun, Moon and Stars obey, and under whose watchful care even Comets perform their stupendous revolutions, pervades the inmost recesses of the heart, and will reward or punish us according to our works.'*

It is true to say that, whilst the symbol may no longer be used, the meaning of it is still present in the reception of the candidate by the Inner Guard in the First Degree.

The Tables of Stone

'The Tables of Stone remind us of that awful period, when they were delivered to Moses, the faithful servant of the Lord, on Mount Sinai, when the rays of Divine Glory shone so brightly that none could behold him without fear and trembling, when Moses descended from the burning mountain his face shone as with Divine Majesty, and the terror of Jehovah preceded him.

The thunders ceased and a voice from on high proclaimed the name of the Lord Jehovah merciful and gracious, long suffering and abundant in goodness and truth, keeping mercy for thousands, forgiving iniquity and transgression and sin, and that will by no means clear the guilty, visiting the iniquity of the fathers upon the children and upon the children's children unto the third and fourth generation. Thou shalt worship no other God, for the Lord whose name is Jealous is a jealous God. Such are the Laws which the Great Architect of the Universe has engraven not only on the marbles of Sinai but on the hearts of men, it is given us to be the rule of our faith.

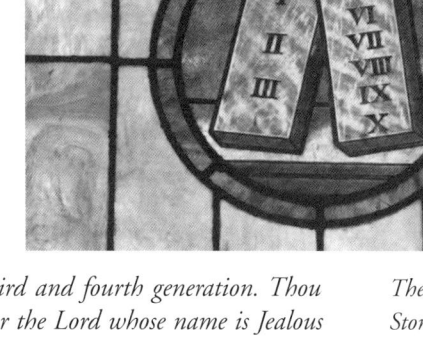

The Tables of Stone

'And we as Masons are taught to regard in them the moral statutes and precepts of our Order which we are bound to obey under the most solemn and awful obligations as ordained for a perpetual decree by our supreme Legislator, the Creator Himself. They are not like other laws and Ordinances commanded by men in His name, which may be altered, but are applicable to all nations, ranks and degrees of men.'

Golden Candlesticks

The Menorah, also called the 'golden lampstand' or 'candlestick', stood at the left side of the Holy Place. It was hammered out of one piece of pure gold. Like for the laver, there were no specific instructions about the size of the Menorah, but the fact that it was fashioned out of one piece of pure gold would have limited its size. The lampstand had a central branch from which three branches extended from each side, forming a total of seven branches. Seven lamps holding olive oil and wicks stood on top of the branches. Each branch looked like that of an almond tree, containing buds, blossoms and flowers. The priests were instructed to keep the lamps burning continuously.

Symbols no longer used

'The Lord said to Moses, Command the Israelites to bring you clear oil of pressed olives for the light so that the lamps may be kept burning continually. Outside the curtain of the Testimony in the Tent of Meeting, Aaron is to tend the lamps before the Lord from evening till morning, continually' (Leviticus, Chapter 24 vv.1-3).

The lampstand was the only source of light in the Holy Place, so without it, the priests would have been moping around in the dark. The light shone upon the table of shewbread and the altar of incense, enabling the priests to fellowship with God and intercede on behalf of God's people.[4]

The Golden Candlesticks

Table of Shewbread

The Table of Shewbread was in the tabernacle of Moses. It was a small table made of Acacia wood and overlaid with pure gold. It measured 3ft by 1.5ft and was 2ft 3in high. It stood on the right side of the Holy Place across from the Menorah or lampstand and held 12 loaves of bread, representing each of the 12 tribes of Israel. The priests baked the bread with fine flour, and it remained on the table before the Lord for a week; every Sabbath Day the priests would remove it and eat it in the Holy Place, then put fresh bread on the table. Only priests could eat the bread, and it could only be eaten in the Holy Place, because it was holy. This was probably a Christian reference because Christ later referred to himself as the Bread of Life: *'And Jesus said unto them, I am the bread of life. He that cometh to me shall never hunger'* (John, Chapter 6 v.35).

Pot of Manna

'The Omer of Manna refers to the Miracle mentioned in the Book of Exodus, when the Children of Israel murmured for bread in the wilderness and the Lord sent Manna to feed them to the full, and Moses said unto Aaron "take a pot and put an omer full of Manna therein and lay it before the Testimony to

be kept as a memorial to after generations of their ingratitude, when they were delivered from famine in the Wilderness by Manna and began to look for flesh". This teaches us not to murmur against the wise dispensation of Providence, but to rely upon the Almighty protection in all our distresses, to follow our Masonic rules, which teach us to guard against innovation and not to introduce unbecoming discourse into the Lodge whereby its harmony may be disturbed.'

Manna was what the Israelites ate in the wilderness while they roamed and lived in tents, whilst travelling to Canaan. It came down from Heaven and sustained them (Exodus, Chapter 16 v.15). They were told to collect an omer (roughly a portion for one person) and that it would go stale after one night. However, the miraculous part was that the manna collected on Fridays lasted two nights so that they would not have to collect any on the Sabbath.

Aaron's Rod

'Aaron's Rod refers to the periods of rebellion of Korah, Nathan, and Abiram, recorded in the 16th and 17th Chapter of the Book of Numbers, when they murmured against Moses, conceiving that his appointment of Aaron as High Priest was more by his own favour than the appointment of the Lord, and Moses spake unto the Children of Israel, "Give me twelve rods, one for every tribe," and they gave him one for each of the Princes, and the rod of Aaron was amongst them. And Moses laid them up in the Tabernacle of Witness before the testimony, and the Lord said unto Moses "and it shall come to pass that the man's rod whom I shall choose shall blossom, and I will make to cease from before me the murmurings of the Children of Israel, whereby they murmur against you". And it came to pass on the morrow that Moses went into the Tabernacle of Witness and Aaron's Rod had bloomed blossoms and yielded almonds; and Aaron was declared High Priest and his rod was laid up before the Tabernacle as a token against the rebellious. We learn from this as Masons that we should never aspire to fill Higher Offices in the Lodge than those to which we are able to do justice by our Masonic Knowledge, and that we should be satisfied with those to which we are chosen by the preference or choice of the Brethren.'

Aaron's Rod

The story of Korah, Nathan (sometimes called Dathan) and Abiram appears (without mention of Aaron's Rod) in the Degree of Grand High Priest within the Order of the Allied Masonic Degrees. The Tables of the Law, the Pot of Manna and Aaron's Rod were contained in the Ark of the Covenant.

Pot of Incense

Some would argue that this should not be listed, even amongst symbols no longer used, given that there are few references to it in English Masonry before the Union. One American Short Talk Bulletin dogmatically avers that the Pot of Incense was never used in England and was brought into American Masonry by Thomas Smith Webb, the author of the American *Webb Monitor* ritual. Sad to say, they are wrong! In Bro T. O. Haunch's recently republished book *Tracing Boards, Their Development & Their Designers*, there is an illustration of a mid-19th century Tracing Board in use in Royal Cumberland Lodge which, some might say unusually for quite a while after 1813, shows several pre-Union symbols including the Pot of Incense.[5]

'The Pot of Incense is an emblem of a pure heart, which is always an acceptable sacrifice to the Deity, and as this glows with fervent heat, so should our hearts glow with gratitude to the Great Author of our Existence for the manifold blessings and comforts we enjoy.'

My own Scottish Lodge – St John Fisherrow No.112 – uses an American ritual for historical reasons. It is interesting to note that the explanation of the Pot of Incense is word for word the same!

The use of incense is, of course, common in places of worship and has been since Old Testament times. Frankincense was presented to the infant Jesus. There is surely some truth in the story we grew up with that it was used in churches to purify the air in days when people weren't able to bathe and shower as they do now, and even more so in the days of the Jewish Temple when animals were being ritually slaughtered for sacrifice. Incense is a symbol of sanctity, not detected as most symbols are by sight, but rather by smell. The Thurifer (or in the Orthodox Church, the Sub-Deacon) will walk backwards in front of the Priest or Bishop swinging his censer from side to side.

A friend of mine, Bro Rt Rev Fr Gerard Crane, writing in *Ye Acon Herald*, the house magazine of the Commemorative Order of St Thomas of Acon, describes the symbolism of incense as '*the path of the ascendant soul or the prayers of the faithful rising from the assembly*'.[6]

In Freemasonry, incense is used at the Consecration of a new lodge, or a new temple. Censing will be done after the consecration elements of corn, wine and oil have been deposited on the lodge board, when the founders are assembled around it. The founders themselves will be censed, according to rank – the Worshipful Master designate three times, the Senior Warden twice and the Junior Warden once. The Consecrating Officer will then pass round the rest of the founders, censing them as well.

Noah's Ark

This symbol is today normally associated with the Degree of Royal Ark Mariner, but it appears among Craft symbols in many 18th century illustrations. The significance of this is explained by Bro R. M. Handfield-Jones in an article about the Royal Ark Mariner degree:

> '*In the first known MS Constitution, the Regius Poem, there occurred on line 537 a passing reference to Noah and the Flood. From then onwards from the Cooke MS every Masonic Constitution contains allusions to Noah, not however to the Flood and the Ark but to his finding the two great pillars inscribed with the seven liberal arts and sciences. The date of the Regius Poem is about 1390 but like the Cooke it bears evidence of being derived from an earlier document written in 1350. Here therefore as early as the middle of the 14th century we have the Noah story appearing in association with Masonry, but the flood and the Ark take a secondary place to the two pillars found by Noah AFTER the Flood.*'[7]

Bro Neville Barker Cryer, in his paper *Craft and Royal Arch Legends*, points to a close working connection between masons and carpenters. In medieval times, when mystery plays were performed, the Guild of Masons generally performed a play about Noah and his Ark. Anderson's Constitutions refer to masons as Noachidae (sons of Noah) and hence this symbol harks back to the earliest traditions of the Craft.[8]

Many Tracing Boards, some dating from before the Union, combine the Ark and the Anchor. Royal Cumberland explains the joint significance thus: *'The Ark and Anchor are emblems of a well grounded hope and of a well spent life. They are emblematical of that (point to the Ark of the Covenant) Divine Ark upon which, if we firmly rest, it will safely bear us over the tempestuous seas of this troubled life, and of that Anchor (point to the Ark of the Covenant) which shall safely moor us in a peaceful harbour where the wicked cease from troubling and the weary are at rest.'*

Key

The Key falls rather into the category of 'Symbols little used', rather than no longer used, because, of course, it continues to be the collar jewel of the lodge Treasurer, although that does not give it the symbolism it formerly had. It is symbolic of the tongue and is still referred to in the Emulation Lectures. In the 1st section of the First Lecture we learn: *'That excellent key, a Freemason's tongue, which should speak well of a brother, absent or present, but when unfortunately that cannot be done with honour and propriety should adopt that excellent virtue of the Craft, which is silence.'*

The Scales

The Scales are a symbol of Justice. We are all familiar with the figure of Justice atop the Central Criminal Court (the Old Bailey) in London. She is blindfold (hoodwinked) and holds a sword in one hand and a pair of scales in the other. Occasionally one finds scales engraved on tombstones of people associated with the legal profession.

In Masonry the Scales are there to remind us that one day our good and bad deeds will be weighed in the balances on the dreaded Day of Judgement. As the Prophet Daniel says to King Belshazzar: *'Thou art weighed in the balances, and art found wanting.'* (Daniel, Chapter 5 v.27).

*Symbol Plaque
belonging to
Cestrian Lodge
No.425*

(The above plaque, showing many symbols no longer used, belongs to Cestrian Lodge No.425 and is preserved in the Masonic Hall, Queen Street, Chester. As with the illustration at the beginning of this chapter, not all of them relate to the Craft.)

1 G. W. Speth – *AQC 11 1889*
2 Harry Carr – *The Freemason at Work*
3 H. Meij – *The Importance of the Scythe*
4 The Tabernacle Place, GoodSeed International
5 T. O. Haunch – *Tracing Boards, Their Development & Their Designers*
6 Rt Rev Fr Gerard Crane – *Ye Acon Herald*
7 R. M. Handfield-Jones – *The Royal Ark Mariner Degree*
8 Neville Barker Cryer – *Craft and Royal Arch Legends* (Cornerstone Society 2000)

Symbols no longer used   197

Endpiece

Sadly we have to stop somewhere. I have tried to cover all the symbols I have come across in a considerable amount of research, but there will be some who will argue that other signs and symbols are connected with Freemasonry. One example would be the signs of the Zodiac. They frequently figure on the walls of European lodge rooms and are not unknown in England.

Bro. Albert Gallatin Mackey said *'Amateur Masonic occultists have attempted to connect Masonry with the Zodiac, one of the conspicuous features of astrologies* (sic); *but here again there is no one zodiac, but many zodiacs throughout the world. The idea of a zodiac itself is one of the largest hoaxes with which men have ever befuddled themselves, and could never have been true to facts. The discovery of dark stars of great magnitude; that what in ancient times was taken for one star was two or more or even a whole galaxy; and the precession of the equinoxes, has made the zodiac meaningless. It is a toy of the mind. There is nothing of the zodiac in the present Masonic ritual; there was never a mention of it in the oldest speculative lodges; in mediaeval times it was a heresy, and operative masons would have abhorred the thought of it.'*

A Typical

Strong stuff, but perhaps it is the current use of zodiacs for fortune-telling that Mackey complains of. He lived from 1807 to 1881, but horoscopes were certainly around then. It is not the first time Freemasonry has been hijacked for the benefit of others. The early 19th century nuisance Richard Carlile, author of The Devil's Freemason, said: *'the Key Stone of the Royal Arch of Freemasonry is the ancient science of the zodiac, with its moral counterpart of human culture made mysterious in its secret and priestly associations; which is also the science of all religions that pretend to revelations; and also of the religion of the Druids, and of all the Pagans from Hindostan to Rome.'* [1]

The other great American Albert, Bro Albert Pike, was certainly keen on planetary motions and the like being depicted in lodge rooms. Most of us in England are content with seven stars in the ceiling. Pike's design for an American (Scottish Rite) temple runs as follows:

'On the ceiling, also, particular Stars and Constellations are painted. In the centre, the three stars in the belt of Orion; and between them and the Northeast, the Pleiades and Hyades, one of which is Aldebaran; half-way between Orion and the Northwest, Regulus in Leo; in the North Ursa Major; in the Northwest, Arcturus; West of Regulus, Spica Virginis; in the West, Antares; in the South, Fomalhaut; over the East, also is Jupiter, and over the West, Venus; Mercury, close to the Sun, and Mars and Saturn, near the centre of the ceiling. The Stars in the belt of Orion represent the number 3; the Hyades 5, the Pleiades and Ursa Major, 7. The five royal Stars are Aldebaran, Arcturus, Regulus, Antares, and Fomalhaut.'

He specifies that Sun should be painted in gold, the Moon in silver, and the stars and constellations in white. Later on he adds:

'Near the horizon in the south is a moderately large five-pointed star, representing Sirius, the dog star. This is the brightest fixed star in the heavens and one of the nearest. It is the nose of the constellation Canis Major, the Great Dog, but the other stars of the constellation are not shown. Between Sirius and the ceiling's center is Fomahault, found in the constellation Piscis Austrinis. The other stars of the constellation have been included to help identify Fomahault.

'Directly over the center of the lodge is the rectangular constellation Orion, the Hunter, raising a shield and club against the attack of Taurus, the bull. Across the middle of Orion are three stars, very near the celestial equator, representing his belt. These three stars could represent the three lights at the altar.

'Still farther north, but well above the horizon, is the Pole Star, the symbolic anchor point of the heavens. Slightly to one side is the Big Dipper or Ursa Major. Pike includes Ursa Major, the

Great Bear, but does not mention the Pole Star. It has been included, however, as a logical part of the arrangement of stars.

'The precise location of the Pole Star above the horizon depends on the geographic location of the lodge. In Minneapolis and other locations at forty-five degrees north latitude, the Pole Star is half way between the north horizon and the center of the ceiling. At the equator it is exactly on the north horizon.

'Ursa Major has seven main stars, including the two pointers used to locate the Pole Star. One of these seven stars is actually a double or pair, Mizar and Alcor. Ursa Major seems to be a primary symbol in the Ecossais Third Degree, where it often appears on the blue sash of that degree.'[2]

So this looks like another example of our not helping ourselves by allowing Masonry to appear to be connected with clairvoyance and the occult, which we are not. For that reason I heartily agree with what Bro Mackey says above. Perhaps we should conclude by considering what Masonry itself symbolises. We have looked at the component parts; we have considered both individual symbols and the story they combine to illustrate. But is there not also a central 'idea' or ideal? Isn't there a basic principle which has inspired all the similar organizations that have existed down through the ages, whether or not we can claim any form of direct descent from them?

I don't think I can better the words of Brother Charles H. Lacquement, Grand Chaplain of the Grand Lodge of Pennsylvania, when he says: *'Freemasonry gets its amazing vitality because its foundation is laid on the great truths from which come the great moral lessons it inculcates. Behind the two great truths, the Fatherhood of God and the Brotherhood of Man, is the chief Masonic virtue, Charity or Brotherly Love. Masons are taught to practice this virtue at all times and to assimilate it into their very lives. It is this virtue that leads Masons to do their duties, to stretch forth a helping hand to a fallen brother, to hold a brother's reputation equally with his own, to whisper good counsel in his ear, and in the most friendly manner, endeavour to bring about the best person this brother can be. In so doing, the Mason is strengthening his own inner self and bringing about the best in himself. Masonry makes in men, strength of character, of thought, and of emotional stability.'*[3]

As our Pro Grand Master, Most Worshipful Bro Lord Northampton, said not long ago: *'So, while it is essential to bring more men into Masonry, it is also essential to put more Masonry into men.'*[4]
Whilst we continue to do that, the 'idea' of societies of good men, doing good and improving their minds at the same time will continue to bear fruit and to symbolise goodness in the human race.

1 Andrew Prescott – *Richard Carlile: The Devil's Freemason* (Centre for Research into Freemasonry, University of Sheffield)
2 Norman D. Peterson – *Astronomical Symbols in Albert Pike's Ornamentation of the Lodge (Scottish Rite Research Society)*
3 MasonWorld.com
4 *MQ Magazine* Issue 15, October 2005

Bibliography

The Holy Bible
The Holy Koran
Emulation Ritual
The Emulation Lectures of the Three Degrees in Craft Masonry
Bottomley Ritual
The Official Ritual of the Heredom of Kilwinning and the Rosy Cross
    Published with the authority of the Grand Lodge of the Royal Order of Scotland
The Ritual of the Mark Degree
The Ritual of the Royal Ark Mariner Degree
The Ritual of the Grade of Zelator – *Societas Rosicruciana in Anglia*
War and Peace by Leo Nikolayevich Tolstoy
Illustrations of Masonry by Bro William Preston
Anderson's Constitutions, 1723 & 1738

Index

24-inch gauge 100
Acacia 52, 163, 165, 168, 169, 192
Address in the North East Corner 39, 99, 160
Address in the South East Corner 134, 135
Admission, candidate seeking
  First Degree 78, 83, 84
  Second Degree 122, 123
  Third Degree 153, 154
Advance from West to East
  First Degree 89
  Second Degree 123, 124
  Third Degree 154, 155
Alchemy 33, 113, 145
Allegory 10, 11, 25, 35
Allied Masonic Degrees, Order of 10, 24, 78, 194
Almoner 52, 54, 55
Amos, the Book of 73, 124
Amphibious Lodge No.258 (Province of Yorks WR) 79
Anaximander 134
Ancient and Accepted Scottish Rite – *see also Scottish Rite* 82, 113, 178
Ancient Mysteries 15, 78
Anderson, Dr James 74, 109, 180
Anticlockwise or Widdershins 40, 123, 124
Antients' Grand Lodge 8, 9, 47, 92, 127, 136, 182
Apron
  Entered Apprentice 48-51, 98
  Fellowcraft 49, 51, 128
  Master Mason 49, 51, 161
  Provincial, Metropolitan or District 49
  Grand Lodge 48, 49
Arabic Numerals 16
Arch of Steel 44
Ark of the Covenant 44, 106, 163, 167, 168, 185, 194, 196
Arms of Grand Lodge 8

Ashlar
  Perfect 72, 73, 99, 134, 135, 136
  Rough 72, 78, 99, 100, 135, 136
Ashmole, Bro Elias 32, 33, 34

Baals Bridge Square 29, 31, 70
Bakers (or Baxters) 32
Balcarres, Lord 33
Ballot 38, 40, 79
Baptismal Font 40, 84
Barrow-in-Furness 72
Birkenhead Priory 32, 33, 34
Bishop Herbert 93
Blazing Star 20, 54, 64-66, 105
Blindfold – *see also Hoodwink* 80, 196
Boaz 46, 92, 139
Boswell, James 157
Bottomley Ritual 57, 127, 159
Bowring, Bro Josiah 66, 105
Breast Jewel (types) 60
Bright Morning Star 160
Bristol 127, 168, 183
Broken Column 55, 62, 63
Burns, Bro Robert 16, 76, 176

Cable Tow 51, 83, 157
Caduceus 20, 55
Calvin, John 19, 92
Candidate, presentation of
  First Degree 88
  Second Degree 123
  Third Degree 155
Carlile, Richard – *The Devil's Freemason* 198
Carr, Bro Harry 44, 49, 52, 56, 105, 124, 127, 153, 160, 163, 172, 173, 186, 187
Cave Paintings 13
Celestial Canopy 37
Chain of Union 6, 68, 115, 139
Chamber of Reflection 82
Chaplain 38, 53, 54, 112

Index 203

Charge 39, 77, 96, 101, 117, 119, 158, 160
Charity 60, 80, 99, 100, 105, 110, 117, 124, 160, 190
Charity Steward 55, 185
Chartres Cathedral 131
Chess 19, 63, 64
Chisel 100, 186, 187
Churchwardens 43
Circumambulation 87
Civil War
  American 62
  English 161
Clockwise 40, 41, 87, 123, 124
Closing the Lodge
  First Degree 111, 112
  Second Degree 144, 145
  Third Degree 172, 173
Clothing 77, 80
Collar 20, 51, 52
Collective Unconsciousness 148
Colne Manuscript 69
Colours, symbolism of 15, 17, 18
Columns 46, 47
Columns, Wardens' 46, 49, 75
Combermere Lodge No.605 60
Communication of Secrets
  First Degree 95-97
  Second Degree 125-128
  Third Degree 160
Constitutional Rolls 47, 137
Cooke MS 28, 92, 131, 195
Coronation Oath 94
Cowan 23, 34, 57
Cross, The 8, 154, 190
Croton 21, 33, 159
Cryer, Neville Barker 43, 91, 111, 195
Cuneiform 14
Cyprus 55, 56, 59, 62, 75, 77, 79, 89, 183

Deacons
  Senior 40, 43, 44, 55, 84, 123, 180, 181
  Junior 40, 43, 44, 55, 84, 89, 95, 98, 99, 123, 180, 181

Dionysian Artificers 24, 26, 28, 35, 139
Directions East, North, South and West 38
Director of Ceremonies 40, 43, 44, 54, 72, 178
Divine Shekinah 65, 167

Ear of Corn 140
East Lancashire 40
Edinburgh House Manuscript 92
Egypt 15, 19, 20, 22, 24, 330
Eleusinian Mysteries 22, 23, 25, 26, 57
Ely, Cambridgeshire 59
Emblem 7-11
Emulation Lodge of Improvement 67, 103, 153, 162, 170
Emulation Ritual 39, 66, 98, 167, 179, 185
Enoch, seventh from Adam 46, 47, 137, 140
Entered Apprentice 39, 48, 49, 50, 51, 74, 84, 98, 108, 117, 118, 120, 121, 123, 136, 155
Essenes 20, 26, 27, 35
Eton College 59
Euclid, 47th Proposition 52, 106
Exhortation, Third Degree 158
Ezekiel, Book of 9

Festive Board 21, 39, 68, 79, 113
First Artificer in Metals 151
First Covenant 15
First Degree 11, 20, 23, 25, 36, 37, 39, 42, 50, 64, 65, 67, 71, 72, 74-116, 119, 122, 138, 141, 148, 152, 171, 181, 190
Five Points of Fellowship 34, 146, 173
Five-pointed star – *see also Pentangle* 32, 34, 146
Flavius Josephus 46, 139, 151
Forget-me-not 61, 62
Four Cardinal Virtues 27, 67, 105, 109, 110, 121
France 41, 44, 58, 59, 66, 82, 86, 108, 130
Free Gardeners, Order of 64, 172

204   A Guide to Masonic Symbolism

GAOTU 115
Garden of Eden, Tree of Knowledge 44
Garter Blue 49, 50, 51
Gateshead 37
Gavel, common 100, 179, 181
Geometry 26, 41, 106, 117, 129, 130-135, 145
Gnomon 134
Grand and Provincial Regalia 49
   Ireland 48, 50
   Scotland 48, 50
Grand Lodge – *see also United Grand Lodge* 8, 9, 47, 55, 63, 69, 76, 92, 101, 127, 154, 180, 182
Grand Lodge Arms 8, 127
Grand Lodge Manuscript 69
Grand Lodge MS No.2 93
Grand Lodge of the Sun 61
Grand Master 32, 54, 117, 146, 177, 180
Grand Tylers of Solomon, Degree of 10
Grande Loge Nationale Française 82
Great Architect of the Universe (GAOTU, TGAOTU) 19, 71, 86, 92, 144, 166, 169, 191
Greece 15, 22, 24, 26, 33, 80, 183
Greek Letter Gamma 41, 145
Gwyllim's *Heraldry* 29

Hele, conceal and never reveal 92
Heraldry 15, 67
Hermes Trismegistus 19, 27
Hermopolis 19, 20, 21
Hieroglyphics 19
Hiram Abif, legend of 10, 23, 59, 104, 138, 149, 151, 158, 162, 163, 186
Holy of Holies 37, 148, 166, 167
Hoodwink 80, 94, 122, 196
Hourglass 82, 187, 188
Huyghebaert, Bro Jacques 41, 45, 118

Immoveable Jewels 11, 71-73, 106
Indented or Tessellated Border 65-68, 105
Individual Consciousness 75
Initiation, Initiate 20, 23, 25, 27, 39, 48, 74-80, 84, 88, 115, 117, 148, 163

Inner Guard 56, 81, 83, 84, 178, 180, 181, 190
Ireland 29, 48, 50, 117, 149, 183

Jachin 46, 139
Jacob's Ladder 65, 71, 105, 107
John Browne's *Master Key* 64, 146, 162, 186
Jones, Bro Bernard 43, 47, 78, 80, 87, 92, 125, 148, 149
Jump Suit 79

Kabbala, the 33
Key 54, 143, 196
King Solomon's Temple 18, 26, 37, 45, 47, 64, 73, 103, 104, 126, 127, 138, 140, 141, 143, 146, 152, 163, 173, 186
Kipling, Bro Rudyard 36, 70, 76, 128, 162
Knights Templar 27, 35, 44, 48, 64, 184
Knocks 83, 84, 88, 122, 153, 172
Koran, the Holy 68, 160

La Houpe Dentelée (lovers' knots) 66
Le Maçon Démasqué – Exposure 44
Letter 'G', the 41, 65, 144, 145
Level 29, 53, 69, 70, 95, 96, 106, 136, 181
Levels (on apron) 49, 50
Lewis 22, 42, 43, 107-109
Light 19, 23, 25, 37, 39, 51, 83, 89, 94, 99, 124, 129, 152, 153, 154, 167, 172, 180, 181, 182
Lighted Candle 82
Lights, Greater and Lesser 11, 45, 47, 48, 52, 69, 75, 89, 94, 95
Lodge of Edinburgh (Mary's Chapel) No.1 3, 74
London Masons' Company 9

Mackey, Bro Albert Gallatin 120, 198, 200
Magic Flute, The 20, 113
Mallet 187
Mark Degree 11, 55, 118, 187, 189
Masonic Charities 60, 115, 190

Index 205

Masonic Hall, Congleton 57
Masonic Hall, Stafford 41
Masons' Marks 31, 32
Master – *see also Worshipful Master* 8, 9, 25, 40, 41, 42, 45, 48, 68, 69, 71, 72, 83, 84, 87, 88, 89, 94, 95, 96, 97, 98, 112, 117, 119, 123, 128, 135, 146, 148, 149, 150, 153, 158, 173, 175, 176, 177, 179, 180, 181, 182
Mecca, Great Mosque at 40
Mercury 20, 43, 55, 130, 199
Middle Chamber 117, 144
Money and metallic substances 79, 80
Moray, Bro Sir Robert 32, 33, 34
Mosaic Lodge No.5028 101
Mosaic Pavement 18, 20, 27, 63, 64, 66, 68, 105, 166
Moses 18, 20, 39, 63, 65, 66, 81, 103, 107, 126, 145, 186, 190, 192, 193
Mother Lodge 81, 99, 115
Mother Lodge, The 36, 70
Mount Sinai 63, 64, 65, 66, 150
Moveable Jewels 11, 52, 53, 69-71
Mozart, Bro Wolfgang Amadeus 16, 17, 20, 76, 113, 133
MS Constitutions 28, 195
Mud Bricks 73

Native Americans 18
Neanderthal Man 14
Network, Lilywork and Pomegranates 139
New Testament Parables 16, 145
Nine Muses, the 63
Noah 15, 46, 55, 106, 151, 195-196
North Munster, Province of 29
North East Corner 39, 99, 160
Numbers, symbolism of 13, 112-113, 145-146, 173-175

Obligation 42, 44, 68, 80, 82, 110, 111, 122, 124-125, 128, 135, 155-158, 179
Old Charges 28, 69, 85, 86, 92, 131
Old Testament, the 10, 63, 67, 68, 194
Oliver, Bro Rev Dr George 36, 67, 163

Opening
  First Degree 74-75
  Second Degree 122
  Third Degree 152-153, 172
Operative masonry 28-32, 35, 59, 64, 69, 78, 92, 163
Operative Craft of Stonemasonry 85
Order of St Patrick 50
Order of the Garter 10, 50, 161
Order of the Secret Monitor 10, 44, 91
Order of the Thistle 50
Ormskirk, Lancashire
  Parish Church 30, 39
  The Dispensary 142
Orphic Schools 22
Ox, Man, Lion and Eagle 8, 9
Oxford 59, 141

Parallelepipedon 36
Past Master 51, 52, 53, 60, 68, 115, 119, 136, 178
Peace and Unity Lodge No.314 48
Pedestals 42
Penalties 93
Pentangle (Pentagram) 32, 34, 145, 146
Pentateuch, the 63
Perambulations 40, 87-88, 123, 154
Personal Unconscious 117
Pike, Bro Albert 28, 37, 58, 149, 199
Pillars 37, 45-47, 103-105, 128, 137, 138, 139, 140, 151, 195
Plato 129
Plott, Dr Robert 58
Plumb Rule 29, 53, 69, 70-71, 96, 106, 136, 181
Plutarch 23
Poignard 84
Prayer 65, 84-87, 100, 112, 122, 123, 125, 154, 166, 172
Premier Grand Lodge (Moderns) 8, 9, 32, 47, 53, 65, 101, 177
Preparation
  First Degree 78-83
  Second Degree 119-122
  Third Degree 153

206 A Guide to Masonic Symbolism

President Lyndon B. Johnson 77
President Tassos Papadopolous 77
Preston, William 85, 130, 136, 152, 171
Private Eye 80
Promulgation, Lodge of 48
Pullinge, VW Bro A. H. 73
Pythagoras 20-22, 27, 33, 35, 52, 53, 89, 106, 111, 133, 134, 146, 159

Quarries, King Solomon's 37
Questions before Passing 119-122
Questions before Raising 150-151

Rainbow 15, 174
Raising 154, 158
Reconciliation, Lodge of 48, 153, 154, 172
Rectified Scottish Rite 12, 38, 48, 152
Red Cross of Constantine, Order of 23
Rees, Bro Julian 18, 80, 84
Regius Poem 28, 85, 131, 195
Regular Step in Freemasonry 95
Renaissance 33
Requirement to wear white 79
Rock Lodge No.1289 36
Roman Numerals 16, 17
Rose Croix 82, 111, 113
Rosettes 49, 50, 51, 128, 139, 161
Rosicrucians 33, 35
Royal and Select Masters, Order of 10, 24
Royal Arch 9, 16, 26, 48, 53, 60, 67, 111, 114, 117, 150, 152, 168, 172, 182, 183, 184, 187, 198
Royal Ark Mariner Degree 195
Royal Master, Degree of 10
Royal Order of Scotland 11, 40, 63, 64, 65, 66, 113, 135, 140, 146
Royal Society 34

St Thomas 70, 195
Schaw, William 34
Scottish Rite 12, 20, 25, 38, 48, 82, 113, 199
Scripture 10, 73, 90, 91, 92, 94, 117, 155, 157

Second Degree 8, 39, 41, 46, 65, 69, 70, 71, 84, 89, 94, 96, 111, 112, 117-147, 148, 150, 161, 171, 173, 175, 177, 178, 181
Secrecy 23, 27, 90, 92, 93, 112
Secretary 38, 40, 54, 99
Secrets, communication of
    First Degree 95-97
    Second Degree 125-128
    Third Degree 160
Select Master, Degree of 10, 24, 183
Seth 137, 139, 140
Seton, Alexander 34
Shepherd of Hermas, the 27
Shibboleth 140
Siva or Shiva, Hindu Goddess 64, 112
Skull 164
Slipper 80, 81
So mote it be 85
Solomonic Degrees 10
Sophocles 23
Speth, Bro G. W. 59, 185
Square 8, 11, 18, 29, 41, 52, 53, 69-70, 94, 99, 106, 109, 122, 136, 145, 153, 179
Square and Compasses 9, 18, 45, 47, 53, 61, 70, 75, 94, 106, 135, 136, 165
Squares, level and perpendiculars 95, 149
Squaring the lodge 66, 124
Stars, in temple ceiling 25, 199
Stations of the Cross 40
Stewards
    Grand and Provincial Grand 49, 50, 57, 161
    Private Lodge 51, 56-57
Stonehenge 14, 15, 143
Succoth and Zaradatha 37
Sun, Moon & Master of the lodge 47, 95
Supreme Being 86, 87, 101, 159
Symbol, nature of 7-12
Symbolism of Three 112-113
Symbolism of Five 145-146
Symbolism of Seven 173-175
Symbolism of the Lodge Room 36-73
Symbols no longer used 184-197

Index   207

Tabernacle of Moses 18, 20, 39, 103, 185, 192, 193
Tassels 15, 49, 67, 98, 109, 161
Templar Beauceant Standard 27, 64
Ten Commandments 63, 65
Text Messaging 16
The five senses 34, 124, 146
Third Degree 10, 19, 23, 39, 51, 68, 84, 107, 117, 123, 129, 135, 136, 138, 141, 148-175, 177, 180, 181, 184, 188, 200
Thoth 19, 20, 21, 22, 92
Three Castles and Square 8
Three distinct knocks 84
Three Great Lights 11, 45, 47, 48, 52, 69, 75, 89, 94, 95
Three Lesser Lights 45, 47, 48, 94, 95
Tools, Operative masons 28, 29, 100
Tower of the Five Orders, Oxford 141, 142
Tracing Board
  First Degree 11, 20, 25, 36, 37, 39, 42, 43, 64, 65, 67, 71, 81, 100, 101, 102, 105, 138, 141, 152, 190
  Second Degree 39, 46, 89, 112, 123, 128, 129, 136, 173, 175
  Third Degree 39, 150, 164, 170, 171
Trade Rolls of Aberdeen 32
Traditional History 160, 161-164
Traditions, lodge 40-41, 77, 127, 183
Treasurer 38, 52, 54, 196
Tree of Life 18
Triangle 44, 50, 51, 52, 53, 54, 98, 112, 113, 143, 146, 161
Tyler 56, 57-58, 66, 83, 122, 153, 156, 180, 181
Tyler's Toast 22

Umbilical chord 83
Union Lodge No.129 (Province of Cumberland & Westmorland) 5, 79
Union of 1813 8, 42, 43, 45, 48, 53, 55, 56, 83, 136, 163, 172, 183, 184, 185, 190, 194
United Grand Lodge of England 8, 10, 43, 99, 180

United Grand Lodges of Germany 61

Vaughan, Thomas 33
Vedas 68
Volume of the Sacred Law 8, 11, 45, 47, 53, 68-69, 71, 73, 75, 82, 89, 92, 101, 105, 107, 121, 123, 159, 168

Wands 43-45, 54
Wardens
  Senior Warden 38, 39, 40, 43, 49, 53, 72, 75, 77, 88, 89, 95, 98, 111, 112, 123, 128, 154, 161, 178, 180, 181, 195
  Junior Warden 38, 40, 42, 43, 49, 53, 72, 75, 88, 95, 98, 141, 152, 178, 180, 181, 195
Warrant 99, 180
Warrington 34
West Lancashire 40, 48, 72, 142, 160, 189
White Gloves 58-60
William Smith's *Mason's Pocket Companion* 92
Winding Staircase 123, 128, 141, 144, 173, 175
Without evasion, equivocation, etc 94
Working Tools
  First Degree 100, 112
  Second Degree 8, 69, 70, 71, 96, 111, 136
  Third Degree 171-172
Worshipful Master 8, 23, 38, 39, 42, 43, 44, 45, 49, 51, 52, 84, 95, 99, 112, 114, 115, 141, 152, 178, 180, 195

Yin-Yang Balance 18
York 30, 31, 59
York Rite 182, 183
Yorkshire (West Riding), Province of 6, 79

Zeldis, Bro Leon 59
Zodiac 25, 198